Risk Analysis and its Applications

David B. Hertz
Formerly a Director and Partner of McKinsey & Co.

and

Howard Thomas
University of Illinois at Urbana — Champaign

JOHN WILEY & SONS

Chichester · New York · Brisbane · Toronto · Singapore

Copyright © 1983 by John Wiley & Sons Ltd.

All rights reserved.

Library of Congress Cataloguing in Publication Data:
Hertz, David Bendel, 1919–
 Risk analysis and its applications.
 Includes bibliographical references and index.
 1. Risk   2. Decision-making.   3. Capital
investments—Evaluation.   I. Thomas, H. (Howard)
II. Title.
HD61.H42   658   81-16382

ISBN 0 471 10145 1   AACR2

British Library Cataloguing in Publication Data:
Hertz, David B.
 Risk analysis and its applications.
 1. Risk management   2. Risk
 I. Title   II. Thomas, Howard
 658.4′03   HD61

ISBN 0 471 10145 1

Typeset by Activity, Salisbury, Wilts.,
and printed by The Pitman Press Ltd., Bath, Avon.

Contents

viii

Preface

This project developed through an association which began in the early 1970s, when David Hertz, then a partner in McKinsey and Co., Management Consultants, and also an adjunct professor at Columbia University, spent two periods as a visiting professor at London Business School (LBS). At that time, Howard Thomas was a faculty member at LBS and Director of the Decision Analysis Group, funded primarily by the UK Social Sciences Research Council. David's assignment at LBS was to teach special elective courses in risk analysis and planning under uncertainty on London's MBA (MSc) program. Howard later became the coordinator and joint instructor for these courses on the basis of his research interests and David's peripatetic consulting schedule.

During this period we were encouraged by various practitioners, businessmen and students who suggested that we should write practically oriented book(s) on our elective subjects. As we discussed the idea, the belief grew that any such text should appeal equally well to business majors, MBAs, and executive program students. Subsequently we met up with Jamie Cameron of John Wiley and Sons, our publishers, who was excited not only about the risk analysis project, but also by the concept of a planning under uncertainty text, which, incidentally, Wiley will also be publishing shortly after the appearance of this volume.

Over the succeeding years we crossed paths many times; for example, whilst jointly conducting a risk analysis seminar at the Spanish business school, IESE, and again while HT was a visiting professor in the United States. During this period, we both had ample opportunity to develop a broadly-based coverage and knowledge of a wide range of applications. This has been possible through such actitivities as consulting, teaching, and research contract work. In addition, during the period of HT's appointment as a Foundation Professor at the Australian Graduate School of Management in Sydney, he was able to develop work within Australian and Far East contexts, while at the same time continuing to work with DH in the American and European environment. Throughout this time, working drafts of case and textual material have been routinely exchanged. The final version of the manuscript is fully consistent with our initial objectives, and has benefited considerably from the extended time horizon between project idea and completion.

Those initial objectives were:

   (i) To develop David's original *Harvard Business Review (HBR)* articles: 'Risk Analysis in Capital Investment' (1964), and 'Investment Policies that Pay Off' (1968). Incidentally, 'Risk Analysis in Capital Investment' was reprinted as an *HBR* classic, not only to mark its importance, but also to acknowledge the sale of 150,000 reprint copies by the *Review*.

  (ii) To present a broad understanding of the risk analysis approach and its potential areas of application. That is, the aim of the book is not to present an argument in relation to the theory of finance, but rather to offer a strategic thinking methodology which might encourage decision-makers to examine carefully the data and assumptions surrounding a decision problem such as an investment project. In other words, the textbook is not intended to serve as a toolkit for financial decision-making.

 (iii) To develop the book's applied perspective through the use of a series of real-life case examples, which have been written up as case histories. This approach has been adopted in an effort to improve the flow of the textual exposition of the risk analysis approach

 (iv) To publish simultaneously a companion volume, entitled *Practical Risk Analysis*, which would provide readers and students with an opportunity to test their mastery of risk analysis in a 'learning by doing' sense.

We believe that risk analysis, viewed as a broad approach for handling uncertainty, is now routine and commonplace in business and public decisions. Indeed, we believe that the approach encourages business and public decision-makers to understand risk more effectively, thereby making them more willing to take some calculated risks. Risk analysis is not aimed at *eliminating* uncertainty, or even *minimizing* it, but rather at encouraging entrepreneurial activity through a better awareness of risk.

Our position is put very clearly by Peter Drucker (1) in this extract from his essay on 'The Manager and the Management Sciences':

The fear of risk-taking

    To try to eliminate risk in business enterprise is futile. Risk is inherent in the commitment of present resources to future expectations. Indeed, economic progress can be defined as the ability to take greater risks. The attempt to eliminate risks, even the attempt to minimize them, can only make them irrational and unbearable. It can only result in the greatest risk of all: rigidity.

    The main goal of a management science must be to enable business to take the right risk. Indeed, it must be to enable business to take *greater* risks — by providing knowledge and understanding of alternative risks and alternative expectations: by identifying the resources and efforts needed for desired results; by mobilizing energies for contribution; and by measuring results against expectations, thereby providing means for early corrections of wrong or inadequate decisions.

All this may sound like mere quibbling over terms. Yet the terminology of risk minimization does induce a decided animus against risk-taking and risk-making — that is, against business enterprise — in the literature of the management sciences. Much of it echoes the tone of the technocrats of a generation ago. For it wants to subordinate business to technique, and it seems to see economic activity as a sphere of phsyical determination rather than as an affirmation and exercise of responsible freedom and decision.

This is worse that being wrong. This is lack of respect for one's subject matter — the one thing no science can afford and no scientist can survive. Even the best and most serious work of good and serious people — and there is no lack of them in the management sciences — is bound to be vitiated by it.

REFERENCES

1. Drucker, P. F., *The Manager and the Management Sciences in Management: Tasks, Responsibilities, Practices,* Harper and Row, London, 1974.

Acknowledgements

Chapter 2 extracts material previously published in the *Harvard Business Review* which is reprinted here by permission of the *Harvard Business Review*. The extracts are adapted from 'Risk Analysis in Captial Investment' by David B. Hertz (September–October, 1979) and 'Investment Policies that Pay-Off' by David B. Hertz (January–February, 1968). Copyright ©, 1979, 1968 by the President and Fellows of Harvard College; all rights reserved.

Chapters 2 and 3 use cases, namely 'Aztech Electronics' and 'Property Development in Caracas' developed primarily by Howard Thomas whilst at London Business School. They were originally published in *Case Studies in Decision Analysis* by P. G. Moore, H. Thomas, D. W. Bunn and J. M. Hampton and are reproduced here by permission of Penguin Books Ltd., London, SW10 0UH, England.

Chapter 4 uses extracts from an article 'Measuring Uncertainty' by P. G. Moore and H. Thomas in *Omega* (1975). They are reproduced here by permission of the Chief Editor of *Omega*, the international journal of management science.

The Mucom Case in Chapter 6 was originally written by Professor Gordon Kaufman of the Sloan School of Management, MIT, and is used here with permission.

Chapter 8 uses extracts from an article 'Management Science and the Chief Executive' by David B. Hertz (*Management Decision*, 1972). It is reproduced here by permission of the Editor, *Management Decision*.

We also owe a great intellectual debt to other scholars with whom we have been associated. Notably, Professor Peter Moore, Deputy Principal of London Business School and joint Director (with H.T.) of the Decision Analysis Unit at L.B.S., Professor Gordon Kaufman of MIT, Professor Larry Phillips of Brunel University and the London School of Economics, Professor Howard Raiffa, Frank P. Ramsey, Professor at Harvard Business School, Professor Robert Winkler of Indiana University, Dr. Rex Brown of Decision Science Consortium, Dr. Michael Menke, formerly of SRI and Dr. Ralph Keeney of Woodward–Clyde. Members of the Decision Analysis Group at London Business School in the 1970s, namely, Derek Bunn, Juliet Hampton, John Hull, Andrew Lock, Paul Morris and Peter Burville, also deserve particular mention. Clearly their influence on our thinking and work has been important, stimulating and valuable.

Introduction: The Book, Issues, Definitions, and Scope

1. WHAT WE UNDERSTAND BY THE TERM 'RISK ANALYSIS'

Decision and Risk Analysis as Strategic Thinking Frameworks

Decision and risk analysis (Hertz (2), Thomas (6), Raiffa (5)) can be viewed as having two major roles. Firstly, it offers a broad perspective for structuring the process of decision-making, and secondly, it provides a set of techniques for evaluating the worth of alternative decision options. Both analytic approaches involve *decomposing and structuring the problem*, assessing the *uncertainties and values* of the possible outcomes, and the *determination of the preferred strategy* in terms of some specified choice criteria.

We believe that within the organizational context there is a close connection between decision and risk analysis, and policy and strategy formulation. Further, we believe that risk analysis should be able to add a valuable contribution in terms of providing strategic thinking input for a process of policy dialogue about the decision situation. Such input should be iterative, adaptive, and flexible, while at the same time providing a 'thinking structure' for policy/strategy problems. It is further contended that there is no meaningful distinction between analytic approaches such as risk analysis — which develops an awareness of the impacts of risk and uncertainty on decision problems — and processes of policy/strategy formulation concerned with the resolution of these problems. They should both be seen as valuable parts of *policy dialogue* prior to final decisions being taken.

Risk Analysis Defined

The term 'risk analysis' is used here to denote methods which aim to develop a comprehensive understanding and awareness of the risk associated with a particular variable of interest (be it a payoff measure, a cash flow profile, or a macroeconomic forecast). In other words, a forecast is obtained for a variable of interest in the form of a probability distribution. Two solution techniques are most commonly used to generate the required forecast probability profile. An analytical approach might be adopted. Using this technique, individual

1

2

forecasts are combined (according to a specified structural model) using statistical distribution theory (often in relation to such standard distributions as the normal distribution) to calculate the mean and variance parameters of the probability distribution of the final criterion variable (usually a payoff measure). The other technique most frequently used is to adopt a Monte-Carlo-type simulation approach using the structural model. This model specifies the set of equations required to combine the input probabilistic variables into the distribution of the final payoff measure.

Typically, not all of the inputs need to be specified as probabilistic variables because a preliminary *sensitivity analysis* is often used to screen and identify those input variables which need to be specified in probabilistic form.

Risk analysis has, perhaps, found the greatest immediate acceptance in the area of investment project appraisal. The reason for this may be that it is in such areas that managers frequently have to confront the possibility of making the wrong decision and experiencing 'negative' outcomes such as financial loss. Although risk analysis is useful in this area, it is possible that many readers of the original Harvard Business Review (HBR) articles (Hertz (2)) wrongly interpreted risk analysis as an argument in methodology about investment decision-making. Unfortunately, by concentrating on this aspect, some people may have missed the broader perspective of risk analysis: that is, as a vehicle for examining the data surrounding a decision problem (which might very often be an investment proposal) in the light of all the pervasive uncertainties of the world, of which business is simply one part. In other words, we see a broad role for risk analysis in terms of strategic thinking about decision problems. Risk analysis is as important a vehicle in planning, forecasting, understanding, and handling uncertainty, as it may seem to be in the area of financial decision-making.

Risk analysis has a valuable role to play in the management of the strategic process through its input into such areas as: *forecasting and planning*, *risk positioning* for the firm, *scanning* of the uncertain business environment, *scenario development* in relation to potential social, political, economic, and technological futures, and the *handling of risk and uncertainty*, which are increasingly stressed in modern strategic management paradigms, e.g. Hofer and Schendel (3).

It should be noted that the risk analysis method emphasizes the value of managerial judgement in both input estimation and decision. Our experience suggests that the variety of information available from a risk analysis is useful in two main areas. Firstly, it is a valuable aid in clarifying managerial assumptions about the nature of the decision problem and consequent implications, and secondly, it is an invaluable tool for improving communication, debate and dialogue about the problem (i.e. its assumptions, structure, etc.) amongst the managerial team, and also between managers and analysts. We believe this improved communication to be one of the major benefits to be gained as a result of using risk analysis.

However, we are not suggesting that risk analysis should ever be considered as a meaningful substitute for managerial judgement. The contribution which risk analysis can make is to help managers' thinking processes, and this is done in the first instance by forcing them to confront the structure of the decision problem in a relatively unemotional manner. After the problem has been defined, a 'first-pass' risk analysis can facilitate various activities: it can successively assess the range of uncertain variables deemed important, gather any information required which bears on the resolution of the problem, exhaustively evaluate the cross-impacts amongst the uncertain variables, and combine key uncertain variables to identify viable decision paths and options for the organization in terms of specified preference and choice criteria. Ultimately, it enables the decision-maker — business executive, government administrator, scientist, legislator — to examine, discuss, and eventually understand why one course of action might be more desirable than another.

2. SOME DEFINITIONS

Meaning of Risk and Uncertainty

As used in this book, *risk* means both uncertainty, and the results of uncertainty. That is, risk refers to a lack of predictability about structure, outcomes or consequences in a decision or planning situation. Risk is therefore related to concepts of chance such as the probability of loss or the probability of ruin.

Some earlier writers in the field drew a distinction between risk and uncertainty in the following manner. A risk situation is argued as one in which a probability distribution for outcomes is made on a meaningful basis, agreed upon by the set of relevant experts, and is, therefore, 'known'. Uncertainty situations arise, therefore, when a consensus agreement amongst the set of experts cannot be achieved, i.e. there is an unknown, undefined probability distribution on the set of outcomes.

Lindley (4) points out that a different and more useful form of distinction is often drawn between events which are *statistical* and those which are not. Statistical events are defined to be capable of very extensive repetition, whereas non-statistical events are essentially unique. However, many decision situations are unique and refer to choice on one occasion, so that decision-makers are not often confronted by repeatable situations. Thus, decision-makers must often make 'non-statistical' or subjective probability assessments which are consistent and coherent in terms of the laws of probability (and can, therefore, be compared with so-called 'statistical' or objective probabilities) in order to represent the uncertainty which exists in decision situations.

The purpose of the above is simply to illustrate that while distinctions between risk and uncertainty, or statistical and non-statistical events, are useful in conceptual terms, they have limited value in the practical process of risk assessment and analysis. Indeed, concepts of strategic risk must reflect the realities of strategic decision situations. That is, they must recognize such issues as the quality of information available to decision-makers and the importance of outcomes and organizational goals.

Therefore, our concept of strategic risk recognizes that strategic decision-making situations involve 'structural uncertainty'. In other words, there is considerable uncertainty about the formulation of the problem in terms of its structure and underlying assumptions. As a result, the definition of risk here is broadened to include both the lack of predictability about outcomes and also *all* of the elements of problem structure. This includes such factors as the relevance of assumptions, the generation of strategic alternatives, the level of organizational information about the problem, the importance of consequences and the ability to attain various organizational goals.

Decision Criteria

In this text we assume that the reader has an acquaintance with such investment decision-making criteria as Net Present Value (NPV), Internal Rate of Return (IRR), and Payback. However, some useful review material can be found in Copeland and Weston (1) and Van Horne (7). In financial decision-making contexts we shall follow the finance literature and adopt NPV as the most appropriate and valuable worth criterion.

We should also point out, however, that as our concept of risk analysis applies to a wide range of decision situations, there may be other criteria which can be used in choosing the most sensible strategy paths. For example, the decision criterion may be multi-attributed, as in cost/benefit analysis applications, or based on a time profile of cash flows as, for example, for an organizational growth strategy path.

3. ISSUES ASSOCIATED WITH THE RISK ANALYSIS APPROACH

Problem Finding and Structuring

The preliminary pre-decisional effort involved in problem identification, i.e. in the modelling and structuring phase, is the most important, worthwhile but often least stressed activity amongst all stages of the decision and risk analysis approach. In our experience, it is clear that well over half the time and effort in any analysis should be spent on structuring the problem.

Reference to earlier writing on decision and risk analysis, including our own, indicates that such structuring skills can often only be 'learned by doing'. That is, such skills may often only be acquired through experience in decision and risk analysis. Such a view suggests that if a taxonomy of problem types, e.g. new product, manufacturing investment, etc. were available, the problem-solver could be aided in his early analysis by having the opportunity to match his particular decision problem with one of the problem types catalogued within the firm or literature. In other words, if more risk analysis applications were presented in the literature, practitioners and problem-solvers could increase their awareness of the available set of problem types and so have a broader base for reference purposes.

However, although the development of a taxonomy of problem applications is useful, it needs to be supported by creative diagnosis, particularly in relation to ill-structured problems. Such creative diagnoses involve identifying combinations of facts to highlight key variables and specify novel alternatives.

Value Preferences, Time Preferences, and Risk Preferences

Three types of preferences are present in most decision problem situations: *value*, *time*, and *risk*. It should be noted that all three represent judgements of the decision-maker, decision-making group, or organization. *Value* preferences are the concern of multi-attribute utility; *time* preferences refer to discounting concepts and rate of return, whereas *risk* preferences are often described as 'risk attitudes', and relate to concepts of the utility of wealth. We consider the design of procedures for establishing such preference judgements as perhaps the most important function of the top management group and board of directors of the organization concerned.

The issue of the corporate or organizational utility and preference structure is treated at length in this book. The contrasting assumptions of subjective expected utility and, for example, asset-pricing theories, lead to different utility structures and ultimately to different decision paths.

Examples of Risk Analysis

Throughout the book we stress case examples, often of the case-history type, in the hope of improving the argument and, at the same time, providing an opportunity to develop the 'learning by doing' concept which is so essential to the effective application of risk analysis.

Risk analysis, in our broadly-based definition, has become routine in business and almost universally adopted in cost/benefit issues. We believe strongly in the value of illustrating applications with as wide a range of examples as possible, and intend to use these examples to support the argument for practical implementation, both in this text and the case-study companion volume.

4. SCOPE OF THE BOOK

Aim of the Book

The book is, therefore, a thorough, applications-oriented treatment of risk analysis. As a result, no-one should misconstrue its role — it is in no sense a text on financial decision-making, or on the application of modern finance theory. Its role is rather to treat risk analysis as an approach for handling and confronting risk. In addition, strategic thinking about alternative decision options should always be supported by appropriate risk analyses, which indicate useful entrepreneurial paths for the organization.

Relationship to Companion Text: *Practical Risk Analysis*

The challenge we forsee in this book is to provide the manager, and the management school student, with an insightful understanding of, and framework for, handling risk in decision problem situations. Therefore, we hope to present the rationale underlying the approach, and present solutions to some associated measurement problems. In addition, through the use of a series of real-life case studies, we hope to give readers a feel for application, as well as offering an indication as to how such approaches fit in relation to the modern theories of finance based upon capital asset pricing concepts. The companion volume will present further case studies, so that readers will have an opportunity to develop risk analysis models, thereby gaining personal experience of applied situations. Finally, we would like to emphasize how strongly we believe in the value and importance of risk analysis in structuring and modelling uncertainty, and it is our hope that some of this enthusiasm will be conveyed to readers in the pages which follow.

Chapter Organization

To set the scene for the book's development, we would now like to provide an outline of the work of succeeding chapters. Chapter 1 examines the nature of risk. Chapters 2 and 3 deal with approaches for assessing and understanding the impacts of risk, both in the context of the individual project, and when viewing combinations of possible projects. In Chapter 2 we examine the underlying rationale of the risk analysis or risk simulation approach, originally developed by David in his work at McKinsey and Company. In an Appendix to Chapter 2, we demonstrate, through the use of a case-study process called the 'Management of Uncertainty', how risk analysis can be developed and implemented within an organization in terms of an oil- and gas-drilling problem. We also treat the process of screening options through risk analysis in an R & D decision situation (Aztech Electronics). In Chapter 3 we examine other, more exact, analytical approaches for the evaluation of investment projects. Detailed consideration is given to approaches, such as Hillier's, which assume a functional form for the distribution of NPV and IRR.

Recognizing that the procedures described in Chapters 2 and 3 impose measurement requirements on the decision-maker, or group of decision-makers, we discuss the measurement issues associated with risk analysis procedures in Chapter 4. Thorough treatment is given to, for example, issues concerning the assessment of subjective probability distributions and the problems of judgement under uncertainty, e.g. about preferences.

In Chapter 5, we try to develop a *total risk* or *firm risk* perspective for the risk analysis approach. Projects are viewed not in terms of their inherent riskiness, but in terms of risk from a corporate perspective. Our aim is to attempt to tie in risk analysis in the context of financial decision-making with the modern capital asset-pricing theories derived from finance.

In Chapter 6 we present several case studies of risk analysis in practice (involving public decisions, manufacturing decisions, resource project decisions, and weapons system acquisitions). Chapter 7 includes consideration of implementation problems associated with risk analysis, and provides a suggested approach for handling risk analysis in the organizational context.

Finally, Chapter 8 attempts both to summarize the book's message and to suggest useful directions for strategic risk analysis in the future. In particular, some pressing applied research issues are delineated.

REFERENCES

1. Copeland, T. E. and Weston, J. F. *Financial Theory and Corporate Policy*, Addison-Wesley, Reading, Mass., 1979.
2. Hertz, D. B. Risk analysis in capital investment, HBR Classic, *Harvard Business Review*, September/October 1979, pp. 169–182.
3. Hofer, C. W. and Schendel, D. *Strategy Formulation: Analytical Concepts*, West Publishing, St. Paul, Minnesota, 1978.
4. Lindley, D. V., *Making Decisions*, John Wiley, London, 1971.
5. Raiffa, H. *Decision Analysis*, Addison-Wesley, Reading, Mass., 1968.
6. Thomas, H. *Decision Theory and the Manager*, Pitman/Times Management Library, London, 1972.
7. Van Horne, J. C. *Financial Management and Policy*, 5th edn., Prentice-Hall, Englewood Cliffs, New Jersey, 1980.

Chapter 1

The Nature of Risk

INTRODUCTION

It would be very hard to find many human activities which are not characterized in some sense or other by the presence of risk and uncertainty. Public sector agencies such as, for example, the Nuclear Regulatory Commission in the United States, must judge the risks of safe operation of nuclear power plants and determine levels of acceptance risks for society (see Fischoff et al. (8)). Businesses also face uncertainty at nearly every phase of their operations, although fortunately, some sources of uncertainty are sufficiently insignificant that they can be ignored. Others, such as the loss of entrepreneurial management talent or the onset of sudden but severe competition, cannot be overlooked, but to a greater or lesser extent can be anticipated. Decisions such as new product launches, company takeovers and major capital investment programs can be categorized as being risky in that their outcomes are difficult to predict accurately, and the consequences of wrong decisions can often prove to be quite costly.

Businesses can sometimes seek ways to reduce the riskiness inherent in their activities. First, they can obviously seek to insure against such risks as fire, accidents, theft, etc. However, in practice, they would hardly ever consider insuring a new product launch precisely because, in so doing, they would transfer the rewards from risk-taking almost entirely to the insurance company. This would, surely, be untenable if the business had confidence and belief in its entrepreneurial talent. Second, the business might seek to share the risks with another group or groups perhaps because of extreme technological uncertainties. Some examples of risk sharing are seen in aerospace and airframe manufacturing contexts. The European Airbus A-300B is just such an example of a joint-venture, risk-sharing activity involving European countries such as France and Great Britain, in different phases of research and development and aircraft manufacture. Third, risk reduction can often be achieved through information and intelligence-gathering programs. New product launches can perhaps be improved by undertaking some form of market research into likely market acceptance. However, market research can be expensive and can delay the launch for a period of time during which a competitor may establish a significant platform and base in the market. It should be clear, therefore, that whilst businesses can reduce risks, make contingency plans, and monitor future events carefully they cannot in any sense get rid of risky consequences entirely.

It is probably true that businesses and public sector agencies have been aware for some time of the potential impact of risk on their activities but until very recently, with the possible exception of insurance and other finance-based companies, they have not formally examined its effects in terms of operational or strategic procedures in any significant detail. The impetus of the less than stable economic conditions of the late 1960s and 1970s has speeded up the incorporation of concepts of risk into business and governmental decision-making procedures.

However, it should be possible to obtain some broad consensus of views about the meaning of risk. In the next section we review some definitions of risk and try to arrive at a sensible synthesis.

WHAT IS RISK?

Some writers, for example Rothkopf (16), turn for immediate guidance to dictionary resources for establishing base definitions of risk. Rothkopf quotes Webster's *Third International Dictionary*, in which risk is defined as 'the possibility of loss, injury, disadvantage or destruction'. Other dictionaries would probably provide similar definitions.

One view of risk that is common in the management literature is that risk can be thought of in terms of variability or uncertainty, however imprecise those latter two terms may be (they often seem from different sources to mean different things to different people). Yet the sense of this view of risk is that, say, a mining exploration investment is seen as risky because it is erratic and because considerable uncertainty about future outcomes arising from exploration is often expressed by managers of exploration projects, i.e. there is a spread of possible future outcomes.

To take another example, the term 'risk' has a specific meaning in the insurance industry. Quite apart from a risk being loosely defined as an item to be insured (e.g. a potential fire, theft, or fraud represents a risk to the insurer underwriting the insurance policy), writers in insurance seek to differentiate two categories of risk, i.e. 'pure' risks and 'speculative' risks. 'Pure' risks exist for business firms when the potential outcomes are the chance of loss or no loss (i.e. no potential gain exists). Examples of such risks include physical damage to assets and losses through fraud or criminal acts. 'Speculative' risks involve the possibility of both gain *and* loss for a business. The rewards for taking such speculative risks are the profits which eventually accrue. Such speculative risks comprise marketing, production, and financial risks faced by firms in the market environment, and consequent potential political and technological risks and changes in the wider economic environment. Typically, businessmen are only interested in insurance against 'pure' risks and even then they increasingly employ risk managers who judge whether firms should self-insure or transfer such risks to an insurance company. It is important to note, however, that the underwriter within an insurance company usually judges a particular risk in terms of concepts such as *probable maximum loss*, i.e. the best estimate of the loss that would occur if the event happened in the period under cover, and *possible maximum loss*, i.e. the largest loss that could occur if the event happened (i.e. the extreme right-hand tail of the distribution of potential losses). The interesting thing about such insurance definitions and particularly probable maximum loss (pml) is that two scales are typically identified in relation to a given risk, i.e. a severity grading (amount of potential loss) and a frequency or probability grading (likelihood of occurrence of loss) as a prelude to determining a pml figure. Rothkopf (16) also argues that many businessmen identify severity and probability. In his dealings with businessmen he suggests that they use the word 'risk' in a manner which implies that the risk of a venture increases if the likelihood of loss increases, or if the magnitude of possible loss increases. He uses this observation to argue that variability in relation to a profit or a worth measure is not, of itself, an adequate definition of risk because a venture may have both a large variation with respect to potential profit but also no possibility whatsoever of making a loss. Rothkopf's position is confirmed by Slovic (18) in a series of psychological experiments. The perceived risk for his subjects was more likely to be determined by the probability of loss and the amount of loss than by the variance of the gamble. In addition, recent studies of attitudes towards risk have pointed out that, if the range of a businessman's utility function for assets includes bankruptcy, then his utility function will be risk-averse for normal business risks, but possibly risk-seeking near to bankruptcy (i.e. ruin).

In this book, we shall be interested primarily in risk expressed in financial or economic terms, i.e. uncertainty in relation to money, profit, or wealth. We would argue that risk is itself a broad concept and believe that it has many dimensions in relation to projects within a firm. Some of these dimensions are listed below:

1. *Risk identification:* For example, what are the most critical variables? How can we forecast future earnings, cash flows, etc.?
2. *Inability to forecast project performance:* Questions which obviously occur in relation to riskiness here are, first, what is the *expected profit* (i.e. a measure which encompasses both the size of potential profit and its potential likelihood of occurrence)? Second, what is the variability of profit, i.e. over what range of profits are potential project outcomes likely to fall? Third, what chances are there of a very unfavorable outcome such as, a loss situation occurring?
3. *Risk varies with the level of the organization:* Looking at a project (e.g. an oil-mining exploration project) on its own merely identifies the business risk associated with a single project. Firms, however, generally hold portfolios of projects in order to spread their risk so that even if one project may seem to be extremely risky at an individual level, it becomes far less risky when viewed in a *total firm* or portfolio context. Risk will, therefore, need to be interpreted both in relation to the *single project* and *total firm* contexts.

In the next section we make some general comments on the process of risk determination, which develop from many of the dimensions of risk identified thus far.

THE PROCESS OF RISK DETERMINATION

In attempting to deal with risk and uncertainty, the manager might follow an analytical approach for practical problem-solving which would typically involve a logical sequence of steps for handling risk as detailed below:

(i) *Risk identification* — developing an understanding of the nature and impact of risk on the current and potential future activities of the organization.

(ii) *Risk measurement* — the assessment and classification of risky situations.

(iii) *Risk evaluation and re-evaluation* — the judgement about actions to handle risk and the possible need to re-evaluate risk options.

Risk Identification

Risk identification is equivalent to risk diagnosis. During this stage, we seek to reduce the uncertainty, in descriptive terms, about the identity and potential impact of the key variables that characterize risk in the problem situation under consideration. In essence, we require to diagnose the problem and develop an understanding of its structure. Given this level of understanding we should then be better able, for example, to determine the role of information gathering as a potential aid both in terms of risk reduction and also in the sensible solution of the problem.

Writers in the area of futures research might also argue, particularly if the decision problem involves either a lengthy time-span or the potential impact of technological, social, or political uncertainty, or perhaps both, that some of the futures planning tools might be needed to identify the key variables and uncertainty impacts. In recent years, the use of written *scenarios* (Chambers (6), Jantsch (10)) as a means for enabling managers to understand complex futures has expanded considerably. This process usually involves the responsible manager in first identifying a series of possible futures, or scenarios, e.g. Best, Most Likely, and Worst scenarios for a particular future business opportunity and then describing, in some detail, the likely events which might occur with each of these contemplated futures. It is often argued that this process, somewhat akin to forced introspection, succeeds in expanding the manager's horizons and abilities precisely because it forces him to develop a wider understanding of future impacts and thus generate a type of 'thinking' algorithm (structure) for confronting the problem. A possible counter-argument is that the procedure might still lead to 'tunnel vision' because the manager will tend to anchor his perceptions about the future closely around his

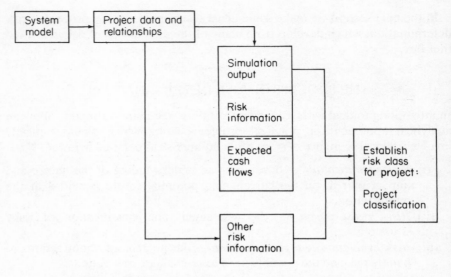

Figure 1 Risk determination and positioning phase for a single project

current concerns, values, and level of information, i.e. he will 'anchor' around the most likely scenario. Tversky and Kahneman (20) for example, develop this point further by identifying some of the common biases which affect managerial judgement and we will summarize their arguments in a later chapter on measurement (Chapter 3).

Other devices, such as the Delphi approach, whose *raison d'être* is to enable a group to reach a consensus view about risky situations, have also been widely used in futures planning. Such procedures and aids ultimately aim to develop better managerial awareness of key variables and uncertainty impacts in business-decision situations. However, it is important to recognize that these procedures are guidelines, and cannot replace those managerial skills of creativity, problem-solving, and entrepreneurial ability that are by their very nature innate. These skills enable managers to take risks and gain rewards in terms of profit. Managers nearly always say, however, that they take calculated risks, i.e. before embarking on any venture they assess the risks involved and also the chances of making a loss. How can they get a better feeling for and understanding of risk?

Risk Estimation ·

Earlier in this chapter we discussed the distinction between the riskiness of an individual project and the 'total risk' or portfolio perspective of a firm.

It seems to us that part of the purpose of risk analysis and assessment is to understand better the risk classification of a particular single project. Figure 1 shows how we characterize this process.

The system model of the business project is obtained from the prior risk identification or diagnosis phase. During this period devices such as logic and decision trees, and futures planning tools, can be used to determine and understand problem structure. The essence of such a model, irrespective of how simple or complex the decision problem may be, is that it attempts to capture all feasible alternatives and specify the nature of risks and uncertainties faced.

Once this model specification has been arrived at in a meaningful manner, the managerial team must assess and estimate project data and specify the nature of relationships amongst key variables. Typically estimated at this stage are subjective probability distributions for chance events and cash flow measures for key economic variables. These are inputs for a full risk analysis of the decision problem in which risk simulation, or a short-cut analytical technique, may be used as a primary solution approach for establishing the project's business risk. Thus, such an approach can give insights into how accurately such factors as future cash flows and earnings can be forecast, and enable a manager to screen the project into risk classes, e.g. high, medium, or low risk. This screening process, very much akin to risk positioning, allows the manager to say whether a given project's individual risk profile is more or less than average, or about the same. However, it does not tell the manager whether or not it is a good deal. Such a judgement must depend upon the firm's total risk and other strategic factors.

Risk Judgement and Evaluation

Managerial judgement about risk must ultimately involve a judgement about the riskiness of the overall portfolio of the firm's activities and, therefore, about the relationship any individual project has to the firm's total risk. If the objective of the firm is to maximize shareholder wealth, then managers entrusted with shareholders' funds should not invest in capital projects unless the expected returns exceed those available to shareholders in the capital markets. The arguments in modern finance theory assume that opportunity rates in the capital market include risk premiums. Capital projects with high risk require high rates of return to be profitable in relation to capital market opportunities. Thus, typical capital projects should be grouped into risk classes according to the exposure to broad economic risks that each represents, and an appropriate risk-adjusted discount rate (i.e. a relevant opportunity rate) should be derived for projects within given risk classes. By using such risk-adjusted rates, management can determine net present value figures which predict the likely net effect of a project on the market value of the firm. In this way, management can be expected to maximize the value of the firm because the procedure explicitly recognizes the relationship of each individual project to the total risk of the firm. Figure 2 shows the essential elements of the risk estimation process.

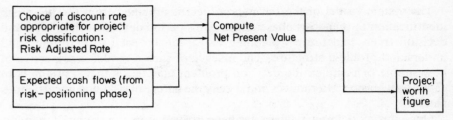

Figure 2 Project evaluation process

The output of the process is a net present value figure for the project, which gives a measure of the project's likely effect on the firm's market value. At this stage, the manager must make an evaluation about the project, and ultimately a decision about its likely acceptance or rejection.

Risk Evaluation

There are a number of issues which confront a manager when judging the worth of a project. Not only is he concerned about its likely effect on market value as measured by the net present value figure, but also about the influence of intangible, unmeasurable factors. In addition, the manager can at this stage test the *sensitivity* of the net present value figure to any or all of the assumptions used in its calculation, e.g. the estimation of project cash flows, or the correctness of the risk classification and its effect upon the discount rate used in the calculation. Ultimately the manager will balance each of these factors and make a judgement about project adoption — in so doing his attitude towards other intangible risky factors will probably assume greater importance. Such factors may relate to organizational strategic aspects, e.g. competitive factors, the desire to develop particular organizational competences, possible social factors, etc. and the inability to plan futures in a meaningful way. Figure 3 shows a conceptualization of the manager's judgemental and evaluation process.

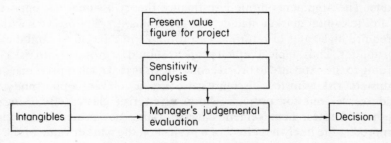

Figure 3 Decision-making

In later chapters, by the use of case studies, we will discuss how managers should handle risk. At this stage it is useful to present the available evidence

...erning the ways in which managers currently appear to make allowance for risk in project appraisal contexts.

EVIDENCE ON PROJECT APPRAISAL METHODS

The accumulated evidence, from surveys and applied articles, appears to indicate that risk simulation is rarely used as a basis for aiding the process of decision-making about investment projects. For example, most articles appear to suggest that risk analysis should only be used in evaluating those larger, more strategic projects (see, for example, Brown (2) and Kryanowski (13) for mining investment applications, Smith and Monkin (19) for petroleum investment applications, and Klausner (12) for shipping investment applications), which are significant to senior management, and which are sufficiently complex that it is difficult to handle them satisfactorily in any other way.

The apparent lack of reported applications of applied risk analysis suggests that we should, at least, try to determine some of the possible reasons. In order to do this, we need to establish the criteria companies currently use in taking financial investment decisions. Extensive surveys have been carried out in Britain, Australia, and the United States by writers such as Williams and Scott (21), Aharoni (1), Burke (3), Carsberg and Hope (4), Rowley (17), Klammer (11), Mao (15), Cheng (7), and Fremgen (9). Without going into detail about their research methods or specific findings, certain general conclusions emerge which merit serious attention from the perspective of the risk analyst. Managerial judgement was very often regarded as being an important feature of the decision-making process. Quotes from Williams and Scott (21) and Aharoni (1) illustrate this. Williams and Scott found that project choice was influenced by:

(a) the policy and strategy of the firm;
(b) managerial and technical resources, experience and 'know-how' in certain types of investment;
(c) a common thread with existing activities.

Aharoni adds that:

(a) managerial time was often at more of a premium than finance;
(b) the cost of additional information could be prohibitive;
(c) 'gut feel' judgement was, therefore, valuable.

Aharoni's last point is given further emphasis in relation to Carsberg and Hope's survey of practice in the United Kingdom (UK) in which managerial judgement was found to be the top-rated criterion for investment decision-making.

Judgement and expertise are managerial qualities which are extremely valuable in confronting uncertainty and which are clearly essential ingredients of the decision-making process. Longbottom and Wade (14) in another survey of UK practice reported that most companies with experience of risk analysis

16

have found considerable difficulty in assessing uncertainty in the for
probability distributions. The problem was perceived to be an educational
one in that non-specialist managers very often had trouble in understanding
the concepts of probability and thus in translating their verbal feelings about
uncertainty into equivalent probabilistic statements. Carter (5) mentions the
same problem but Kryanowski (13) emphasizes that with some prior
discussion and training such assessments can generally be obtained.

Another general conclusion to emerge from these surveys of capital
investment decision-making is that it has taken twenty years for the 'advanced
theories' of the 1950s in finance (i.e. discounting mathematics; DCF, NPV,
etc.) to become the practice of the 1970s. Managers in the 1960s favored
payback because they understood it and saw it as a very simple liquidity
criterion. There was also evidence in the 1960s of a lack of understanding of
discounting concepts, which many popular articles sought to alleviate. The
development of concise, readable managerial statements of discounting
concepts and the simultaneous advent of computer technology which quickly
provided such discounting calculations, forced executives to reconsider the
value of DCF techniques and promote implementation within their own
organizations. By the 1970s therefore, with this educational impetus, DCF
approaches had supplanted payback, although the latter was still often used
as a subsidiary liquidity criterion and an aid for managerial judgement.

The overriding impression from the evidence is that managers tend to look
for decision criteria with which they feel comfortable, can understand and
which also leave some room for the exercise of managerial judgement. Given
this view, the lesson for the proponents of risk analysis is that the potential
impact of risk and uncertainty on managerial decision-making in the 1980s,
(e.g. unpredictable economic and technological environments, high inflation
rates, etc.) is so important and far-reaching that educational and other
initiatives must be taken to persuade and encourage managers to implement
sensible procedures for incorporating risk and other probabilistic concepts
into the decision-making process. More case studies of successful risk
analyses and better managerial treatments of risk analysis applications in
areas such as finance need to be presented in the management literature. Risk
analysis also needs to be explained in such a way that managers perceive that
the procedure formalizes their judgements about uncertainty and value in a
precise way, and also allows them to modify their judgements in the light of
new information or 'second thoughts'. In addition, the positive advantages of
risk simulation, outlined in current literature, have also to be stressed. For
example:

(a) in assisting managers to understand the nature of cross-impacts
between uncertain factors in their decision problems;
(b) in enabling managers to confront, relatively easily, changes in the
assumptions underlying a project's viability, i.e. 'what if' analysis and
other types of sensitivity analyses;

conc) in developing an understanding of the nature of the risk inherent in the single project, i.e. being better able to determine a risk classification for projects.

Problems in implementing risk assessment and analytical procedures have also to be overcome. The human and organizational problems associated with the use of any management approach are sufficiently challenging that solutions can be found. It may be that risk analysis procedures would be more beneficial to some companies and organizational situations than to others — the judgement on that issue is left to the reader although some case evidence will provide guidelines.

REFERENCES

1. Aharoni, Y., *The Foreign Investment Decision Process*, Division of Research, Harvard Business School, Boston, 1966.
2. Brown, R. V., 'Do Managers Find Decision Theory Useful', *Harvard Business Review*, May **1970**, 78–89.
3. Burke, E. J., *A Survey of Capital Budgeting Practices by Australian Companies*, 1970–71, University of Newcastle Research Associates, 1972.
4. Carsberg, B. V., and Hope, A., *Business Investment Decisions Under Inflation*, Institute of Chartered Accountants in England and Wales, London, 1976.
5. Carter, E. E., 'What are the Risks in Risk Analysis, *Harvard Business Review*, July/August **1972**, 72–82.
6. Chambers, J. C., Mullick, S. K., and Smith, D. D., *An Executive's Guide to Forecasting*, Wiley, New York, 1974.
7. Cheng, P. C., 'An Evaluation of Planning for Facility Acquisition', *Managerial Planning*, March/April, **1973**, 16–17.
8. Fischoff, B., Lichtenstein, S., Slovic, P., Derby, S. L., and Keeney, R. L., *Acceptable Risk,* Cambridge University Press, Cambridge, 1981.
9. Fremgen, J. M., 'Capital Budgeting Practices: A Survey', *Management Accounting*, May **1973**, 20–21.
10. Jantsch, E., *Technological Forecasting in Perspective*, OECD, Paris, 1967.
11. Klammer, T., 'Empirical Evidence of the Adoption of Sophisticated Capital Budgeting Techniques', *Journal of Business*, **45**, July 1972, 387–397.
12. Klausner, R. F., 'The Evaluation of Risk in Marine Capital Investments', *Engineering Economist*, **14**, No. 4, 1968, 183–214.
13. Kryanowski, L., Lusztig, P. A., and Schwab, B., 'Monte-Carlo Simulation and, Capital Expenditure Decisions — A Case Study', *Engineering Economist*, **18**, Fall 1972, 31–48.
14. Longbottom, D. A., and Wade, G., 'An Investigation into the Application of Decision Analysis in UK Companies', *Omega*, **1**, No. 2, 1973, 207–215.
15. Mao, J. C. T., 'Survey of Capital Budgeting: Theory and Practice', *Journal of Finance*, May **1970**, 349–360.
16. Rothkopf, M. H., 'On Measuring Risk', *Working Paper*, 1975, Xerox Palo Alto Research Center.
17. Rowley, C. S., 'Methods of Capital Project Selection', *Managerial Planning*, March/April **1973**, 23–34.
18. Slovic, P., 'The Relative Influence of Probabilities and Payoffs upon Perceived Risks of a Gamble', *Psychonomic Science*, **9**, 1967.
19. Smith, M. B., and Monkin, B., 'Probability Models for Petroleum Investment Decisions', *J. Petroleum Technology*, **22**, May 1970, 543–550.

18

20. Tversky, A., and Kahneman, D., 'Judgement Under Uncertainty: Heuristics and Biases', *Science*, **185**, 1974, 1124–1131.
21. Williams, B. R., and Scott, W. P., *Investment Proposals and Decisions*, Allen and Unwin, London, 1965.

Chapter 2

The Basis of the
Risk Analysis Approach

INTRODUCTION

Risk analysis was proposed originally by David Hertz, who regarded it as a natural and logical extension of the sensitivity analysis approach (Rappaport (21)). By using risk analysis, managers can contemplate and confront the future uncertain environment in which they operate. Whilst the enlightened manager has for some time investigated the effects of assumptions about uncertain futures on decision alternatives, the broadly-based approach offered by risk analysis provides another 'lens' for examining and understanding the alternative decision options.

The essence of this classical risk analysis approach is to provide a means by which the decision-maker can look ahead to the totality of possible future outcomes in evaluating whether he ought to approve some investment or new-product proposal, or whether he should adopt some particular corporate strategy with regard to the future. Most frequently, the decisions at hand are financial decisions and typically the decision-maker will make the judgement about the worth of possible future outcomes in terms of criteria such as the *internal rate of return* or *net present value.* The differentiating feature of risk analysis arises from the fact that the decision-maker is presented with the information about the financial criterion (*net present value*, or *payback*, or *internal rate of return*) in the form of a probability distribution for that criterion. This is accomplished, as we shall see in detail from our subsequent discussion, by first asking the decision-maker to nominate experts within the organization who will both structure the essence of the decision problem, and try to identify the events which might happen over some uncertain future time horizon. These areas are evaluated as a prelude to estimating the likelihood of occurrence of those events. Thus, if forecasts of future cash flows are developed in probabilistic terms, the decision analyst can provide the decision-maker with an assessment of the probability distribution for the financial worth of the project.

In this chapter we concentrate upon identifying the nature of the risk analysis approach, its relationship to investment policy and its potential drawbacks. This discussion should help to establish the framework for the remainder of the book, mainly by indicating some of the adaptations and modifications to the risk analysis approach which have been suggested in recent years. These adaptations, treated in detail in later chapters, lead us during the course of the book, to develop preferred routes for carrying out risk analyses within organizations.

WHAT IS RISK ANALYSIS?

It is useful at this early stage of our study of the risk analysis approach to develop a framework, albeit a conceptual model, for the process of investment decision-making. We can first identify the basic, deterministic, single project appraisal process at the firm level, which is well treated in the finance literature. (For examples, see Van Horne (24), Weston and Brigham (26), Merrett and Sykes (18), Levy and Sarnat (15), Farrar (7), and additional references quoted in the introduction.) The diagram in Figure 1 shows the essence of project appraisal.

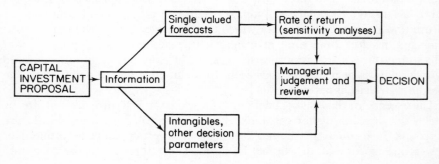

Figure 1 Basic project appraisal

Typically the relevant uncertain variables in the proposed project, e.g. costs, prices, economic factors, etc., can be identified and quantified in terms of single best-guess estimates. From these estimates cash flow figures are calculated and rate of return figures (NPV (net present value) or IRR (internal rate of return) or payback) are generated. These rate of return figures can then be recalculated in a sensitivity analysis phase during which the estimates for any of the quantifiable variables can be amended (particularly those which may be crucial in relation to the proposal's acceptance) and any cash flow figures thus modified. The final decision normally emerges from a review and judgement phase during which the manager and the decision-making group consider the rate of return calculations in relation not only to the sensitivity analyses, but also to other investment possibilities and intangible and immeasurable factors not considered in the formal calculation.

The risk analysis approach builds upon the basic project appraisal framework by explicitly recognizing the uncertainty which exists in all decision problems. It does this by building up uncertainty estimates for the decision variables and eventually generating a probability distribution for the rate of return variables. The outline flow diagram of the approach is shown in Figure 2.

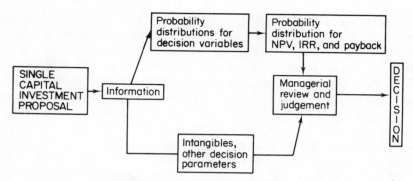

Figure 2 The risk analysis process

In the risk analysis process, therefore, the manager's understanding about the effects of uncertainty upon the project improves and, as a result, his role also changes. As he is confronted with output information on the rate of return in probabilistic terms, he has better information about such factors as future cash flow forecasts and the investment proposal's likely future potential. This means that his judgement about project worth and any decision about project acceptance will reflect his and the decision-making group's risk attitude in relation to this uncertain future (which, we may note in passing, may not necessarily be in one-to-one correspondence with the firm's goals and risk-taking propensities). In this judgement, the attitude towards risk is often based upon some form of intuitive trade-off between the mean or average rate of return and the project's likely variability as measured by the standard deviation of the rate of return. Decision analysts ((Raiffa (20), Moore and Thomas (19), Howard (14), Brown, Kahr, and Peterson (5)), have argued that the risk analysis approach is a special case of the more general framework offered by decision analysis. It differs from decision analysis in its use of risk simulation as a solution technique and by its intuitive, rather than formal (i.e. not using the utility function apparatus) incorporation of the decision-maker's risk attitude (i.e. his preference function for payoffs) into the decision-making process. The structure of the decision analysis approach is shown in Figure 3.

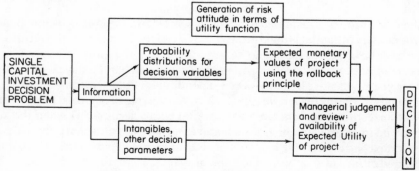

Figure 3 The decision analysis process

The expected utility criterion (see Swalm (23), Hammond (10)) provides a ranking of projects as the output of the process, instead of an informal managerial review of probability distributions of net present value for those projects. It is thus a form of uncertainty reduction. This 'first-pass' expected utility ranking provides a 'screen' before the manager considers the influence of intangibles and other factors on his choice amongst the various options. At a later point in the text we will show that normative procedures exist to help a decision-maker incorporate such multiple conflicting objectives into the decision process through the assessment of multi-attribute utility functions.

In many ways the three approaches outlined in Figures 1, 2, and 3 really form a sequential and interactive approach. In current practice perhaps one-half to two-thirds of major decision problems are analysed by the basic deterministic analysis route of Figure 1. Of the remaining one-third to one-half that may require probabilistic evaluation because of their perceived size, complexity, and strategic nature, around two out of three and possibly considerably more, can be adequately handled by the risk analysis approach alone. Therefore, one could speculate that in practice probably 10 percent of all problems will require the total decision analysis apparatus. Put simply, and there is evidence for this view from practitioner surveys (Carter (6)), managers may baulk at the formalization of risk attitudes via a utility function (Swalm (23), Hammond (10), Grayson (9)) and may feel uncomfortable with the concept.

However, the important point to draw from this consideration of the rationale of decision analysis appraisal processes is that they must be interactive. A pilot or basic analysis will yield insights into the problem, particularly through the sensitivity analysis phase, which, in turn, will yield information about the need to take the analysis further by explicitly incorporating probabilistic notions and risk analysis into the appraisal process.

In the remainder of this chapter we examine the probabilistic phase in considerable detail. We will give a detailed explanation of the risk analysis approach, and in so doing, review disadvantages of alternative appraisal methods.

Need for a New Concept

The evaluation of a capital investment project starts with the principle that the productivity of capital is measured by the rate of return we expect to receive and the cash flow (value) we expect to generate over some future period. A dollar received next year is worth less to us than a dollar in hand today. Expenditures three years hence are less costly than expenditures of equal magnitude two years from now. For this reason we cannot calculate the rate of return or present value of an investment realistically unless we take into account (a) when the sums involved in an investment are spent and (b) when the returns are received.

Comparing alternative investments is thus complicated by the fact that they usually differ, not only in size, but also in the length of time over which expenditures will have to be made and benefits returned.

It is these facts of investment life that long ago made apparent the shortcomings of approaches which simply averaged expenditures and benefits or lumped them, as in the number-of-years-to-pay-out (the so-called Payback) method. These shortcomings stimulated students of decision-making to explore more precise methods for determining whether one investment would leave a company better off in the long run than would another course of action.

It is not surprising, then, that much effort has been applied to the development of ways to improve our ability to discriminate among investment alternatives. The focus of all these investigations has been to sharpen the definition of the value of the capital investments to the company. The controversy and furor that once came out in the business press over the most appropriate way of calculating these values has largely been resolved in favor of the discounted cash flow methods (net present value, in particular) as a reasonable means of measuring the rate of return that can be expected in the future from an investment made today.

Thus we have methods which, in general, are more or less elaborate mathematical formulas for comparing the outcomes of various investments and the combinations of the variables that will affect the investments. As these techniques have progressed, the mathematics involved has become more and more precise, so that we can now calculate discounted returns and present values very accurately. However, the sophisticated businessman knows that behind these precise calculations is information which may not be very precise. At best, the discounted cash flow information he is provided with is based on an average of different opinions, with varying reliabilities and different ranges of probability. When the expected returns and present values on two investments are close, he is likely to be influenced by the 'intangibles' — a somewhat precarious pursuit. Even when the figures for two investments are far apart, and the choice seems clear, there may well lurk, in the back of the businessman's mind, memories of Rolls-Royce, Penn Central, the RB211, the Edsel Car and other ill-fated ventures.

In short, the decision-maker realizes that there is something more he ought to know, something in addition to the expected net present value. He suspects that what is missing has to do with the nature of the data on which the expected value is calculated, and with the way those data are processed. It has something to do with uncertainty, with possibilities and probabilities extending across a wide range of rewards and risks.

The Achilles Heel

The fatal weakness of past approaches thus has nothing to do with the mathematics of discounted cash flow (DCF) calculations. We have pushed along this path so far that the precision of our calculation is, if anything, something illusory. The fact is, that no matter what mathematics is used, each of the variables entering into the calculation of rate of return is subject to a high level of uncertainty. For example:

The useful life of a new piece of capital equipment is rarely known in advance with any degree of certainty. It may be affected by variations in obsolescence or deterioration, and relatively small changes in useful life can lead to large changes in return. Yet an expected value for the life of the equipment — based on a great deal of data from which a single best possible forecast has been developed — is entered into the DCF calculation. The same is done for the other factors that have a significant bearing on the decision at hand.

Let us look how this works out in a simple case — one in which the odds appear to be all in favor of a particular decision:

The executives of a food company must decide whether to launch a new packaged cereal. They have come to the conclusion that five factors are the determining variables: advertising and promotion expense, total cereal market, share of market for this product, operating costs, and new capital investment. On the basis of the 'most likely' estimate for each of these variables the picture looks very bright — a healthy 30 percent return indicating a significantly positive expected net present value. This future, however, depends on each of the 'most likely' estimates coming true in the actual case. If each of these 'educated guesses' has, for example a 60 percent chance of being correct, there is only an 8 percent chance that all five will be correct ($.60 \times .60 \times .60 \times .60 \times .60$) if the factors are assumed to be independent. So the 'expected' return or present value measure is actually dependent on a rather unlikely coincidence. The decision-maker needs to know a great deal more about the other values used to make each of the five estimates and about what he stands to gain or lose from various combinations of these values.

This simple example illustrates that the rate of return, or value measure, actually depends on a specific combination of values of a great many different variables. But only the expected levels of ranges (e.g. worst, average, best; or pessimistic, most likely, optimistic) of these variables are used in formal mathematical ways to provide the figures given to management. Thus, predicting a single most likely rate of return gives precise numbers that do not tell the whole story.

The 'expected' rate of return, or present value, represents only a few points on a continuous curve of possible combinations of future happenings. It is rather like trying to predict the outcome in a dice game by saying that the most likely outcome is a '7'. The description is incomplete because it does not tell us about all the other things that could happen. In Figure 4, for instance, we see the odds on throws of only two dice having six sides. Now suppose that each die has a hundred sides and there are eight of them! This is a situation more comparable to business investment, where the company's market share might become any one of a hundred different sizes and where there are eight

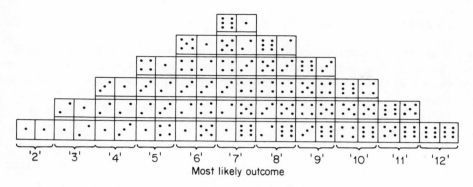

Figure 4 Describing uncertainty — a throw of the dice

different factors (pricing, promotion, and so on) that can have an effect on the outcome.

Nor is this the only trouble. Our willingness to bet on a roll of the dice depends not only on the odds but also on the stakes. Since the probability of rolling a '7' is 1 in 6, we might be quite willing to risk a few dollars on that outcome at suitable odds. But would we be equally willing to wager $10,000 or $100,000 at those same odds, or even at better odds? In short, risk is influenced both by the odds on various events occurring and by the magnitude of the rewards or penalties which are involved when they do occur. To illustrate again:

Suppose that a company is considering an investment of $1 million. The 'best estimate' of the probable return is $200,000 a year over a specified time horizon. It could well be that this estimate is the average of three possible returns — a 1-in-3 chance of getting no return at all, a 1-in-3 chance of getting $200,000 per year, a 1-in-3 chance of getting $400,000 per year. Suppose that getting no return at all would put the company out of business. Then, by accepting this proposal, management is taking a 1-in-3 chance of going bankrupt.

If only the 'best estimate' analysis is used, management might go ahead, however, unaware that it is taking a big chance. If all of the available information were examined, management might prefer an alternative proposal, with a smaller, but more certain (i.e. less variable) expectation.

Such considerations have led almost all advocates of the use of modern capital-investment-index calculations to plead for a recognition of the elements of uncertainty. Perhaps Walker (25) sums up current thinking when he speaks of 'the almost impenetrable mists of any forecast'.

How can the executive penetrate the mists of uncertainty that surround the choices among alternatives?

Limited Improvements

A number of approaches to cope with uncertainty, including ignoring its existence, (see Hogarth (13), MacCrimmon and Taylor (16)) have been successful up to a point, but all seem to fall short of the mark in one way or another.

(1) More Accurate Forecasts

Reducing the error in estimates is a worthy objective. But no matter how many estimates of the future go into a capital investment decision, when all is said and done, the future is still the future. Therefore, however well we forecast, we are still left with the certain knowledge that we cannot eliminate all uncertainty.

(2) Empirical Adjustments

Adjusting the factors influencing the outcome of a decision is subject to serious difficulties. We would like to adjust them so as to reduce the likelihood that we will make a 'bad' investment, but how can we do that without at the same time spoiling our chances to make a 'good' one? In any case, what is the basis for adjustment? We adjust, not for uncertainty, but for bias.

For example, construction estimates are often exceeded. If a company's history of construction costs is that 90 percent of its estimates have been exceeded by 15 percent, then in a capital estimate there is every justification for increasing the value of this factor by 15 percent. This is a matter of improving the accuracy of the estimate.

However, suppose that new-product sales estimates have been exceeded by more than 75 percent in one-fourth of all historical cases, and have not reached 50 percent of the estimate in one-sixth of all such cases? Penalties for overestimating are very tangible, and so management is apt to reduce the sales estimate to 'cover' the one case in six — thereby reducing the calculated rate of return. In doing so, it is possibly missing some of its best opportunities.

(3) Revising Cutoff Rates

Selecting higher cutoff rates for protecting against uncertainty is attempting much the same thing. Management would like to have a possibility of return in proportion to the risk it takes. Where there is much uncertainty involved in the various estimates of sales, costs, prices and so on, a high calculated return from the investment provides some incentive for taking the risk. This is, in fact, a perfectly sound position. The trouble is that the decision-maker still needs to know explicitly what risks he is taking (i.e. what premium he needs to earn as a reward for risk-taking) and what the odds are on achieving the expected return.

(4) Three-level Estimates

A start at spelling out risks is sometimes made by taking the high, medium, and low values of the estimated factors and calculating value measures based on various combinations of the pessimistic, average, and optimistic estimates. These calculations give a picture of the range of possible results but do not tell the executive whether the pessimistic result is more likely than the optimistic one — or in fact, whether the average result is much more likely to occur than either of the extremes. So, although this is a step in the right direction, it still does not give a clear enough picture for comparing alternatives.

(5) Selected Probabilities

Various methods have been used to include the probabilities of specific factors in the return calculation. Grant (8) discusses a program for forecasting discounted cash flow rates of return where the service life is subject to obsolescence and deterioration. He calculated the odds that the investment will terminate at any time after it is made depending on the probability distribution of the service-life factor. After calculating these factors for each year through maximum service life, he then determines an overall expected rate of return.

Bennion suggests the use of game theory to take into account alternative market growth rates as they would determine the rate of return for various alternatives. He uses the estimated probabilities that specific growth rates will occur to develop optimum strategies. Bennion points out:

> Forecasting can result in a negative contribution to capital budgeting decisions unless it goes further than merely providing a single most probable prediction ... [with] an estimated probability coefficient for the forecast, plus knowledge of the payoffs for the company's alternative investments and calculation of indifference probabilities ... the margin of error may be substantially reduced, and the businessman can tell just how far off his forecast may be before it leads him to a wrong decision (Bennion (3))

Note that both of these methods yield an expected return, each based on only one uncertain input factor — service life in the first case, market growth in the second. Both are helpful, and both tend to improve the clarity with which the executive can view investment alternatives. But neither sharpens up the range of 'risk taken' or 'return hoped for' sufficiently to help very much in the complex decisions of capital planning.

Sharpening the Picture

Since every one of the many factors that enter into the evaluation of a specific decision is subject to some uncertainty, the executive needs a helpful portrayal of the effects that the uncertainty surrounding each of the significant factors has on the returns he is likely to achieve. Therefore, the method that was developed at McKinsey & Company combines the variabilities inherent in all the relevant factors. Our objective is to give a clear picture of the relative risk and the probable odds of coming out ahead or behind in the light of uncertain foreknowledge.

A simulation of the way these factors may combine as the future unfolds is the key to extracting the maximum information from the available forecasts. In fact, the approach is very simple, using a computer program to do the necessary arithmetic. (Recently a computer program to do this was suggested by Hess and Quigley for chemical process investments (11)).

To carry out the analysis, a company must follow three steps. First, estimate the range of values for each of the factors (e.g. range of selling price, and so on) and within that range the likelihood of occurrence of each value.

Second, select at random from the distribution of values for each factor one particular value. Then combine the values for all of the factors and compute the rate of return (or present value) from that combination. For instance, the lowest in the range of prices might be combined with the highest in the range of growth rate and other factors. (The fact that the factors are dependent should be taken into account, as we shall see later.)

Finally, do this over and over again to define and evaluate the odds of the occurrence of each possible rate of return (or present value). Since there are literally millions of possible combinations of values, we need to test the likelihood that various specific returns on the investment will occur. This is like finding out by recording the results of a great many throws what percent of '7's or other combinations we may expect in tossing dice. The result will be a listing of the rates of return (or present values) we might achieve, ranging from a loss (if the factors go against us) to whatever maximum gain is possible with the estimates that have been made.

For each of these rates the chances that it may occur are determined. (Note that a specific return can usually be achieved through more than one combination of events. The more combinations for a given rate, the higher the chances of achieving it — as with '7's in tossing dice.) The average expectation is the average of the values of all outcomes weighted by the chances of each occurring.

The variability of outcome values from the average is also determined. This is important since, all other factors being equal, management would presumably prefer lower variability for the same expected present value (or return) if given the choice. This concept has already been applied to investment portfolios (Markowitz (17), Sharpe (22)).

When the expected value and variability of each of a series of investments have been determined, the same techniques may be used to examine the effectiveness of various combinations of them in meeting management objectives.

Practical Test

To see how this new approach works in practice, let us take the experience of a management that has already analyzed a specific investment proposal by conventional techniques. Taking the same investment schedule and the same expected values actually used, we can find what results the new method would produce and compare them with the results obtained when conventional methods were applied. As we shall see, the new picture of risks and returns is different from the old one. Yet the differences are attributable in no way to changes in the basic data — *only to the increased sensitivity of the method to management's uncertainties about the key factors.*

Investment Proposal

In this case a medium-sized industrial chemical producer is considering a $10 million extension to its processing plant. The estimated service life of the facility is ten years; the engineers expect to be able to utilize 250,000 tons of processed material worth $510 per ton at an average processing cost of $435 per ton. Is this investment a good bet? In fact, what is the return that the company may expect? What are the risks? We need to make the best and fullest use we can of all the market research and financial analyses that have been developed, so as to give management a clear picture of this project in an uncertain world.

The key input factors management has decided to use are:

1. Market size.
2. Selling prices.
3. Market growth rate.
4. Share of market (which results in physical sales volume).
5. Investment required.
6. Residual value of investment.
7. Operating costs.
8. Fixed costs.
9. Useful life of facilities.

These factors are typical of those in many company projects that must be analyzed and combined to obtain a measure of the attractiveness of a proposed capital facilities investment.

Obtaining Estimates

How do we make the recommended type of analysis of this proposal? Our aim is to develop for each of the nine factors listed a frequency distribution or probability curve. The information we need includes the possible range of values for each factor, the average, and some ideas as to the likelihood that the various possible values will be reached. It has been our experience that for major capital proposals, managements usually make a significant investment in time and funds to pinpoint information about each of the relevant factors. An objective analysis of the values to be assigned to each can, with little additional effort, yield a subjective probability distribution.

Specifically, it is necessary to probe and question each of the experts involved — to find out, for example, whether the estimated cost of production really can be said to be exactly a certain value or whether, as is more likely, it should be estimated to lie within a certain range of values. It is that range which is ignored in the analysis management usually makes. The range is relatively easy to determine; if a guess has to be made — as it often does —it is easier to guess with some accuracy a range rather than a specific single value. We have found from past experience at McKinsey & Company that a series of meetings with management is most helpful in getting at realistic answers to the *a priori* questions. (The term 'realistic answers' implies all the information management does *not* have, as well as all that it does have.)

The ranges are directly related to the degree of confidence that the estimator has in his estimate. Thus, certain estimates may be known to be quite accurate. They would be represented by probability distributions stating, for instance, that there is only one chance in ten that the actual value will be different from the best estimate by more than 10 percent. Others may have as much as 100 percent ranges above and below the best estimate.

Thus we treat the factor of selling price for the finished product by asking executives who are responsible for the original estimates these questions:

1. Given that $510 is the expected sales price, what is the probability that the price will exceed $550?
2. Is there any chance that the price will exceed $650?
3. How likely is it that the price will drop below $475?

Managements must ask similar questions for each of the other factors, until they can construct a curve for each. Experience shows that this is not as difficult as it might sound. Often information on the degree of variation in factors is readily available, as in, for instance, historical information on variations in the price of a commodity. Similarly, management can estimate the variability of sales from industry sales records. Even for factors that have no history, such as operating costs for a new product, the person who makes the 'average' estimate must have some idea of the degree of confidence he has in his prediction, and therefore he is usually only too glad to express his feelings. Likewise, the less confidence he has in his estimate, the greater will be the range of possible values that the variable will assume.

This last point is likely to trouble businessmen. Does it really make sense to seek estimates of variations? It cannot be emphasized too strongly that the less certainty there is in an 'average' estimate, *the more important it is to consider the possible variation in that estimate.*

Further, an estimate of the variation possible in a factor, no matter how judgemental it may be, is always better than a simple 'average' estimate, since it includes more information about what is known and what is not known. It is, in fact, this very *lack* of knowledge which may distinguish one investment possibility from another, so that for rational decision-making it *must* be taken into account.

This lack of knowledge is in itself important information about the proposed investment. To throw any information away simply because it is highly uncertain is a serious error in analysis which the new approach is designed to correct.

Computer Runs

The next step in the proposed approach is to determine the returns, or present values, that will result from random combinations of the factors involved. This requires realistic restrictions, such as not allowing the total market to vary more than some reasonable amount from year to year. Of course, any method of rating the return which is suitable to the company may be used at this point; in the actual case, management preferred internal rate of return, so that method is followed here.

A computer can be used to carry out the trials for the simulation method in very little time and at very little expense. Thus, for one trial actually made in this case, 3,600 discounted cash flow calculations, each based on a selection of the nine input factors, were run in a relatively short period of time at a very low cost figure. The resulting rate-of-return probabilities were read out immediately and graphed. The process is shown schematically in Figure 5.

Data Comparisons

The nine input factors described earlier fall into three categories:

1. *Market analyses.* Included are market size, market growth rate, the firm's share of the market, and selling prices. For a given combination of these factors sales revenue may be determined for a particular business.
2. *Investment cost analyses.* Being tied to the kinds of service-life and operating-cost characteristics expected, these are subject to various kinds of error and uncertainty; for instance, automation progress makes service life uncertain.

32

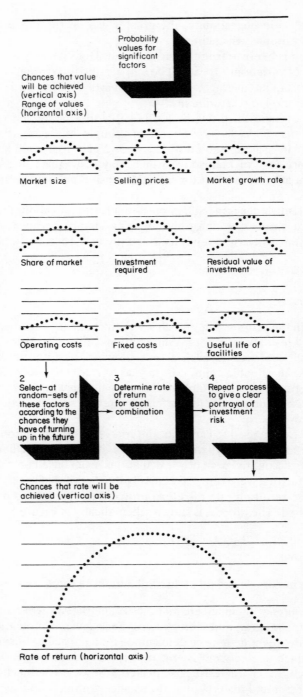

Figure 5 Simulation for investment planning

3. *Operating and fixed costs.* These also are subject to uncertainty, but are perhaps the easiest to estimate.

These categories are not independent, and for realistic results our approach allows the various factors to be tied together. Thus, if price determines the total market, we first select from a probability distribution the price for the specific computer run and then use for the total market a probability distribution that is logically related to the price selected.

We are now ready to compare the values obtained under the new approach with the values obtained under the old. This comparison is shown in Figure 6.

Valuable Results

How do the results under the new and old approaches compare? In this case, management has been informed, on the basis of the 'one best estimate' approach, that the expected internal rate return was 25.2 percent before taxes. When we ran the new set of data through the computer program however, the result was an expected internal rate of return of only 14.6 percent before taxes. This surprising difference is due not only to the fact that under the new approach we use a range of values; it also reflects the fact that we have weighted each value in the range by the chances of its occurrence.

Our new analysis therefore may help management to avoid unwise investment. In fact, the general result of carefully weighing the information and lack of information in the manner we have suggested is to indicate the true nature of otherwise seemingly satisfactory investment proposals. If this practice were followed by managements, much regretted overcapacity might be avoided.

The computer program developed to carry out the simulation allows for easy insertion of new variables — in fact, some programs have previously been suggested that take variability into account (Hillier (12)). But most programs do not allow for dependence relationships between the various input factors. Further, the program used here permits the choice of a value for price from one distribution, which value determines a particular probability distribution (from among several) that will be used to determine the value for sales volume. The following scenario shows how this important technique works:

> Suppose we have a wheel, as in roulette, with the numbers from 0 to 15 representing one price for the product or material, the numbers 16 to 30 representing a second price, the numbers 31 to 45 a third price and so on. For each of these segments we would have a different range of expected market volumes; e.g. $150,000–$200,000 for the first, $100,000–$150,000 for the second, $75,000–$100,000 for the third, and so forth. Now suppose that we spin the wheel and the ball falls in 37. This would mean that we pick a sales volume in the $75,000–$100,000 range. If the ball goes in 11, we have a different price and we turn to the $150,000–$200,000 range for a sales volume.

	Conventional 'best estimate' approach	New approach
Market analyses		
1. Market size		
Expected value (in tons)	250,000	250,000
Range	—	100,000–340,000
2. Selling prices		
Expected value (in dollars/ton)	$510	$510
Range	—	$385–575
3. Market growth rate		
Expected value	3%	3%
Range	—	0–6%
4. Eventual share of market		
Expected value	12%	12%
Range	—	3%–17%
Investment cost analyses		
5. Total investment required		
Expected value (in $ millions)	$9.5	$9.5
Range	—	$7.0–$10.5
6. Useful life of facilities		
Expected value (in years)	10	10
Range	—	5–15
7. Residual value (at 10 years)		
Expected value (in $ millions)	$4.5	$4.5
Range	—	$3.5–$5.0

	Conventional 'best estimate' approach	New approach
Market analyses		
Other costs		
8. Operating costs		
Expected value (in dollars/ton)	$435	$435
Range	—	$370–$545
9. Fixed costs		
Expected value (in $thousands)	$300	$300
Range	—	$250–$375

Note: Range figures in right-hand column represent approximately 1% to 99% probabilities. That is, there is only a 1-in-100 chance that the value actually achieved will be respectively greater or less than the range.

Figure 6 Comparison of expected values under new and old approaches

Most significant, perhaps, is the fact that the program allows management to ascertain the sensitivity of the results to each or all of the input factors. Simply by running the program with changes in the distribution of an input factor, it is possible to determine the effect of added or changed information (or of the lack of information). It may turn out that fairly large changes in some factors do not significantly affect the outcomes. In this case, as a matter of fact, management was particularly concerned about the difficulty of estimating market growth. Running the program with variations in this factor quickly demonstrated to us that for average annual growth rates from 3 and 5 percent there was no significant difference in the expected outcome.

In addition, let us see what the implications are of the detailed knowledge the simulation method gives us. Under the method using single expected values, management arrives only at a hoped-for expectation of 25.2 percent after taxes (which, as we have seen, is wrong unless there is no variability in the various input factors — a highly unlikely event). On the other hand, with the method we propose, the uncertainties are clearly portrayed:

36

Percent return	Probabilities of achieving at least the return shown (percent)
0	96.5
5	80.6
10	75.2
15	53.8
20	43.0
25	12.6
30	0

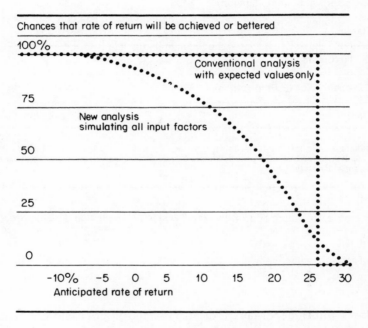

Figure 7 Anticipated rates of return under old and new approaches

This profile is shown in Figure 7. Note the contrast with the profile obtained under the conventional approach. This concept has been used also for evaluation of new product introductions, acquisition of businesses, and plant modernization.

Comparing Opportunities

From a decision-making point of view one of the most significant advantages of the new method of determining rate of return is that it allows management to discriminate between measures of (i) expected return based on weighted probabilities of all possible returns, (ii) variability of return, and (iii) risks.

To visualize this advantage, let us take an example which is based on another actual case but simplified for purposes of explanation. The example involves two investments under consideration, A and B.

When the investments are analyzed, we obtain the data tabulated and plotted in Figure 8. We see that:

(1) Investment B has a higher expected return than Investment A.
(2) Investment B also has substantially more variability than Investment A. There is a good chance that Investment B will earn a return which is quite different from the expected return of 6.8 percent, possibly as high as 15 percent or as low as a loss of 5 percent. Investment A is not likely to vary greatly from the anticipated 5 percent return.
(3) Investment B involves far more risk than does Investment A. There is virtually no chance of incurring a loss on Investment A. However, there is one chance in ten of losing money on Investment B. If such a loss occurs, its expected size is approximately $200,000.

Clearly, the new method of evaluating investments provides management with far more information on which to base a decision. Investment decisions made only on the basis of maximum expected return are not unequivocally the best decisions.

It can be seen that in using risk profiles, management is availing itself of all, not just part of the quantitative information that can be put together on the investment possibilities. And more information in the hands of management should mean better decisions. However, the question of how to use this information remains. Management clearly needs guidance in selecting the 'best' portfolio of investment possibilities from the alternatives available. In essence, management faced with a set of alternatives and an attitude and perspective towards risk must determine what *investment policy* will maximize the earnings-per-share performance of its investments over some defined period.

It is useful at this stage to get a clear conception of the nature and function of an investment policy.

NATURE OF POLICY

Any investment policy, if it is to guide management's choices among available investment alternatives, must embody two components: (i) *one or more criteria* by which to measure the relative economic attributes of investment alternatives, and (ii) *decision rules* — which may or may not make use of risk analysis or otherwise seek to take uncertainty into account — for selecting 'acceptable' investments.

The criteria have been the subject of much analysis and discussion. They include, as we pointed out earlier, the payback period, which is simply the number of years required for the investment to return its costs; average annual percent return on average funds employed; net present value measures; and

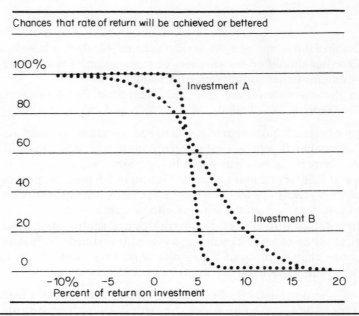

Selected statistics	Investment A	Investment B
Amount of investment	$10,000,000	$10,000,000
Life of investment (in years)	10	10
Expected annual net cash inflow	$1,300,000	$1,400,000
Variability of cash inflow		
1 chance in 50 of being *greater than*	$1,700,000	$3,400,000
1 chance in 50 of being *less than**	$900,000	($600,000)
Expected return on investment	5.0%	6.8%
Variability of return on investment		
1 chance in 50 of being *greater than*	7.0%	15.5%
1 chance in 50 of being *less than**	3.0%	(4.0%)
Risk of investment		
Chances of a loss	Negligible	1 in 10
Expected size of loss	Negligible	$200,000

*In the case of negative figures (indicated by parentheses) *less than* means *worse than*.

Figure 8 Comparison of two investment opportunities

internal rates of return, calculated on a discounted cash flow basis (Bierman and Schmidt (4)). On the other hand, the rules for making choices, particularly under uncertainty, have been largely left up in the air (Adelson (1)). Of course, no pre-established policy can take into account all the considerations — human, organizational, strategic, and financial — that typically enter into a major capital investment decision. Here, however, the concern is strictly with the question of financial policy, which does lend itself to rigorous formulation.

Dual Role

A consistent and adequate investment policy has a double function. In the short run, it should indicate which investments should be chosen to achieve the financial objectives of the corporation. In the long run, it should serve as a basis for identifying or developing investment alternatives that are likely to match the policies selected. In other words, it serves as a basis for both (a) *acting on*, and (b) *communicating about*, investment alternatives.

Screening Proposals

In the first instance, an investment policy may be regarded as a screen which will 'pass' certain investment proposals and reject others. The screen may be coarse or fine, tight or loose, high-risk or low-risk — depending on management's knowing or unknowing choice. Through the screen will pass the acceptable investment proposals that will form management's 'investment set'.

Once it is understood that a risk profile attaches, willy nilly, to all investments and that this profile varies with the criteria chosen, even though based on the same estimates of underlying world phenomena, it becomes clear that a policy with a 'determinate' or single-point-based, decision-rule component is a very coarse screen indeed — if it can be called a screen at all. In any case, as we shall see, such a 'determinate' policy is ineffective, it will not guide management to making the best use of its investment funds, no matter what the company's financial objectives may be.

Risk-based policies, on the other hand, may specify risk-return trade-offs, i.e. how management would prefer to trade off the chances of low return against the chances of high return. For example, would it prefer a virtual certainty of no loss coupled with a virtual ceiling on gains over 20 percent after taxes — or would it accept a one-in-ten chance of significant loss for the sake of a one-in-ten chance of a very high gain? (Note that such risk-based policies should be formulated in terms of the corporation's objectives and risk-attitudes — i.e. the utility function of the corporation may differ from those of the senior managers.)

40

1. Criterion to be used as a measure of investment worth:
   Before-tax return on investments, on a discounted cash flow
   basis

2. Rules to be used to screen investments based on risk profiles
   of proposed projects:
   Accept proposals that have —
   a. Expected value (average of all outcomes) of 5% or greater
   b. One chance in ten that the ROI will exceed 25%
   c. Nine chances in ten that the ROI will exceed 0%

Figure 9 Example of risk-based investment policy

Figure 9 shows how one specific policy may be defined by the criterion to be used and the rules to be followed in screening investments in terms of their risk profiles. These rules, which make explicit management's entrepreneurial or risk-taking attitudes, do allow consistent investment choices (Swalm (23)). The methods described here assume that uncertainty — i.e. the spread of distribution of potential returns around the 'expected value', or average of all outcomes — is a useful measure of risk. It is generally accepted that the further the return might exceed the expected value, the further it could also fall short — and lucky indeed is the company to which this principle does not apply.

Communicating Alternatives

In the second instance, an investment policy can be a powerful communications tool. It enables top management to make known in advance to those responsible for developing investment proposals what sort of projects the company seeks. The object is to control the selection and development of alternatives so that they reflect the gains the company wants to make and the risks it is willing to undergo to achieve them.

In theory of course, this function could be served by policy statements such as: 'All investments must have an estimated average return on capital employed of 12% or more after taxes'.* On the practical level, the complexity of most present-day investment projects and the multitude of future variables to which they are subject, rob such statements of most of their usefulness. This is why top management today, confronted with requests for capital, so often finds that the only significant response it can make is to approve the results of all the analyses that have previously taken place at divisional and staff levels.

With a risk-based policy, using one or more criteria and such rules as are shown in Figure 9, management still has no guarantee that all or any of the available investments will pass through the screen. But it does have a better, more specific means for discriminating among proposed investments. It also

*This statement raises the question as to whether decisions are better made on a pre- or post-tax basis. In general, we believe that the answer is situation-specific, and therefore probably varies from firm to firm. If we had to choose we would opt for a pre-tax basis on the grounds that the tax vagaries/incentives of this and other projects are thereby eliminated.

has a tool for testing out its own procedures for developing investment proposals and for checking out alternative policies. To analyze its own past investments and requests for capital, a company can estimate the risk profiles of these past investments and determine (a) whether it has been consistent in its past selections and (b) what changes in the mix selected would be indicated by different policy choices.

This analysis, however, still will not indicate what is the best investment policy overall — i.e. what impact the choice of a particular criterion, such as net present value, payback, or return on investment, has on the likely outcome of specific real-world variables, such as costs and revenues, or what differences there are (again, in terms of real-world financial results) between high-risk and low-risk screens. In this connection, we think it is important to note that the criteria are mathematically derived in fairly complicated ways from real-world events, such as sales, price changes, equipment installations, and so on. Since the uncertainty profiles of the events must be used to determine the final risk profile of the criterion, simulation methods are often required. In addition, we should also recognize that different approaches and theories would tend to specify somewhat different investment policies — a point taken up in later chapters of this book.

'Efficiency' Concept

Most managements would like to have investment policies that both maximize financial results over the long run and minimize uncertainty or risk. Seeking additional returns, however, normally entails accepting additional uncertainty — i.e. risk. If two policies produce the same average result (e.g. the same average earnings per share over a five-year period), the one that involves less 'variability' (or uncertainty as to the outcome) for the same yield is a more desirable or 'efficient' policy. Conversely, of two policies entailing the same variability, the one producing the higher expected return ('expected' meaning the average of all outcomes) is obviously the better policy. Variability is best measured in terms of the probability distribution of the values within which the actual results are likely to fall.

Standard Deviation

The spread or variability of a risk profile can be measured by the size of the standard deviation, which represents the spread around the expected value of the criterion encompassing two-thirds of all the actual outcomes (in the case of a symmetrical distribution such as the Normal Distribution). Thus, if it is possible to simulate the financial results of investments selected on the basis of a particular policy, the expected return measure — along with the standard deviation* of the financial results obtained with that policy — will indicate the

*Note: this standard deviation measure is calculated making allowances for intercorrelation between investment projects, i.e. covariance effects. Thus, it is often valuable to have projects with negative cross-correlations in a portfolio.

'efficiency' of the investment project set selected under that policy. (With this simulation, the distributions of the uncertainty profiles of revenues, costs, and investments (together with any correlation or covariance effects between projects) in a specific year are combined. These combinations are linear, and we can reasonably expect the results to be normally distributed. Some evidence on this point is presented in Chapter 3.)

The expected return and the standard deviation can be plotted on a graph to show the effectiveness of any policy, and a line can then be drawn through the points of greatest yield for a given standard deviation. This line is called the *efficiency frontier* because it represents the best return management can get for a given variance — unless of course, management either (a) finds a policy that will yield a greater return on investment for no more variance, or (b) develops investment proposals with different uncertainty profiles that provide project choices with less variance for equivalent returns.

Figure 10 illustrates how the average returns — in this case, earnings per share — are plotted against the standard deviation of those earnings to give an efficiency frontier, in the sense of a trade-off between the mean and standard deviation (see Markowitz (17)). Each point on the graph represents the financial results to be expected from a combination of investments selected by passing the same group of proposals through the screen of a particular investment policy. (The results shown in this exhibit were obtained by simulating the operation of a company using this policy for fifteen years.)

Policies A, B, and C lie on the efficiency frontier because each produces the maximum earnings per share for a given degree of risk. Policies D, E, and F do not lie on the frontier because none of them produces, for a given standard deviation, as much earnings as management could obtain by using a different policy. Policy F for example, is better than E because it earns $4.00 against $2.95 for the same risk (15 percent standard deviation); but it is worse than A, which produces earnings of $6.50 at a standard deviation of 16 percent. An efficient policy at 15 percent standard deviation should produce average earnings of approximately $6.25 per share.

Specific policies can, of course, be developed to fill in the entire efficiency frontier curve. For example, the simulation can take into account the capital structure of a real or hypothetical firm, both currently and in the (uncertain) future, thereby dealing effectively with the problem of the marginal cost of capital.

If the objective of an investment policy is to maximize average long-term earnings or yield for a given variation of those earnings or that yield, there are literally no reasons why a management that has calculated its own efficiency frontier should use a policy that is not on that frontier. By definition, such a policy entails more variability in investment results and/or a lower expected return than the company is in fact obliged to accept. A management that wants to invest rationally — that is, wants to optimize results — has every reason, therefore, to locate its efficiency frontier* and continually strive to improve it.

*Note: the efficiency frontier can be defined on a different basis than the mean/standard deviation frontier presented here. Chapter 5 takes up this point in greater detail.

43

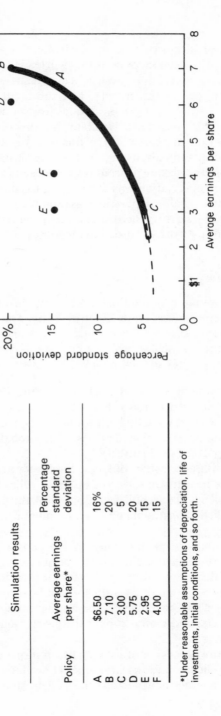

Simulation results

Policy	Average earnings per share*	Percentage standard deviation
A	$6.50	16%
B	7.10	20
C	3.00	5
D	5.75	20
E	2.95	15
F	4.00	15

*Under reasonable assumptions of depreciation, life of investments, initial conditions, and so forth.

Figure 10 Comparing investment policies

Research Results

How practical is the concept of efficient investments sets (on the efficiency frontier) and effective investment policies that will lead to a choice of such sets? In terms of actual investment results, what light does it throw on such issues as the choice of particular investment criteria, and the conduct of the resource allocation process? To help answer these questions, a computer model was developed that made it possible to simulate the effects of various policies, operating over a period of years, on the financial results of a hypothetical company which selects annually from a wide range of investment proposals. Generally acceptable accounting procedures were used to determine financial results. Straight-line depreciation was used, and a fixed percentage dividend, along with a constant allowable debt ratio, was required to be paid where profits were available. At initial start-up each simulation run had standard conditions of assets, earnings, and so forth, and used the McKinsey risk-analysis package.

Seven-step Simulation

As input to the computer simulation model, we developed three sets of thirty-seven hypothetical investments. Each of the hypothetical investments, in turn, was characterized by uncertainty profiles for each of the three key variables for each year of the particular investment: sales, costs, and investment requirements. The computer simulation involved seven steps:

1. Choose an investment policy by (a) selecting financial criterion (or criteria) and (b) establishing decision rules. Except in the case of single-point estimates, these rules specified criterion values, along with a minimum expected value, at the 10 and 90 percent probability points on the criterion-risk profile (see Figure 9).
2. From the uncertainty profiles of key variables for each investment given in the available investment set, develop risk profiles for each.
3. Screen investments against policy, and accept all those that pass the screen, subject to realistic constraints on size and number of investments to be made in a given year.
4. Simulate the financial performance of the chosen investments over a fifteen-year period, selecting at random the operating results for each year from the individual uncertainty profiles for the investment project in order to obtain one set of operating results for that investment for each year.
5. Combine the various revenues, costs, and investment requirements for each of the years, and then compute the yearly financial results for this investment set.
6. Repeat the entire process until a stable distribution of the financial results for the policy chosen and the investments available has been built up. Determine the average or expected value and the standard deviation of the key financial results.

7. Repeat for other policies and other sets of investment alternatives.

Policies Tested

For each of the three investment sets, investment policies covering conservative, medium-risk, and high-risk screens were tested. The conservative ones required a very high probability of no loss along with moderate expectations, while the high-risk ones accepted significant chances of loss but required good chances of high gains.

Figure 11 shows the nature of the policies used for the test, illustrating the low-risk and high-risk policies. (Note that single-point determinate policies — not shown on the figure — were also included in the tests.) The investments available were varied, ranging from short-term to longer term payouts, with cash investment requirements sometimes extending into later years.* The simulation was repeated 500 times for each policy and each set of investments, and the financial results were calculated for each year of a fifteen-year period. The average of each financial result and its standard deviation was determined for each year and for the combination of the last five years of the runs.

GENERAL FINDINGS

Figure 12 shows the results of all the runs, plotted on a standard index basis, for the new investments selected. As can be seen, these results permit us to draw at least four general conclusions.

First, there is a wide gap in financial performance between some commonly used investment policies and those policies that lie on the efficiency frontier.

Second, risk-based policies consistently give better results than those using single-point, determinate decision rules. Using determinate decision rules, one cannot compensate for high risk by raising the level-of-return hurdle; single-point estimates produce, at best, half the return for a given degree of risk, no matter how the required return level is raised or lowered.

Third, long-term financial results are highly dependent on the risk accepted for a given return or on the return achieved for a given degree of risk. Thus, on the efficiency frontier, to get a long-term average of $6 per share, management would have to accept fluctuations on the order of 45 percent in two years out of three, whereas it could get only $3 if it decided to accept a probable fluctuation no greater than 10 percent.

Fourth, some investment criteria are empirically better than others. Whenever growth is a goal — that is, whenever results are measured on an earnings-per-share (EPS) basis — net present value (NPV) and internal rate of return (ROI-dcf), both of which are based on discounting future returns, are

*Note: On a single-point basis, the investments ranged from 1.9 years to 6.8 years for payback, and from 16.9 to 47.2 percent average annual return, and from 7.5 to 77 percent ROI-dcf (internal rate of return).

Criterion	Conservative policy			High-risk policy		
	90% probability of doing better than	Expected value better than	10% probability of doing better than	90% probability of doing better than	Expected value better than	10% probability of doing better than
1. Payback (years to recover investment)	7	5	—	10	4	2
2. Average annual proceeds/investment (percent)	15%	20%	—	-5%	15%	45%
3. ROI-dcf (percent)	10%	15%	—	-10%	10%	35%
4. NPV-dcf* Discount rate:						
10	1.0					
15		1.0			1.0	
45						1.0

Figure 11 Examples of investment policies (after tax)

*The indicated values are ratios of NPV of cash flow at the specified discount rates, divided by the present value of the investments.

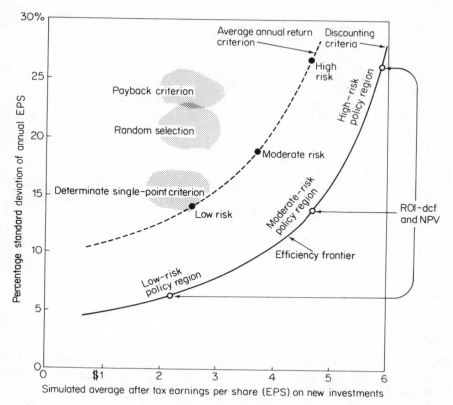

Figure 12 Investment policy simulation

superior to criteria, such as average annual return, which do not take the *time value of money* into account. At 25 percent annual standard deviation, for example — that is accepting one chance in three of the results falling outside ±25 percent of the expected values in any given year — the discounting criterion gives expected EPS of $5.50 while the non-discounted criterion gives $4.10, or 25 percent less.

(Policies that produce equivalent financial results for NPV and internal rate of return criteria can also be developed. That is, by specifying appropriate value for (a) the discount rate and (b) the probability of achieving a particular ratio of the NPV of the cash flow stream to the NPV of the investment, one can obtain exactly the same screen for investments as is provided by specific risk-based values of the internal rate of return criterion.)

Although payback period is still an extremely popular criterion (largely because it is seen as a useful liquidity measure), it turns out to be an extremely crude, inconsistent, and inefficient yardstick from the standpoint of actual financial results. Thus all the investments selected with payback criteria showed higher variances and lower returns than the others.

48

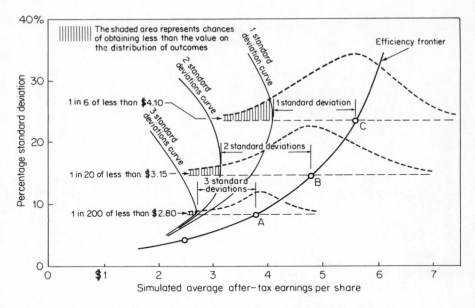

Figure 13 Determining risk boundaries on the efficiency frontier

A more general conclusion to be drawn from this simulation project is that the same approach can profitably be used by management to evaluate its past investments, to determine its efficiency frontier, and to select efficient investment policies that more accurately reflect its risk preferences.

Note that the results shown in Figure 12 are charted in terms of standard deviation — i.e. the vertical coordinate of any point on the chart represents the range of variation that may be expected two-thirds of the time in the results of a particular policy. If management is unwilling to accept one chance in six of results falling below this range, it will have to accept a lower average return.

How much lower depends, of course, on what odds are acceptable. If, for example, assurance is wanted that results will fall above a given boundary five-sixths of the time, one standard deviation must be subtracted from average earnings per share for each policy on the efficiency frontier, thereby creating a new curve inside the efficiency frontier as shown in Figure 13. Or, if management has a still more conservative attitude toward risk and wants a 19-to-1 probability of a given range of results — i.e. an assurance that results will fall below the range indicated for a given return only 1 time in 20 — two standard deviations may be subtracted, giving still another curve along which the returns offered by particular policies can be located.

Of significance here is the fact that different risk preferences, as exemplified by different risk boundaries, dictate different investment policy choices. Thus, in the situation illustrated by Figure 13, Policy C provides an expected return of $5.50 with a ± 25 percent standard deviation. Since these are typical Gaussian or Normal Distributions, we know that one standard deviation (25 percent × $5.50) subtracted from the mean will give a value — approximately $4.10 in this case — below which no more than one-sixth of the possible future values may be expected to fall. Two standard deviations subtracted would mean no more than a 1-in-20 chance of getting less than $2.70.

In the example, a *very* conservative management might wish to accept no more than a 1-in-200 risk. In this case, Policy A would offer the best return possible; all others would give less after subtracting three standard deviations. For a management inclined to moderate risk, however, Policy B is the best choice; it offers a 19-in-20 chance of getting $3.15 or better (see Baumol (2) for a similar approach).

Which risk boundary is used determines which investment policy is best; which boundary to select depends on management's willingness to assume risk. Moreover, the risk aversion inherent in any policy can be assessed by determining the risk boundary on which that policy gives better results than all others. The fewer standard deviations one must subtract to define a frontier on which a given policy is best, the greater is the indicated willingness to accept risk.

CONCLUSION

Investment policy simulation offers corporate management a strategic tool that will enable it to examine the risk consequences of various investment policies. As the methods reported here show, the development of a good investment policy involves four requirements:

1. The determination of risk profiles for all investments, using the risk analysis approach.
2. The use of a discounting measure (either discounted internal rate of return or preferably an equivalent net present value) for assessing the merit of an investment proposal.
3. The establishment of alternative screening rules for investment proposals.
4. The determination of risk boundaries for the alternative policies.

It should be clear that the same policy will not necessarily show the same risk characteristics (or risk boundaries) when used to screen different classes of investments. In one application, for example, a diversified chemical company found that the projects proposed by various divisions — overseas, heavy chemical, and so on — varied widely in their efficiency frontiers, and therefore entailed different risks for the same policies. Having decided what level of risk it wished to assume for each of the businesses, management was able to choose its policies accordingly.

Moreover, the company was able to determine the level of investment in each class of projects that would combine with investment levels and risks in other classes to maximize its chances of achieving its long-range growth goals. With the aid of simulation, it was able to establish ceilings and targets in the various investment classes and to describe in detail the screens or policies to be used to make choices in each of them. This enabled division management and staff personnel to understand management's objectives and to develop more appropriate and promising investment alternatives.

Using the same approach, other companies can now examine in detail the kind of investment opportunities generated by various segments of their businesses and select investment policies that will give them firmer control over their long-term growth. Top executives can analyze their own prejudices, develop understanding about uncertainty impacts, and test out the historical effects of inconsistent and irrational choices on their companies' long-term financial results. In short, top management can get back in the driver's seat, in charge of the most important element of the corporate future — effective investment for growth.

POTENTIAL IMPLEMENTATION OF THE
RISK ANALYSIS APPROACH

Outlining the philosophy and rationale of the approach and emphasizing its value in formulating strategy and managing strategic activity is not sufficient. It is necessary to look in detail at every feature of the approach, and assess the extent to which the approach holds up and appears to be valuable to management.

In subsequent chapters, we will consider such topics as measurement problems in the application of risk analysis, and examine alternative approaches for dealing with risk and uncertainty. For example, is it possible to develop guidelines for making probability assessments? Can such guidelines and procedures be tailored to existing information systems, or do such systems inhibit probabilistic-type thinking? In addition, can risk analysis approaches provide an answer for managers about the questions of the appropriate trade-off between risk and return? Can modern finance theory and theories of capital asset pricing help to provide better answers to questions of investment policy, such as how much higher a return a company should demand in order to compensate for a proportionately greater increase in volatility? In other words, should the focus of the policy be at the firm or corporate level rather than from the perspective of the individual decision-maker.

Further, there are a series of technical issues which must be investigated in relation to risk analysis. For example, what guidelines can be used in building financial models for projects, thereby sensibly accounting for possible correlation between the project's economic variables? Are there simpler and equally effective solution techniques other than risk simulation?

We address these risk analysis issues in detail in subsequent chapters, and provide a wide range of examples of practical applications of risk analysis. We also hope to provide an examination of the problems occurring in applications, as well as giving an appreciation of situations in which it has been successfully implemented. Such contexts include cash flow forecasting, and strategic portfolio analysis.

In order to reinforce the discussion in this chapter, two further case histories of risk analysis applications are presented in the following Appendix. The first example, Aztech Electronics, examines the 'first-pass' application of risk analysis simulation to project selection in electronics research and development. It gives an early insight into measurement difficulties that can occur in implementing the approach. The second example develops the strategy issues raised in the second half of the chapter, and ties risk analysis together with strategic planning under uncertainty in the context of oil exploration. It also shows the step-by-step detail of the construction of a model structure for the oil-exploration situation — a problem-structuring task which we believe is often the most creative, but difficult, phase of the risk analysis process. Above all, the second example seeks to demonstrate the role which risk analysis can play in relation to the management of uncertainty.

REFERENCES

1. Adelson, R. M., 'Criteria for Capital Investment: An Approach Through Decision Theory', *Operational Research Quarterly*, **16**, 1964, 19–50.
2. Baumol, W. J., 'An Expected Gain — Confidence Limit Criterion for Portfolio Selection', *Management Science*, October **1963**, 174.
3. Bennion, E. G., 'Capital Budgeting and Game Theory', *Harvard Business Review*, November/December **1956**, 125.
4. Bierman Jr., H., and Smidt, S., *The Capital Budgeting Decision*, Macmillan, New York, 4th edn., 1976.
5. Brown, R. V., Kahr, A. S., and Peterson, C. R., *Decision Analysis for the Manager*, Holt, Rinehart, Winston, New York, 1974.
6. Carter, E. E., 'What are the Risks in Risk Analysis', *Harvard Business Review*, July/August **1972**, 72–82.
7. Farrar, D. E., *The Investment Decision Under Uncertainty*, Prentice-Hall, Englewood Cliffs, NJ, 1962.
8. Grant, L. E., 'Monitoring Capital Investments', *Financial Executive*, April **1963**, 19.
9. Grayson Jr., C. J., 'Decisions Under Uncertainty: Drilling Decisions by Oil and Gas Operators', Division of Research, Harvard Business School, Boston, 1960.
10. Hammond III, J. S., 'Better Decisions Through Preference Theory', *Harvard Business Review*, November-December **1967**, 123–141.
11. Hess, S. W., and Quigley, H. A., 'Analysis of Risk in Investments Using the Monte-Carlo Technique', *Chemical Engineering Progress*, Symposium Series, **42**, American Institute of Chemical Engineering, 1963, p.55.
12. Hillier, F. S., The Evaluation of Risky Interrelated Investments, North-Holland Publishing, Amsterdam, 1969.
13. Hogarth, R. M., 'Cognitive Processes and the Assessment of Subjective Probability Distributions', *Jour. Amer. Stat. Assoc.*, **70**, No. 350, June 1975, 271–294.
14. Howard, R. A., 'Decision Analysis: Applied Decision Theory', Proceedings IFORS Conference, Boston, 1966.
15. Levy, H., and Sarnat, M., *Capital Investment and Financial Decisions*, Prentice-Hall, Englewood Cliffs, NJ, 1978.
16. MacCrimmon, K. R., and Taylor, R. N., 'Decision-Making and Problem-Solving', in M. D. Dunnette (ed.), *Handbook of Industrial and Organisational Psychology*, Rand-McNally, Chicago, 1976.

52

17. Markowitz, H. M., *Portfolio Selection, Efficient Diversification of Investments*, John Wiley, New York, 1959.
18. Merrett, A. J., and Sykes, A., *The Finance and Analysis of Capital Projects*, Longmans, London, 2nd edn., 1973.
19. Moore, P. G., and Thomas, H., *The Anatomy of Decisions*, Penguin Books, London, 1976.
20. Raiffa, H., *Decision Analysis*, Addison-Wesley, Reading, Mass., 1968.
21. Rappaport, A., 'Sensitivity Analysis for Decision-Making', *Accounting Review*, **XLII**, No. 3, July 1967, 441–56.
22. Sharpe, W. F., 'A Simplified Model for Portfolio Analysis', *Management Science*, January **1963**, 277.
23. Swalm, R. O., 'Utility Theory: Insights into Risk-Taking', *Harvard Business Review*, **44**, Nov/Dec 1966, 123–36.
24. Van Horne, J. C., *Financial Management and Policy*, 5th edn., Prentice-Hall, Englewood Cliffs, NJ, 1980.
25. Walker, R. G., 'The Judgement Factor in Investment Decisions', *Harvard Business Review*, Mar/April **1961**, 99.
26. Weston, J. F., and Brigham, E. E., *Managerial Finance*, 6th edn., The Dryden Press, Hinsdale, Ill., 1978.

Appendix

CASE (A): AZTECH ELECTRONICS

GENERAL COMMENTS

The Aztech case considers the process of assessing project worth in the context of the investment in research and development activity in the electronics industry. In the write-up two basic models are used.

(a) A Risk Analysis/Risk Simulation Model of the Hertz-type (Discussed Earlier in Chapter 2)

Based on subjective probability assessments from four senior managers (decision-makers) the risk simulation output is presented in terms of probability distributions for the NPV, IRR, and payback criteria.

The case shows the probability distributions derived from each manager's assessments in order to illustrate the consensus problems which arise in reconciling the separately produced decision criteria obtained from each individual. We could develop heuristics to deal with the consensus problem but as yet there is no practical theory. A consensus for a particular estimate is comparatively easier to obtain, as each individual can exchange and substantiate the information base used to form the estimate. Thus, in the project evaluation process, consensus estimates should be used as inputs into a decision criterion, rather than attempting to formulate a consensus of decision criteria. This latter point is extremely important in applications of risk analysis.

Further, the NPV, IRR, and payback output is presented only to demonstrate the versatility of the risk analysis approach. We would prefer in *all cases of practical implementation* to use NPV but we recognize that some appraisal procedures still use IRR and payback criteria.

(b) A Churchman–Ackoff Type of Multi-attributed Project Screen

To some extent this screening type of procedure is added as an alternative means of project appraisal which does not require formal financial analysis. Instead, the decision-maker ranks or screens the projects in terms of a number of attributes considered desirable by the firm. The rationale underlying such procedures is taken up in Chapter 3.

53

BACKGROUND TO AZTECH

Aztech Electronics is a comparatively large and well-established company with its principal activities in the micro-electronics industry. It is a subsidiary of an international electronics organization, but has considerable autonomy in its British operations.

The main reason for undertaking research and development work is defined by corporate management as being the need to provide the principal base on which the long-term growth of the company can be developed. In operational terms this implies that research and development work has to achieve a sufficient level of profitability to maintain the future growth of the firm out of internally generated funds. It is not surprising, therefore, that the research and development work in the firm is applied in nature and oriented towards the development of both new and existing products.

Research and development is organized on a departmental basis with a manager appointed to direct its operations. The links between the managing director, the head of R & D, and the heads of the various sub-departments within R & D are close, and weekly management meetings at which the R & D manager and sub-managers are present are held. There has always been a special relationship between the R & D manager and the managing director because of the strategic importance of R & D work to the firm. Their joint philosophy is basically that, without good R & D, they might as well go out of business. This philosophy is offensive rather than defensive; R & D is there to develop new areas of technical competence in advance of competitors.

The research and development manager controls a skilled research staff, whose overall size is about 7 per cent of the total employment of the firm in all functional areas. He has a number of senior project engineers directly under him who are responsible for the day-to-day operations of the various projects which make up the research department's portfolio of projects. The process by which project ideas are generated within the firm is unsystematic, the search process for new project ideas being delegated to all the project engineers and sales engineers. In fact most project ideas are generated from the research and development staff with a number of improvements in design, i.e. applied design projects being suggested by production engineers. Sales engineers often stumble upon untapped market demands and are responsible for putting firms who want a special instrument designed and made in touch with the R & D manager. A few ideas come also from other sub-departments in the company; but the major source is the R & D laboratory itself.

THE HANDLING OF NEW PROJECTS

The firm divides a new project idea once generated into four phases of research:

   (i) Investigation.
   (ii) Laboratory Prototype.

(iii) Production Prototype.

(iv) Pilot Run.

The investigation phase is the most interesting and is the one discussed in this case, because it is at this phase that decisions about possible adoption of projects are made. It comprises three more or less separate stages which can be described as follows:

(a) Preliminary Product Survey

In this stage a broad definition of the technical features of the project is required. In the light of this definition a list of possible technical approaches for the product is drawn up and critical technical areas are identified and evaluated. A preliminary evaluation of the market for the eventual product and its likely costs is also made. This preliminary survey is generally carried out by the engineer who put forward the initial idea.

(b) Detailed Design Study

This presupposes a satisfactory outcome for the preliminary study. The outcome of the initial study is reviewed at a meeting of the R & D manager with the senior project engineers. A detailed study of possible project designs is then carried out by teams of research and design engineers to ascertain the design which is most feasible in terms of overcoming major technical problems at a given cost level.

(c) Project Proposal

Stage (b) is an essential prerequisite for (c). In (c) a complete technical specification is prepared for the project and, where possible, preliminary circuit diagrams are provided. The specification is accompanied by a formal market estimate, i.e. an evaluation of economic factors and a time schedule for the development project.

This detailed project proposal is most often carried out by a senior project engineer who coordinates the opinions of the project initiator and the research and design teams employed on the project.

THE SECOND STAGE OF EVALUATION

Once this initial review has been carried out by the project initiator, the project idea is passed on to the research manager for action. He generally convenes a meeting of his senior project engineers to evaluate the areas in which greater information about the feasibility of the project is needed. Once the areas are defined, a working party of research and design engineers is set up to evaluate the project in detail and this team is encouraged to maintain close liaison with

56

the marketing, sales, production, and financial areas of the firm. The process of reviewing projects occurs regularly in the R & D department, and projects are formally reviewed as and when they are generated. One of the main elements of the formal review is the judgement of the potential worth of a proposed development in terms of financial criteria, such as the likely return on the R & D investment. The calculation of such criteria is not regarded as being the sole basis on which the decision to adopt a particular project is made. Occasionally overriding technical or other reasons influence decisions and alter the weighting given to financial evaluations. Nevertheless, financial criteria are given the greatest importance by the research and development manager in his project selection decision.

THE CONSIDERATION OF TEN PROJECTS

Following the above principles, ten projects had recently come up for evaluation. Four senior project engineers made their separate assessments on whether each of these projects was worth investing in.

Project 1

One of a projected family of instruments for electronic measurement. The objective of pursuing the concept of the family of instruments was a result of a company plan to produce a range of test instruments in an area not previously exploited by the company. Market potential was considered by the company to be considerable and the expertise was available within the research and development laboratory to carry out the work.

Project 2

A complementary instrument to Project 1 produced to extend the product line.

Project 3

The final member of the first phase of a series of instruments defined by Projects 1, 2, and 3. The latter was produced to provide a complete measurement system for the customer and to provide training for existing engineers in the technical area before the launching of the second phase of this system of instruments. Again, market potential for the system was estimated to be considerable.

Project 4

A measurement instrument sponsored and planned by the laboratory management to follow on and replace an existing instrument. The modifications were designed to improve the capability and performance of the device. The market potential was thought to be large.

Project 5

A re-design of an existing instrument for a specific customer. The request for the research to be done emanated from the sales division who considered that the market offered was profitable to the company.

Project 6

An instrument specifically planned by the laboratory management to place the firm in a new area of electronic measurement. Again, the market was considered to be very large and the measurement area one with great long-term potential. As a result the project was felt to be a learning exercise to some extent as well as a profitable venture for the company and its technical staff.

Project 7

An electronic measurement instrument designed to meet known existing demand. Again a family of instruments was planned and in this case it is considered reasonable to view them as one, rather than three distinct projects. The idea for the project was generated within the laboratory.

Project 8

An instrument designed and planned to be used as a complementary instrument to an existing successful product marketed by the firm. The market for the instrument was thus considered to be steady but not great.

Project 9

An instrument designed as a result of technical 'fall-out' from the series of Projects 1 to 3. Considered to have a useful market potential and overall benefit for the firm.

Project 10

An instrument designed specifically to a special contract from a customer. Sales department considered the development would be extremely profitable for the firm, and the laboratory regarded the development work as being a fairly simple task.

THE EVALUATION OF THE PROJECTS

As a first stage in the project evaluation, an analysis on a purely financial basis was carried out. The simulation approach was adopted since distributions of the internal rates of return (IRR) could easily be obtained in addition to those of net present value (NPV). A structural flow chart for the procedure is shown in Figure 1. Net cash flows per period were assumed to be independent and assessed as Normal probability distributions. Each of the four decision-makers made assessments under various assumptions of the project's life. Tables 1, 2, 3, and 4 summarize the financial assessments obtained from each decision-maker. It will be noted that the four decision-makers did not make assessments of all the projects concerned.

However, for reasons mentioned earlier, such a purely financial analysis was considered too narrow in view of the other objectives which the company set for its research and development programs. The complete set of objectives that were considered relevant by Aztech were as follows:

  (i) Profitability.
 (ii) Growth and diversity of the product line.
(iii) Offensive research mounted to anticipate competition.
(iv) Increased market share.
 (v) Maintained technical capability.
(vi) Increase in firm's reputation and image.
(vii) Provision of interesting research work to maintain engineer creativity.

A practical way of dealing with these objectives is via the Churchman–Ackoff model, the basis of which is described in the Appendix. Each decision-maker is asked to give the projects some weight (between 0 and 1) according to the extent to which it satisfies each of the seven objectives given above. He is also required to give a weight (again between 0 and 1) to each of the seven objectives, assessing its importance and subject to the restriction that the sum of the weights for all the seven objectives must be 1. A weighted objective score is obtained as described in the Appendix, and these scores for the ten projects, over the seven objectives, from each of the four decision-makers, are summarized in Table 5. Table 6 gives the decision-makers' consensus estimates of the costs anticipated for each project.

As there were no immediate capital-rationing constraints, the primary problem was not to determine which of the projects should be undertaken, but to assess the worth of each project as a R & D investment. Aztech's process of project evaluation had left them with the task of reconciling on the one hand the alternative approaches to assessing project worth and on the other hand the differing views of the four senior project engineers.

ISSUES FOR DISCUSSION

(1) Which of the ten projects discussed should be accepted? Which of the financial criteria discussed (i.e. NPV, IRR, payback) are appropriate for decision-making in this context?

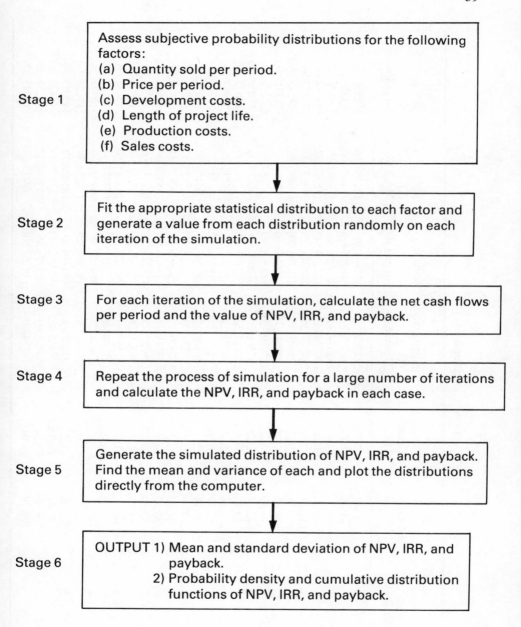

Figure 1 The risk simulation program

Table 1 Decision-Maker 1

Project	Length of life (years)	IRR (%) Mean (SD)	Payback (Years) Mean (SD)	NPV at 10% (£) Mean (SD)	NPV at 15% (£) Mean (SD)	NPV at 20% (£) Mean (SD)	NPV at 25% (£) Mean (SD)
1	7	126.40 (3.95)	2.53 (0.04)	224750.25 (7735.27)	177891.06 (6273.63)	142163.16 (5183.60)	114536.31 (4320.83)
2	4	—	1.70 (0.08)	241574.81 (207515.5)	204928.81 (18364.87)	174653.19 (16398.62)	149435.62 (14734.66)
2	5	140.23 (12.68)	1.68 (0.07)	287407.25 (21601.30)	241748.12 (18795.00)	204526.37 (16795.46)	173893.94 (14393.09)
2	6	138.82 (13.31)	1.70 (0.08)	307244.75 (21980.25)	256668.00 (19343.36)	215831.25 (17182.66)	182512.06 (15371.20)
3	7	242.27 (8.50)	2.25 (0.02)	847168.69 (27414.72)	679080.06 (22103.64)	550615.00 (13148.94)	451069.50 (15077.94)
4	7	61.18 (3.37)	3.40 (0.09)	30023.27 (1573.22)	22404.97 (1321.43)	16711.98 (1119.31)	12407.14 (964.13)
5	5	79.19 (3.98)	2.70 (0.05)	103578.75 (7232.00)	82895.75 (6128.98)	66458.50 (5225.32)	53278.18 (4489.47)
5	6	85.92 (3.63)	2.72 (0.08)	143929.81 (7545.21)	114851.12 (6303.92)	90930.81 (5358.06)	72630.19 (4592.86)
5	7	92.30 (3.33)	2.72 (0.08)	196037.75 (8536.27)	153748.25 (6994.76)	121417.06 (5839.66)	96383.62 (4939.21)
8	3	>500	1.07 (0.01)	332566.69 (21526.84)	298725.56 (19312.31)	269625.50 (17424.93)	244434.06 (15827.29)
8	4	>500	1.07 (0.01)	442844.25 (24098.02)	390890.56 (21349.54)	347231.00 (14034.38)	310231.25 (17125.23)
10	3	506.50 (31.47)	1.21 (0.02)	207502.81 (8913.48)	183480.50 (8002.81)	163081.12 (7171.43)	145635.50 (6435.10)
10	4	526.50 (22.72)	1.21 (0.01)	350226.00 (12544.0)	302973.31 (10752.00)	263977.62 (9413.00)	231254.50 (8245.32)

Table 2 Decision-Maker 2

Project	Length of life (years)	IRR (%) Mean (SD)	Payback (Years) Mean (SD)	NPV at 10% (£) Mean (SD)	NPV at 15% (£) Mean (SD)	NPV at 20% (£) Mean (SD)	NPV at 25% (£) Mean (SD)
2	3	41·62 (15·34)	2·06 (0·23)	26018·14 (12486·37)	19787·99 (11304·25)	14579·86 (10286·72)	10202·60 (9404·92)
2	4	77·60 (13·53)	1·99 (0·15)	79432·81 (15143·40)	65463·97 (13451·82)	53921·07 (12035·66)	44312·50 (10837·70)
2	5	90·38 (11·73)	2·00 (0·15)	126438·06 (16084·64)	103774·00 (14105·86)	85424·94 (12485·58)	70432·00 (11142·25)
2	6	97·86 (11·77)	1·99 (0·15)	172256·19 (19827·09)	139829·06 (17093·75)	114128·62 (14897·57)	93528·50 (13122·81)
2	7	36·97 (1·89)	4·35 (0·09)	96308·12 (7548·20)	64575·75 (5944·60)	41542·98 (4777·04)	24644·39 (3917·91)
3	7	233·75 (6·65)	2·28 (0·02)	782198·87 (27117·88)	627294·50 (21951·91)	508785·87 (18074·76)	416867·19 (15077·94)
4	7	178·46 (8·05)	2·43 (0·03)	129682·19 (4132·34)	103423·44 (3349·47)	83377·06 (2793·66)	67863·94 (2343·66)
5	7	92·35 (3·34)	2·65 (0·08)	227217·06 (8804·82)	177733·19 (7248·40)	140046·27 (6084·37)	110968·37 (5158·25)

Table 3 Decision-Maker 3

Project	Length of life (years)	IRR (%) Mean (SD)	Payback (Years) Mean (SD)	NPV at 10% (£) Mean (SD)	NPV at 15% (£) Mean (SD)	NPV at 20% (£) Mean (SD)	NPV at 25% (£) Mean (SD)
6	4	40.59 (16.93)	3.03 (0.32)	177776.81 (102635.19)	131073.44 (88110.25)	93835.56 (76202.87)	63949.38 (66354.44)
6	5	56.92 (10.78)	3.00 (0.26)	361974.50 (89755.25)	278682.62 (76475.44)	213245.81 (65711.44)	161390.37 (56898.52)
6	6	64.11 (10.03)	2.97 (0.27)	525625.25 (106396.25)	404049.44 (89080.62)	310412.00 (75410.12)	237517.19 (64440.73)
6	7	67.18 (9.69)	3.01 (0.28)	671624.62 (125638.06)	510521.87 (103083.12)	389032.50 (85735.60)	296221.06 (72133.37)
6	8	101.44 (5.49)	2.59 (0.12)	149818.00 (89117.37)	1157742.00 (72675.12)	903978.00 (60124.58)	711898.00 (50450.84)

(2) If there were a financial constraint of £50,000 on the amount that Aztech could spend on R & D, would the selection problem be altered? If so, in what respects?

(3) Has Aztech's process of project evaluation introduced decision-making problems which would be avoided with an alternative project review structure?

(4) How would you allow for risk in the selection of projects, either with or without a financial constraint?

APPENDIX   CHURCHMAN–ACKOFF MODEL FOR MULTI-DIMENSIONAL OBJECTIVES

The following is a concise description of the Churchman–Ackoff model for evaluating a set of projects on a basis of multiple objectives.

1. Suppose that, at some moment in time, the decision-maker assigns a relevant set of objectives $(O_1 \ldots , O_n)$ for his decision problem.

2. Suppose also that he has a number of alternative research projects $(R_1 \ldots , R_k)$ which need to be evaluated.

3. The decision-maker then constructs a $(k \times n)$ matrix with alternative projects as rows and objectives as columns.

	O_1	$\ldots$	O_n
Weights	W_1	$\ldots$	W_n

R_1 $\ldots$

. $\ldots$ $= (M)$

. $\ldots$

. $\ldots$

R_k $\ldots$

4. The cells in the matrix are assigned values between 0 and 1 according to the extent to which each R_i satisfies each of the objectives.

5. The decision-maker is also asked to estimate a positive weight W_i to each objective subject to the restriction that

$$\sum_{i=1}^{n} W_i = 1$$

in order to establish the priority between objectives. Let W be the $(n \times 1)$ column vector of weights.

6. A weighted objective score is then calculated for each project R_i by obtaining the $(k \times 1)$ column vector S by matrix multiplication, i.e.

$$S = M \times W$$
$$(k \times 1) = (k \times n)(n \times 1)$$

This weighted objective score is the criterion by which preliminary project decisions should be made.

Readers are referred to C. W. Churchman, *Introduction to Operations Research*, Wiley, 1951, for fuller details of this multidimensional model.

Table 4 Decision-Maker 4

Project	Length of life (years)	IRR (%) Mean (SD)	Payback (Years) Mean (SD)	NPV at 10% (£) Mean (SD)	NPV at 15% (£) Mean (SD)	NPV at 20% (£) Mean (SD)	NPV at 25% (£) Mean (SD)
2 (run 1)*	3	-4.08 (18.14)	2.87 (0.16)	-11219.93 (14719.70)	-14719.54 (12968.23)	-16259.61 (11495.42)	-18394.79 (10247.88)
2 (run 2)	3	-2.20 (5.91)	2.96 (0.07)	-11040.69 (5422.57)	-14022.69 (4437.91)	-16391.54 (4523.93)	-18272.62 (4167.37)
2 (run 1)*	4	12.37 (11.74)	3.22 (0.5)	3014.63 (12825.58)	-2198.90 (11289.07)	-6387.83 (10000.25)	-9714.16 (8911.28)
2 (run 2)	4	12.63 (4.99)	3.14 (0.24)	2894.92 (5373.44)	-2364.92 (5170.44)	-6513.96 (4372.76)	-9843.42 (4018.66)
2 (run 1)*	5	15.13 (11.10)	3.49 (0.74)	6497.69 (13557.10)	404.28 (11893.68)	-4419.11 (10502.84)	-8256.21 (9330.85)
2 (run2)	5	16.96 (4.81)	3.23 (0.28)	943.49 (5118.80)	-4114.52 (4579.48)	-8148.22 (4126.45)	-11376.18 (3742.35)
6	5	105.30 (6.65)	2.57 (0.07)	881574.37 (81321.00)	713935.87 (67848.69)	581270.87 (57180.34)	475253.94 (48656.84)
6	6	107.89 (5.92)	2.58 (0.07)	1036561.37 (79089.06)	832361.12 (65442.43)	672758.25 (54782.20)	546645.44 (46323.98)

6	7	107.94	2.58	1109396.00	884228.44	710084.44	573755.25
		(6.62)	(0.07)	(92040.44)	(76304.69)	(63947.75)	(54106.92)
7	3	4.07	2.88	−5680.40	−9542.51	−12639.83	−15127.84
		(7.68)	(0.12)	(7785.22)	(6672.34)	(5988.22)	(5408.16)
7	5	28.26	2.91	47110.27	33957.37	23515.70	15162.16
		(5.80)	(0.17)	(9928.05)	(8625.91)	(7563.82)	(6688.96)
7	6	27.49	3.28	31532.95	19676.25	10373.49	3026.40
		(5.44)	(0.20)	(9708.32)	(8494.93)	(7500.94)	(6678.80)
10	3	26.74	2.53	12655.69	7652.96	3547.03	161.34
		(14.67)	(0.20)	(10654.57)	(9902.01)	(9256.92)	(8698.27)
10	4	54.30	2.51	50789.48	39636.50	30578.67	23169.31
		(14.70)	(0.18)	(11301.14)	(10354.18)	(9572.68)	(8918.00)
10	5	61.31	2.51	70762.37	55647.80	43543.93	23766.78
		(12.29)	(0.18)	(10233.80)	(9288.67)	(8527.65)	(7904.26)

*The table gives for project 2 the simulation results from two runs of the same model. This provides some guidelines for the accuracy of the results from simulation experiments.

Notes on Tables 1 to 4
(a) SD = standard deviation.
(b) IRR = internal rate of return.
(c) NPV = net present value.

Table 5 Project Scores over Seven Objectives

Project	*DM 1 Score	Rank	DM 2 Score	Rank	DM 3 Score	Rank	DM 4 Score	Rank
1	28.34	5 =	42.59	2	30.40	5	39.68	4 =
2	23.51	7	31.03	7	35.15	3	19.93	8
3	38.91	2	35.34	4	37.31	2	41.85	3
4	18.35	8	32.14	6	—		57.54	2
5	28.34	5 =	39.64	3	—		39.68	4 =
6	31.20	4	28.88	8	31.62	4	38.28	6
7	—		12.29	10	40.11	1	16.26	9
8	44.57	1	44.25	1	—		58.60	1
9	—		34.97	5	23.09	6	—	
10	35.95	3	23.51	9	—		24.92	7

*DM = Decision-maker. Scores expressed as percentages.

Table 6 Estimated Costs for Each Project

Project	1	2	3	4	5	6	7	8	9	10
Cost (£0000)	2.76	2.74	2.72	1.05	0.7	3.66	1.11	1.53	2.54	3.77

NOTES ON THE ANALYSIS

(1) On the purely financial analysis, the decision-makers would accept all ten projects except for the specific case of decision-maker 4 who would reject project 2.

(2) As the financial analysis was carried out first, its results would have been used in the Churchman–Ackoff score. Specifically, the score for each project on objective 1 ('To ensure profitability') would rationally be based upon the financial analysis. Hence the C–A score embeds the financial analysis.

(3) Aztech's project evaluation process leads inevitably to a consensus problem in reconciling the separately produced decision criteria obtained from each individual. As noted earlier a consensus on particular estimates (e.g. costs, sales, etc.) is comparatively easier to obtain as each individual can exchange and substantiate the information base he used to form the estimate. Thus, in the project evaluation process, consensus estimates should be used as inputs into a decision criterion, rather than attempting to formulate a consensus of decision criteria.

Table 7

Project	Total ranking	Average ranking	Aggregate rank
1	17	4.25	3
2	25	6.25	8
3	11	2.75	2
4	16	5.33	5
5	13	4.33	4
6	22	5.50	6 =
7	20	6.66	10
8	3	1.00	1
9	11	5.50	6 =
10	19	6.33	9

Table 8

Projects in rank order	8	3	(1)	5
Cumulative cost	15.3	42.5	(>50)	49.5

(4) If we attach equal weight to each of the 4 decision-makers in aggregating the C–A scores, we obtain aggregate ranks for the projects as in Table 7. Assigning the projects in value order up to the £50,000 constraint indicates that projects 8, 3 and 5 should be selected (see Table 8).

CASE (B) STRATEGIES FOR OIL EXPLORATION

THE MANAGEMENT OF UNCERTAINTY

The future is always uncertain. The results of critical decisions in exploration often hinged on the values of extremely wide-ranging variables. However, this very uncertainty provides the challenge to build new and profitable reserves through taking risks. But uncertainty brings on real costs as well as potential profits. While the problem of risk cannot be eliminated, it can be attacked through systematic analysis of the uncertainties surrounding potential reserves, their costs and profitability and the range of outcomes of alternative strategies of exploration.

This case is concerned with the uncertainties and risks of exploration and how they can be managed to improve the profitability of exploration.

1 STRATEGIC PLANNING IN EXPLORATION

To gain perspective on the planning problem under uncertainty, it will be useful to review its meaning and to deal with an example. This case, therefore:

(1) Outlines briefly the need for and nature of planning uncertainty
(2) Suggests an example in oil exploration.

A Concept of Strategy for Exploration

The purpose of corporate planning is to coordinate and focus company resources on attractive opportunities for further growth and profitability, by capitalizing on the skills and other resources available. The corporate operating plan is expressed in a strategy for each of the major operating functions, defining their relative longer term roles in the company as a whole. The five major United States international petroleum companies have seen their opportunities quite differently over the last several years, and have therefore followed quite different strategies. This is readily apparent from the very different concentrations of fixed assets and the rates of asset growth in the various functional areas for these companies (Exhibit I).

Such operating strategies should be based on careful analysis of economic factors, existing skills and potential future opportunities. The particular role that exploration in an oil company, for example, will play should reflect:

1. The need for crude and natural gas reserves by the corporation.
2. The availability of these reserves from outside sources at an attractive price.
3. Opportunities for exploration available to the company, and expected success of possible exploratory activities.
4. Resources (e.g. geologists, etc.) for carrying out exploration activities.
5. Competing demands for risk capital in the other functional areas.

The strategic plan should specify a course of action for a function that will contribute in a significant way to the realization of the corporation's objectives. The plan should give focus and direction not only to the broad aspects of activities, but also, in the context of overall opportunities, to shorter term situations (such as a lease sale in which there are choices of blocks for which to bid).

Selecting a Strategy

A strategy is thus a portfolio of opportunities selected on the basis of certain

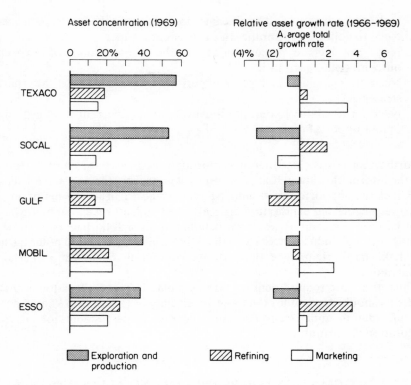

Exhibit I Major US oil companies follow different functional strategies

qualifying criteria for each individual opportunity. It is implicit in the strategic planning process that not all combinations thus defined are equally desirable. Alternative strategies should be evaluated on the basis of:

1. Feasibility (e.g. are resources available?).
2. Contribution to objectives (e.g. do expected returns and ratios meet objectives?).
3. Risk (e.g. what are the chances of not meeting desired goals?).

The final choice of opportunities should balance these considerations.

Making such a choice is complicated by the seemingly large number of combinations of options available, and by the difficulty of properly evaluating and dealing with the risk aspects of each combination.

Key Requirements for Strategic Planning

To be effective in defining a strategy, the planning process should reflect the key requirements for each function. These requirements can be summarized as follows:

1. Need for inclusion of all significant opportunities in the selection process.
2. Need to define opportunities in a consistent manner.
3. Need to include uncertainties in the presentation of expected outcomes of opportunities.
4. Need to recognize and present performance tradeoffs of alternative strategies.
5. Need for flexibility to permit rapid evaluation of current strategy in light of new opportunities.

Furthermore, it is clear that as exploration progresses for an opportunity, and the information about that opportunity is improved, the decision to include or reject that opportunity should be reanalyzed in order to maintain the priorities underlying exploration programs and budgets on a systematic basis. That is, if an opportunity not now included in a portfolio begins to show — perhaps through industry activity — that it has considerably more potential and less risk than originally estimated, its continuing exclusion is certainly unwarranted.

Thus, the basic requirement for strategic planning in exploration is that it explicitly should account for the basic uncertainty or lack of firm knowledge in the information underlying economic and reserve assessments of different exploration opportunities.

2 INFORMATION FOR PLANNING AND ALLOCATION

The purpose of exploration is to identify the presence and magnitude of previously untested additional reserves suited for development and production. In general, this is a problem of improving the information about an area, and continually evaluating it as to what it promises in terms of future reserves. The basic information largely is geological and geophysical. It is translated into economic terms for evaluation and planning through a specific exploration program. The program outlines the timing and magnitude of an exploration effort deemed necessary to pursue the opportunity (Exhibit II). For strategic planning and resource allocation purposes, the large amount of information describing an opportunity can be characterized by three key attributes: risk capital required, potential reserves, and expected profit. Estimates of these attributes are always uncertain to a degree that depends on the completeness and quality of the information upon which they are based.

Uncertainty and Probabilistic Representation

Many complex considerations enter into the geological and economic assessments of an exploration opportunuity. Attempts to identify all directly

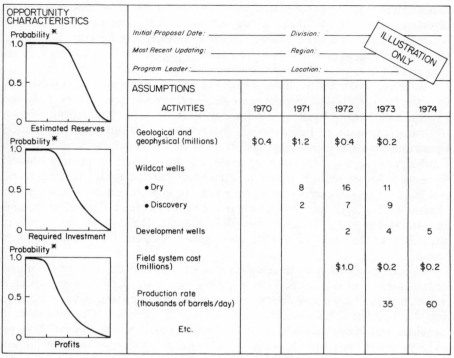

Exhibit II Exploration program summary

measurable parameters relevant to such assessments and to correlate them statistically through regression analysis, for example, in order to predict the outcome of an exploration program, have been attempted on several occasions but have known little success. The estimates underlying an exploration program are still always subjective in nature. That is, they represent a professional explorationist's interpretation of available data on a given piece of untested acreage.

Since available data is always incomplete — it becomes complete only when the exploration program is complete and the presence of hydrocarbon deposits has been proven or disproven — these subjective estimates of the value and resource requirements of an exploration opportunity necessarily are uncertain. In fact, the degree of uncertainty is related directly to the quality and completeness of the available data. And, clearly, knowledge of the uncertainties underlying the estimates he uses is crucial information for the decision-maker. Thus, two opportunities having the same 'best (subjective) estimate' values for future potential and profitability are not equivalent if one has a much wider range of possible results than the other — i.e. if the uncertainties surrounding the best estimates are very different. The decision-maker ordinarily does not and probably should not have the detailed data at hand when he chooses between alternative opportunities. But he must be able to differentiate between opportunities not only on the basis of their expected outcomes, but also on the uncertainties surrounding these outcomes.

Traditional quantitative analyses have not provided adequate representations of uncertainty. Risk, if evaluated at all, typically has represented only the expected chance of success or failure in drilling wells, based primarily on historical experience. Estimates of characteristic attributes of exploration opportunities are typically single-point, 'best guess' estimates. In addition, the estimator sometimes discounts estimates for uncertainty to protect himself from an unfavorable later outcome. Analyses based on such information are not likely to be satisfactory in the long run. To improve on analytical results, sensitivity analysis is used frequently to evaluate the effect of possible changes in estimated inputs. This approach, while helpful, does not, however, reflect the effects of the whole range of uncertainties associated with every estimated value.

Explicit recognition of uncertainty can be attained through probabilistic representation of estimates. That is, rather than estimating only an expected value, a probability density (or cumulative distribution) function is estimated for the key variables entering into an overall estimate. This distribution provides a portrayal of the *specific probabilities* that the variable will take on over values in its range. In such an estimate, the shape of the distribution reveals the quality of the information on which the estimate is based — the more good information that is available, the less spread (or uncertainty) the estimate will possess.

Exhibit III demonstrates this relationship. The exhibit presents estimates of

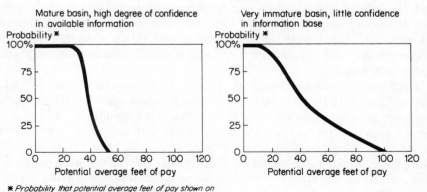

ESTIMATED AVERAGE FEET OF PAY

* *Probability that potential average feet of pay shown on horizontal axis will be equalled or exceeded.*

Exhibit III The level of information is directly reflected in the 'spread' of the estimated profile

average reservoir thickness — in feet of pay — for two basins. (The estimates were obtained as part of the input required to develop estimates of future hydrocarbon potential for these basins.) One is a very mature basin, the largest part of which has been explored in detail, and the basin possesses significant production. Based on this experience, explorationists are confident in estimating an average, expected reservoir thickness of about 40 feet. This confidence is reflected in the fact that they are 90 percent certain that pay thickness will exceed 30 feet, while they see only a 10 percent chance that it will exceed 50 feet. The steep cumulative distribution function over this range demonstrates this confidence. The other, however, is a very immature basin with no existing production and little factual information available as to pay thickness of its potential reservoirs. The cumulative distribution function of estimated average pay thickness correspondingly is flat over the relatively wide range of 10 to 100 feet.

Analytic handling of probabilistic information poses no real problems on present-day computers. The conceptual problems in dealing with probabilistic information are more serious. They are largely a matter of education and training. Estimation and interpretation of probabilities can, however, be made easier through careful structuring of the estimation task.

Models that provide such structures for estimating the characteristic attributes of an exploration opportunity have been developed and, in the case of estimating potential reserves, successfully tested.

Estimating Potential Reserves

The key attribute characterizing an exploration opportunity is its estimated potential reserve. This single attribute underlies all other considerations relating to an opportunity. Estimating potential reserves is, therefore, the starting point for assessing an opportunity.

The approach taken to assessment of basin potential was to identify the major informational building blocks which formed the basis of an estimate of future reserves. Probabilistic estimates were then defined for a variable representing the synthesis of all geologic, geophysical, and experimental data contributing to each of these information areas. The estimates were combined by means of a computerized Monte Carlo simulation to arrive at a probabilistic estimate of a basin's future hydrocarbon potential.* The resulting estimate is developed as a cumulative distribution of future potential.

A flow chart of the basin evaluation model is shown in Exhibit IV. The model requires the estimate of seven inputs, six of them probabilistic. One factor requires only a single point estimate. The questionnaire used in the data collection procedure is attached as Appendix A. Exhibit V shows sample basin potential input estimates, and Exhibit VI presents a sample of the resulting future hydrocarbon potential profile.

---

*Natural gas and gas liquid reserves are converted to BOE on an equivalent value basis to yield BOE reserves.

The potential reserve model can be used for any size exploration opportunity. The estimation logic and procedures developed for basin evaluation that the model incorporates can be applied equally well to a specific opportunity.

Estimating Economic Attributes of an Opportunity

Based on the estimate of potential hydrocarbon reserves for an exploration opportunity, an estimate can be made of the risk capital requirements necessary to find this potential, and of its economic value if found. These estimates usually are based on a specific exploration, development, and production program keyed to the discovery of the estimated potential.

The economic evaluations of such programs are not new. Much effort has gone into developing methods for assessing economics of new opportunities. However, the presently available tools for such evaluations are not necessarily geared to the problems of strategic planning and allocation. The most frequently used evaluation model is structured along accounting lines. Though, in general, this structure is not incorrect, the model relies on inputs that are 'necessary for economic success' (e.g. 500 million BOE for international offshore opportunities) and seldom includes more than a very crude subjective assessment of the likelihood of such reserves occurring. In addition, this economic evaluation relies on historically based unit finding and development costs. In many situations, these costs do not reflect local geological and environmental conditions, which may make their use for all opportunities questionable. And, of course, this evaluation method is not based on probabilistic information, and thus does not reflect explicitly the relative uncertainties underlying different opportunities. Corporate planning and evaluation staff have recognized these problems, but have not been able to deal with them effectively.

A Risk Analysis Model would utilize geologically based reserve estimates and a fairly detailed exploration program as the basis for evaluating risk capital requirements and payoffs of an opportunity. A shortcoming of the R/A approach for strategic planning purposes is its operational complexity. Highly detailed data outputs from a study of an opportunity are required prior to its evaluation using the Risk Analysis Model. And this level of input information required is typically not available for many opportunities in their early stages, especially in the international area. Using the R/A approach is not likely to be feasible for the development of an exploration strategy where many opportunities must be evaluated and compared — frequently with little information.

A more useful approach to economic evaluation would be one that combines the probabilistic nature and geologic realism of the R/A model with the ease of manipulation and relatively smaller information requirements of the accounting-type model now used by the planning groups. Exhibit VII presents

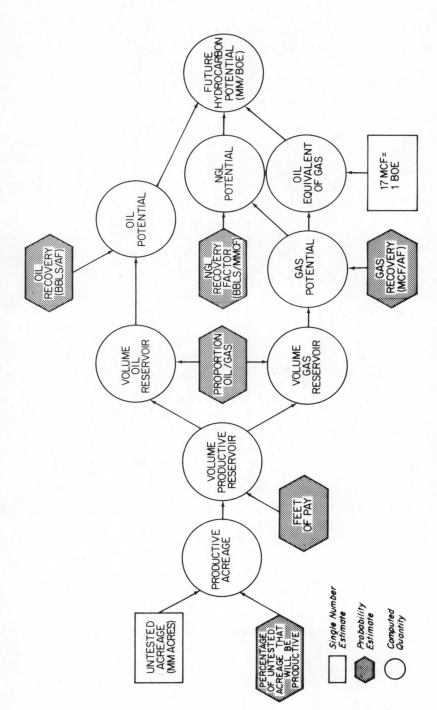

Exhibit IV Final flow chart basin evaluation model

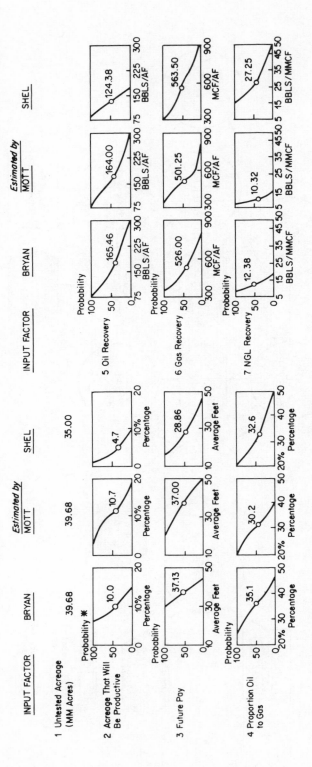

Exhibit V Basin potential input estimates

o Represents the expected value of the input variable

* All probabilities represent the probability that numbers on the horizontal axes will be equalled or exceeded.

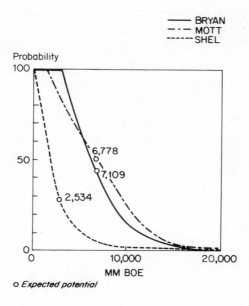

Exhibit VI Future hydrocarbon potential
profile

an economic estimation model in flow chart form that possesses these
characteristics. The model requires input estimates for:

1. Geological and geophysical expenditures, timed over the life of the
    exploration play.
2. The number of wildcat wells that are to be drilled, and their timing.
3. The well cost for wildcatting.
4. Average expected reservoir depth.
5. Expected land costs (bonus plus rentals).
6. The most likely field production pattern to be used.
7. Initial well productivity that can be expected.
8. The well cost for development drilling.
9. Average field production system costs.
10. The unit well-head value of hydrocarbons.
11. Unit operating costs for production.
12. The expected government share of revenue.

In addition, the model assumes the availability of a probabilistic estimate of
future potential, such as the profile obtained from the Reserve Estimation
Model.

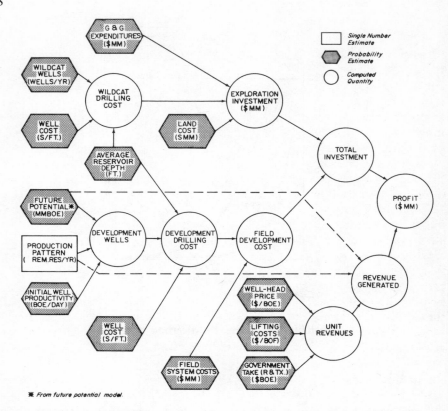

Exhibit VII Flow chart. Proposed economic evaluation model

The application of the model results in probabilistic profiles for risk investment and profitability* of an opportunity. Inputs to the model will reflect directly a specific exploration program for the opportunity. Estimates useful for evaluation can be derived even if only a general and very informal exploration program exists. To operate the model will require coordination between explorationists who furnish the geologic base information and planners who must estimate the financial characteristics. A suggested questionnaire for data collection is attached as Appendix B.

This model can be implemented directly since it is based almost exclusively on information presently being utilized for economic evaluation. The next section puts these estimates into a framework for the selection of combinations of sets of opportunities to form an exploration strategy.

_____

*Profitability may be measured directly as gross profit accumulated over some time horizon (e.g. 5 or 10 years), or it may be expressed as dollar-per-dollar return — the ratio of gross profit to investment, discounted ROI, or DCF rate of return. The necessary modifications are simple technical accounting changes.

3 DEVELOPING A STRATEGY

Strategic decision-making can be improved by the use of consistent quantifications of an exploration opportunity's geologic and economic attributes that convey not only the expected values of the attributes, but also the associated uncertainty. For the first time, the risks involved and benefits obtainable in tradeoff decisions between opportunities are made explicit. And the decision-maker can attain, given his own preference for risk, a rational balance for the exploration portfolio.

Making risk-based tradeoffs does, however, require a carefully structured process for developing strategies. Since alternative strategies simply are different combinations of exploration opportunities, these combinations should be defined in a way that reflects correctly the uncertainties characterizing their component opportunities. Furthermore, the representation of a strategy should be flexible enough to allow evaluation along several related dimensions as exploration objectives change. For example, whether the decision-maker's interest is focused on the total expected profit a strategy promises to generate over some number of years, or on the expected hydrocarbon reserves found, will depend on specific corporate concerns at the time of evaluation. The first step in formulating a strategy then is to find a representation of it that contains those uncertainty characteristics of the constituent opportunities most relevant for evaluation and selection of a 'suitable' strategy.

The selection process itself should reflect explicitly the conflicting goals of reserves or profits versus required investment. It must allow for clear and rapid assessment of the impact of specifying alternative risk acceptance levels that may be desired for a strategy and/or of alternative levels of risk capital that may be available. Only if the decision-maker can test the effects of changing such constraints, can the process aid him in selecting the most appropriate strategy.

Formulating Strategies

The starting point for developing a strategy is the set of all exploration opportunities available. Alternative strategies are formed by selecting different combinations of opportunities from this set. Each resulting strategy, in reflecting its constituent opportunities, will have its own unique attributes — i.e. expected reserves, expected profit, risk investment requirements and the uncertainties associated with these.

The Set of Opportunities

At any point in time, as many as 200 (untested) exploration opportunities around the world may be recognized by a company. Each of these represents an area about which a qualified indiviual or group of individuals in the company has some information leading to the belief that the area may possess significant hydrocarbon potential. The opportunity may represent a completely new area for the company's exploration effort — e.g. the Gulf of Thailand — or it may be only a new target in a relatively mature exploration area — e.g. the deep formations in the Anadarko Basin. It may be an area readily accessible to the company — i.e. concessions are already held, or easily obtainable, or it may be an area where participation must be sought on a partnership basis. Of course, areas where exploration is not possible at the time of evaluation for reasons of land availability, technology, or political realities do not represent real opportunities. The functional exploration activities (e.g. magnetics, seismic, drilling, etc.) that would result from the inclusion of any specific areas in such a diverse set of opportunities obviously would differ. That is significant to the extent that the skills and manpower resources for them must be available. However, for strategic selection, opportunities should be considered along comparable dimensions only — their potential contribution to exploration objectives, and their expected risk investment requirement.

Forming Alternative Strategies

The feasible set of exploration opportunities consists of those opportunities which are acceptable based on non-quantifiable criteria such as land availability, geopolitical and technical considerations. Thus, for example, a company may not now consider opportunities in Algeria because of that country's strong stand against what it considers 'exploitation of its natural resources' by foreign petroleum companies.

In theory, every possible combination of the feasible opportunities represents a strategy. Aspects that will distinguish one strategy from the next are:

1. Mix of potentially large and small opportunities.
2. Emphasis on the development of particular territories.
3. Mix of opportunities with different maturity.

Moreover, management, based on its professional and managerial experience, usually will have guidelines on these aspects that an acceptable strategy should meet. Only a relatively small number of the potentially many feasible strategies will therefore require further analysis.

Representing a Strategy

Each feasible strategy that might be considered will consist of a combination of individual opportunities to be exploited in whole or in part (partial exploitation may be achieved through partnerships). The strategy can be described by the same attributes and in the same form as an individual exploration opportunity. Thus, a strategy may be characterized by probabilistic result profiles of reserves, risk capital, and profit generated.*

To make strategies comparable for evaluation, investment and profit profiles should represent results over a common time period. Since alternative strategies can consist of widely different combinations of exploration opportunities having various different life cycles, they can exhibit varying patterns of investment requirement and revenue generation over time. Rather than discounting financial results to their present value, thereby unduly penalizing larger and longer term opportunities, strategies may be compared on their cumulative results at specific points in their life cycle. To accommodate the typical exploration cycle of 4 to 6 years, analyses of 5- and 10-year profiles, respectively, may be appropriate.

On the basis of such profiles, a strategy may be represented as a specific outcome of the expected total profit (undiscounted), for some specific risk capital investment.

The use of gross profit over a given time period as the key attribute of a specific strategy's outcome may need some explanation. Expected reserve has in the past often taken precedence in evaluating alternative strategies. However, the expected reserve criterion does not reflect effectively the economic value of a strategy — although indirectly it suggests a relation between reserves and revenue. In an attempt to overcome this shortcoming, earlier strategic plans have considered strategies whose component opportunities were screened on profitability (or unit profit). Such screening raises a serious problem when strategies are represented probabilistically. Profitability estimates, being based on reserve and cost estimates — both of which are uncertain — are subject to a great amount of uncertainty. The resulting wide profiles for profitability estimates almost certainly will ensure that many opportunities will have a significant number of profitability levels in common. It is difficult to distinguish adequately between opportunities on the basis of unit profitability.

Estimates of gross profit also are based on estimates of reserves and costs to find and exploit these opportunities. They, therefore, also will have much uncertainty associated with them. Since gross profit, however, does reflect directly both potential reserves and their economic value, it is well suited as the primary criterion for evaluating strategies. It is not necesary to screen opportunities that may enter into alternative strategies required, although pre-screening can take place according to the wishes of the decision-maker.

Accepting gross profit over specific time periods as the primary evaluation criterion, each strategy or set of opportunities then can be described as a

*Since each of these characteristics typically is the sum of the corresponding characteristics of several opportunities, the attributes for the strategy can be assumed distributed normally in the typical 'bell-shaped curve.' The expected value of the attributes for any strategy then will be the sum of the expected values of the corresponding attributes of the opportunities included in that strategy, and the variance will be the sum of the corresponding variances.

point on a profit/risk investment graph. This point represents the expected values of the risk capital required and the profits generated as a result of following that strategy. Moreover, as we have seen in the previous chapter, each of these values has a probability distribution associated with it. Combining these distributions and representing the uncertainties attached to profits and risk investment for a strategy produces an 'oval of uncertainty' within which possible outcomes of the strategy will fall (Exhibit VIII). Specifying different levels of risk — i.e. one, two, or three standard deviations in the investment and profit dimensions — will result in ever larger concentric ovals containing all possible outcomes of that strategy with 68, 95, and 99 percent certainty respectively. The decision-maker, by choosing levels of risk acceptable to him for both profit and investment requirement, then explicitly chooses a set of outcomes he wishes to consider for a strategy.

Increased expected profits of a particular strategy or combination of opportunities ordinarily will be directly related to higher investments. Additionally, both higher profits and higher investments usually entail greater risks. Where this is the case, the oval areas of uncertainty become larger for larger profit expectations.

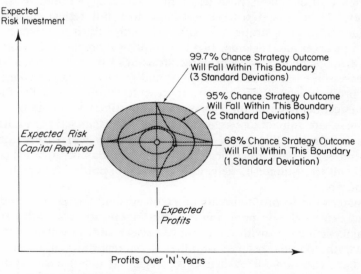

Exhibit VIII Strategy definition on investment-profit graph

Selecting a Suitable Strategy

Measuring variability, or risk, of strategy outcomes in terms of the probability distribution over the values which are likely to occur makes the problem of choosing between alternative strategies more complex. Strategies are no longer as easily distinguishable as when they were characterized by a single set of estimates of expected profit outcomes and capital requirements. The risk versus return tradeoff now must be considered in conjunction with the return versus investment choice that traditionally is made.

Exploration management, of course, would like to select a strategy that both maximizes exploration results (i.e. profits and reserves found) at acceptable risk capital investment and minimizes the uncertainty or risk. Seeking additional returns, however, often entails accepting additional uncertainty — that is, risk. If two strategies produce the same average profit results, the one that involves a lower risk capital expenditure and/or involves less 'variability' (or uncertainty as to the outcome) for the same yield clearly is a more desirable strategy. Conversely, of two strategies entailing the same risk (i.e. same size 'ovals'), the one producing the higher expected profit return for equivalent risk investment obviously is the better strategy.

Thus, in Exhibit IX (showing the expectations and risk for several hypothetical combinations of opportunities), strategy *one* probably is preferable to strategy *seven* (since it provides a greater profit for approximately the same risk capital at any risk level), and strategy *four* certainly would be preferred to strategy *seven* (since it promises nearly the same profit at substantially lower investment). Such tradeoffs become more difficult to visualize when one strategy does not clearly dominate another — e.g. strategy *one* promises greater profit than does strategy *two*, but at a price of higher risk investment.

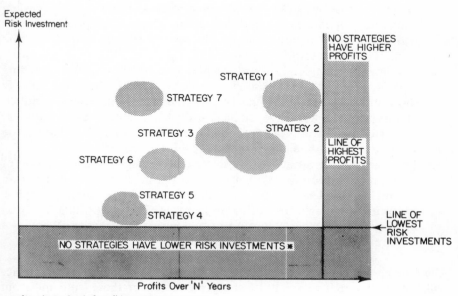

* At a chosen level of confidence that results will fall within boundaries shown.

Exhibit IX Selecting a suitable strategy

Based on this concept of suitable use of risk capital investment, the set of available strategies can be reduced to only those that promise the most attractive return for a given level of risk investment. A suitable strategy will belong to this smaller group.

Selection from the group of attractive strategies will be guided primarily by available risk capital. But, within any range of investment, several strategies may seem attractive. And these may not, in fact, be clearly distinguishable from one another (e.g. strategies *four* and *five* in Exhibit IX). Two strategies are distinguished on the profit/investment graph by: (1) the distance between their expected outcomes; and (2) the amount of overlap of their 'ovals of uncertainty' — or number of possible outcomes they have in common. Strategies *four* and *five* are difficult to distinguish on both counts. A third characteristic for comparison is the relative sizes of the uncertain areas of the two strategies. Here strategy *four* begins to look better than *five*. A choice may thus still be definable.

It is clear that on occasion two or more strategies can appear indistinguishable on all counts. At that point, selection of a 'suitable' strategy becomes an exercise of managerial preference. No quantifiable logic can simplify such a choice.

To summarize, the process for selecting a suitable strategy based on probabilistic representation of the uncertainties underlying exploration proceeds as follows:

1. Generate possible strategies as combinations of the set of feasible exploration opportunities, and evaluate their associated profit, reserve, and risk capital requirements profiles over a specific period, or time periods (e.g. 5 years and 10 years).
2. For any possible level of risk capital investment over the planning horizon (e.g. $25 to $50 million, $50 to $75 million, etc.) identify those strategies promising highest expected profits. Strategies identified in this way are attractive in their use of available risk capital (e.g. strategies, one, two, three, four, and five in Exhibit IX). Selection of the suitable strategy should be from among this set.
3. From among the attractive set, select that strategy (or combination of exploration opportunities) that best meets expected profit goals at an acceptable risk level. If the corresponding expected required capital exposure is too high, tradeoffs must be made. This can be done easily by moving down in expected profit to a strategy in the attractive set having a lower expected risk capital requirement.

The final choice between investment, profit, and risk of alternative strategies will not be determined solely by the presentation of these outcomes, but bringing out the differences and sharpening understanding of the tradeoffs as this process allows, will certainly lead to more consistent and better strategic decisions.

APPENDIX A ESTIMATE OF FUTURE HYDROCARBON POTENTIAL

Province: _____ Estimator: _____ Date: ____
Assumption: This province *does have* future potential.

A. Untested Acreage

You may enter here the total untested acreage or, if you have an anomaly count, the untested acreage lying within traps. For more information, see 'definitions' at the end of questionnaire.   ___ MM acres

B. Percentage of Untested Acreage (A)
That will be Productive

There are at least three ways to estimate this factor:

1. Find a mature analogous basin and use its 'percentage of the total basin that *is* productive.'
2. Extrapolate from one part of a basin to another: take the percent of the presently tested area that is productive and apply this percent to the entire untested area.
3. If you have used untested acreage in traps in A, you should use the product of: percent of total number of traps which are expected to be productive X percent 'fillup' of the productive traps. See 'fillup' in definitions.

No more than 1% chance productive acreage will reach __ % of untested acreage
No more than 25% chance productive acreage will reach __ % of untested acreage
There is a 50/50 chance productive acreage will be __ % of untested acreage
No more than 25% chance productive acreage will be only __ % of untested acreage
No more than 1% chance productive acreage will be only __ % of untested acreage

C. Average Feet of Pay Expected in the Future
(See definitions)

No more than 1% chance the average feet of pay will be as *high* as   __ feet
No more than 25% chance the average feet of pay will be as *high* as   __ feet
There is a 50/50 chance the average feet of pay will be   __ feet
No more than 25% chance the average feet of pay will be as *low* as   __ feet
No more than 1% chance the average feet of pay will be as *low* as   __ feet

D. Proportion of Oil Versus Gas

What is the percentage of oil in the total plus gas BOE? You may use an analogous basin or projection of the present oil/gas mix in the basin. See definitions for some present oil/gas mix values.

No more than 1% chance oil percentage will be as *high* as ____ percent
No more than 25% chance oil percentage will be as *high* as ____ percent
There is a 50/50 chance oil percentage will be ____ percent
No more than 25% chance oil percentage will be as *low* as ____ percent
No more than 1% chance oil percentage will be as *low* as ____ percent

E. Oil Recovery Expected in the Future

No more than 1% chance the average oil recovery will be as
   high as __ Bbls/AF
No more than 25% chance the average oil recovery will be as
   high as __ Bbls/AF
There is a 50/50 chance the average oil recovery will be __ Bbls/AF
No more than 25% chance the average oil recovery will be as
   low as __ Bbls/AF
No more than 1% chance the average oil recovery will be as
   low as __ Bbls/AF

F. Gas Recovery Expected in the Future

No more than 1% chance gas recovery will be as *high* as ____ MCF/AF
No more than 25% chance gas recovery will be as *high* as ____ MCF/AF
There is a 50/50 chance gas recovery will be ____ MCF/AF
No more than 25% chance gas recovery will be as *low* as ____ MCF/AF
No more than 1% chance gas recovery will be as *low* as ____ MCF/AF

G. NGL Recovery Expected in the Future

No more than 1% chance NGL recovery will be as *high* as ____ Bbls/MMCF
No more than 25% chance NGL recovery will be as *high* as ____ Bbls/MMCF
There is a 50/50 chance NGL recovery will be ____ Bbls/MMCF
No more than 25% chance NGL recovery will be as *low* as ____ Bbls/MMCF
No more than 1% chance NGL recovery will be as *low* as ____ Bbls/MMCF

Major Factor Definitions

Untested Acreage

Determination of untested acreage depends on many factors and cannot be closely defined, but basically untested acreage is acreage where no wells have been drilled. The amount of acreage tested by a well may range from less than 40 acres to more than a township. Untested acreage as used in the questionnaire applies in *three* dimensions.

'Fillup'

'Fillup' (with quotation marks) is the percentage of the total area of closure that lies above the oil–water contact. To most geologists, fillup (without quotation marks) refers to height of fillup relative to total height of closure. The percentage fillup in height may be greatly different from the percentage 'fillup' in area; for example, consider a dome with equally-spaced contours, 1/3 fillup on height covers only 1/9 of the area of closure ('fillup'). This 1/3–1/9 relationship occurs because the area of a circle is proportional to the *square* of the radius. In linear structures, fillup and 'fillup' may be similar.

Average Feet of Pay

This is the weighted average of oil and gas pays expected to be productive in the future. For example: if 30 percent of the productive acreage is expected to have 100 feet of pay and the remaining 70 percent of the acreage to have 20 feet of pay, the weighted average is 30 percent × 100 feet + 70 percent × 20 feet = 44 feet.

Portion of Oil Versus Gas

This applies to reserves which will be discovered in the future and is: ultimate barrels of oil divided by ultimate barrels of oil plus ultimate barrels of oil equivalent to gas

$$\text{i.e.} \left(\frac{\text{oil}}{\text{oil } + \text{ oil equivalent}} \right)$$

Gas is converted at 17 MCF per equivalent barrel. We have found that the oil versus gas BOE ratio is what most geologists answer when asked about oil–gas mix; therefore, this is the question in Section D of the questionnaire.

The volume of oil productive reservoirs versus volume of gas productive reservoirs is specifically *not* asked for in Section D. This is calculated by the computer program.

APPENDIX B ECONOMIC EVALUATION OF
EXPLORATION OPPORTUNITY

Opportunity: _____   Estimator: _____   Date: ____

Assumption: 1. This opportunity has future potentials of a magnitude and probability shown in the attached estimate.*
2. A full-cycle and development program can be developed to obtain the estimated future potential.

Note: All expenditure estimates should be made without regard to their final treatment.

A. Geological and Geophysical (G & G) Expenditures

Estimate the number of dollars that must still be spent on geological and geophysical activities in order to reasonably be able to identify promising geologic anomalies. (This estimate should cover any expenditures for gravity surveys, aeromagnetic surveys and all semidetailed and detailed geophysics that must be done prior to wildcat drilling.)

No more than a 1% chance that as much as $ __ million must still be spent on G & G

No more than a 25% chance that as much as $ __ million must still be spent on G & G

A 50/50 chance that $ __ million must still be spent on G & G

No more than a 25% chance that only $ __ million must still be spent on G & G

No more than a 1% chance that only $ __ million must still be spent on G & G

For optimum exploration pace, estimate at what rate geological and geophysical expenditures should occur once exploration is begun. (When answering this question, assume that whatever resources are required to sustain the desired exploration pace are available. Your estimate of pace should reflect concern for competitive realities, lease terms, and resource balance allowing effective management of the play.)

__ percent of total G & G expenditures will occur in the first 2 years
__ percent of total G & G expenditures will occur in the third and fourth years
__ percent of total G & G expenditures will occur in the fifth and sixth years

B. Wildcat Wells

Estimate the number of wildcat wells that will have to be drilled in order to evaluate the potentially interesting anomalies for this opportunity.

No more than a 1% chance that as many as __ wildcat wells will be drilled
No more than a 25% chance that as many as __ wildcat wells will be drilled

*Result of potential estimating model should be available at start of an economic evaluation.

A 50/50 chance that ___ wildcat wells will be drilled
No more than a 25% chance that only ___ wildcat wells will be drilled
No more than a 1% chance that only ___ wildcat wells will be drilled

Furthermore, assume that full evaluation of potentially interesting anomalies will be carried out over a 6-year period. This period may be shortened of course if the exploration pace permits it — i.e. if lease terms or competitive pressures require it, or if relatively few wildcats need to be drilled.

What percentage of wildcat wells will be drilled in:

First year of play:	___ percent
Second year of play:	___ percent
Third year of play:	___ percent
Fourth year of play:	___ percent
Fifth year of play:	___ percent
Sixth year of play:	___ percent

C. Wildcat Drilling Costs

Estimate expected wildcat drilling costs for this opportunity. (Experience in this or an analogous basin — analogous with regard to environment and technology required — should be considered in estimating this cost.)

No more than a 1% chance that wildcat drilling cost will exceed ___ $/foot
No more than a 25% chance that wildcat drilling cost will exceed ___ $/foot
A 50/50 chance that wildcat drilling cost will equal ___ $/foot
No more than a 25% chance that wildcat cost will be only ___ $/foot
No more than a 1% chance that wildcat cost will be only ___ $/foot

D. Average Reservoir Depth

Estimate average expected reservoir depth that will be encountered in this opportunity. This estimate should be a weighted average of depths at which the major reservoirs are expected to be for the untested acreage — e.g. for an opportunity with three reservoirs at 10,000, 12,000, and 16,000 feet containing about 1/2, 1/4, and 1/4 of expected reservoir volume respectively, the average reservoir depth would be estimated as 12,000 feet (1/2 times 10,000 plus 1/4 times 12,000 plus 1/4 times 16,000).

No more than a 1% chance that reservoir depth will exceed ___ feet
No more than a 25% chance that reservoir depth will exceed ___ feet
A 50/50 chance that average reservoir depth will be ___ feet
No more than a 25% chance that reservoir depth will be only ___ feet
No more than a 1% chance that reservoir depth will be only ___ feet

E. Land Cost

Estimate expected land costs that will be incurred in pursuing this opportunity. (This estimate should cover both rentals and lease bonuses as required.)

No more than a 1% chance that land cost will exceed$ ___ MM
No more than a 25% chance that land cost will exceed $ ___ MM
A 50/50 chance that land cost will equal $ ___ MM
No more than a 25% chance that land costs will be only $ ___ MM
No more than a 1% chance that land costs will be only $ ___ MM

Furthermore, estimate the rate at which this expense will be incurred.

In the first 2 years, ___ % will be spent
In the third and fourth years, ___ % will be spent
In the fifth and sixth years, ___ % will be spent
Beyond the sixth year, ___ % will be spent
Note: If no further land costs need be incurred for this opportunity, the question should be omitted.

F. Production Pattern

Estimate which of the following three average depletion patterns will be most appropriate for production of fields that may be discovered with this opportunity. (Circle one.):

    A. Most efficient producing rate
    B. Prorated to 50% of most efficient
    C. Natural gas (contract delivery)

G. Initial Well Productivity

What would you estimate well productivity to be?

No more than a 1% chance that initial well productivity will exceed ___ BOE/day
No more than a 25% chance that initial well productivity will exceed ___ BOE/day
A 50/50 chance that initial productivity will equal ___ BOE/day
No more than a 25% chance that initial well productivity will be only ___ BOE/day
No more than a 1% chance that initial well productivity will be only ___ BOE/day

H. Development Drilling Cost*

Estimate expected development drilling cost for this opportunity.

*Need not be estimated if expected to be same as wildcat drilling cost.

No more than a 1% chance that development drilling cost will exceed ___ $/foot

No more than a 25% chance that development drilling cost will exceed ___ $/foot

A 50/50 chance that development drilling cost will exceed ___ $/foot

No more than a 25% chance that development drilling cost will be only ___ $/foot

No more than a 1% chance that development drilling cost will only be ___ $/foot

I. Field System Costs

For the most likely well spacing to be used for this opportunity, estimate the total expected costs for a field production system — e.g. pumps, piping, storage, platforms as appropriate. To obtain this estimate, a hypothetical field system must be visualized for an average-sized field that can be expected in this basin.

No more than a 1% chance that average field systems costs will exceed $ ___

No more than a 25% chance that average field systems costs will exceed $ ___

A 50/50 chance that average field systems costs will equal $ ___

No more than a 25% chance that average field systems costs will only be $ ___

No more than a 1% chance that average field systems costs will only be $ ___

J. Development Pace

Estimate the percentage of development that will take place in the:

First year of play: ___ percent	Fifth year of play: ___ percent	
Second year of play: ___ percent	Sixth year of play: ___ percent	
Third year of play: ___ percent	Seventh year of play: ___ percent	
Fourth year of play: ___ percent	Eighth year of play: ___ percent	

In estimating the development pace, assume that all fields will be developed as rapidly as technological and environmental (transportation) conditions permit. Development will generally begin within a year of discovery, and primary development should not take more than 1 to 2 years per field.

K. Well-Head Price

Estimate well-head value of hydrocarbons. This requires estimating market value and then deducting expected transportation charges.

No more than a 1% chance that well-head value will exceed $ ___ per barrel

No more than a 25% chance that well-head value will exceed $ ___ per barrel

A 50/50 chance that well-head value will exceed $ __ per barrel
No more than a 25% chance that well-head value will be only $ __ per barrel
No more than a 1% chance that well-head value will be only $ __ per barrel

L. Lifting Costs

Estimate the direct operating costs per barrel of daily production.

No more than a 1% chance that the lifting cost will exceed __ $/BOE
No more than a 25% chance that the lifting cost will exceed __ $/BOE
A 50/50 chance that lifting cost will equal __ $/BOE
No more than a 25% chance that the lifting cost will only be __ $/BOE
No more than a 1% chance that the lifting cost will only be __ $/BOE

M. Royalties and Taxes

Estimate the government take (royalties and taxes) that will have to be paid on production.

No more than a 1% chance that government take will exceed __ cents/barrel
No more than a 25% chance that government take will exceed __ cents/barrel
A 50/50 chance that government take will be only __ cents/barrel
No more than a 25% chance that government take will be only __ cents/barrel
No more than a 1% chance that government take will be only __ cents/barrel

Chapter 3

The Treatment of Uncertainty in Decision-Making: Alternative Approaches

INTRODUCTION

We can see from the discussion of the risk analysis approach in Chapter 2 that it is but one of a series of possible approaches for dealing with uncertainty in relation to the appraisal of an individual project. One of our aims in this chapter is to provide a concise review of such methods and indicate their level of practical application. It is important to remember that there is no one best approach. It is only through a thorough understanding of the assumptions and implications of each method that a reader can judge which is the most sensible approach to adopt in the context of a particular decision problem.

Certainly, words like risk analysis and decision analysis are used interchangeably in the literature, but there is a real difference between them. Decision analysis requires that the decision-maker must formally articulate his preferences (utilities) for outcomes and choose that option (project) which maximizes expected utility; Figure 3 in Chapter 2 illustrates this point. Risk analysis, on the other hand, does not require such a formal assessment of preference measures for outcomes and leaves the decision-maker to judge and choose between options whose outcomes are depicted in terms of probability distributions. Individual judgement is thus the procedure by which decision-makers choose the preferred option. Managers may adopt heuristics or rules of thumb which involve some form of trade-off between the mean of the distribution and some measure of spread, e.g. the standard deviation. On the other hand, the manager might be interested in estimating for each option the probability that, say, the NPV might be less than zero and in choosing the particular option which minimizes this probability value. Therefore, it is important to examine differences in decision approaches, rules and their implications for the final option choice process, and these topics will be discussed in this chapter.

The other main aim of the chapter is to fit risk analysis within the spectrum of the now increasingly acceptable toolkit of approaches afforded by applied decision analysis. In this way the reader will be better equipped to synthesize a seemingly endless range of alternative approaches and view them as variations of applied decision analysis methodology.

94

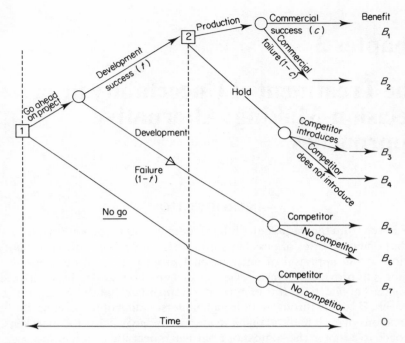

Figure 1 A decision-tree representation of an idealized R & D project
Note: t = probability of development success
c = probability of commercial success
B_1 through B_7 denote financial benefits (outcomes)

THE ASSESSMENT OF PROJECT WORTH

Many models have been proposed in the literature for simplifying appraisals of
project worth. These range from check lists of attractive properties that a
project should possess and from which a score is obtained, to more
sophisticated financial appraisals. The common thread in these approaches is
the recognition of the need to take account of uncertainty and to evaluate the
project in terms of some decision objective(s) or goal(s).

We assume, initially, that a single financial objective, say NPV (net present
value) is reasonable for most project analyses and consider ways of
incorporating and allowing for uncertainty in our financial measures of project
worth. Before we do this we should outline the logic of our procedure in terms
of an idealized decision-tree diagram. The decision tree (Figure 1) shows a set
of possible decisions (indicated by boxes) and chance events (indicated by
circles) which might occur during the life of an R & D investment project. A
diagram such as Figure 1 depicts no more than the futurity of possible decisions
and chance events that the decision-maker feels may occur during the life of the
R & D project. In other words, it is a logical flow diagram of future
possibilities, and is especially useful for the decision-analyst in identifying

uncertain quantities such as technical success, cost, price, sales, etc. for which marginal and conditional probability assessments will have to be obtained from the decision-maker. However, whilst there are often severe problems in obtaining such subjective marginal and conditional probability measures, we shall not consider them here (see Chapter 4).

With the decision-tree diagram as a logical basis for our present discussion, we turn now to a consideration of how we can incorporate uncertainty into project analysis. Uncertainty to the firm is the possibility of unpredicted fluctuations in the cash flow pattern occurring on a given project, thus making financial forecasting extremely difficult. Hertz (12) in a classic article discusses a number of efforts which have been made to cope with uncertainty, the theme of which was covered in broad outline in the previous chapter. To recapitulate:

(i) more accurate forecasts of cash flows;
(ii) empirical, subjective adjustments to some of the factors influencing the outcome of a decision;
(iii) setting a high rate of return standard for a potentially risky project;
(iv) applying a type of sensitivity analysis (see Rappaport (27)) to the factors influencing the outcome of a decision by assessing range forecasts, say, low, most likely, and highest values, of the factors.

He points out that none of these approaches is completely satisfactory, even though such approaches as *sensitivity* analyses are commonly applied in practical situations. The main aim should be to characterize the effect of uncertainty on the criterion measure of worth. This is best achieved by trying to find the probability distribution of the worth measure, so that the variability about the expected value of the measure can be assessed. There are clearly two possible ways in which information about the shape of the distribution of the worth measure can be obtained, namely, either by means of an exact analytic solution, or a simulation approach (see Chapter 2). The two ways are examined in the approaches of Hillier (14) and Hertz (12). Both methods require the identification of the set of key variables on a project which affect the cash flow pattern. Once this set is known, then each of the approaches can produce an approximation to the distribution of the worth measure.

Which Measure of Worth Should Be Analysed?

Since our stated aim is to assess the project's risk profile we also have to address the problem of which worth measure or criterion is most appropriate for such an assessment. Indeed, there are many possible criterion probability distributions which could be devised – ranging from distributions of the payback period (see Weingartner (32)) to distributions of benefit/cost ratios (see Thomas (29)).

One common choice for characterizing a project's risk profile (and our preferred criterion) is the *distribution of net present values* (NPV) obtained by discounting future cash flow projections by a discount rate which reflects the firm's opportunity cost of capital. There are, of course, disadvantages with using the NPV risk profile approach:

(i) If the project involves significant outlays in terms of the firm's resources, then the chance of large fluctuations in the cash flow distribution in a particular year may invalidate the assumption of a constant rate for investment and borrowing. Fluctuations such as this might, in addition, highlight interdependencies between projects dependent on common resources and further complicate the joint problem of investment and financing (see Chambers (3)).

(ii) Changes in a cash flow pattern on a project often cause greater than proportionate changes in the net present value figures. For example: it can be shown that the NPV of a million dollar investment project discounted at, say, a 10 percent rate will be double in the situation where it returns $120,000 per annum for many years into the future than when it returns $110,000 per annum over the same future period.

(iii) In such schema, the choice of cost of capital also affects the expected value and standard deviation of the NPV distribution. In fact, higher discount rates tend to reduce the NPV standard deviation yet, intuitively, higher discount rates imply that the firm requires higher risk premiums (risk adjustments) to compensate for risk.

(iv) Perhaps the most compelling disadvantage is that businessmen often find it difficult to understand the nature of risk when confronted with a project NPV risk profile. For example, the range of present values depicted will often swamp the expected present value and destroy its credibility as a choice criterion. Carter (2) and others (e.g. Hayes (11)) have voiced this managerial reaction in terms such as 'Now that we have the project's risk profile – so what? What do we do with it?'.

The fourth point emphasizes very clearly that managers tend to be very uncomfortable when presented with risk profiles but yet are concerned with dealing with project riskiness. They more often express their risk attitudes in terms such as: 'the need for smooth, consistent, non-fluctuating cash flow patterns' thus echoing some of the cash flow concepts such as 'cash cows' attributed to the Boston Consulting Group or 'the perceived extent of downside risk', i.e. ensuring a virtually 100 percent chance of getting a positive 'bottom line' result for a project. Therefore, any analytical approach must address itself to the issue of the risk-averse attitudes of managers and provide some operational guidelines for incorporating risk aversion into risk profile analysis.

In summary, NPV has clear advantages over other approaches because it gives an unambiguous measure of the value of the incremental project for the firm. If a project, when discounted at the firm's opportunity cost rate, returns a positive NPV, then it should be accepted as it increases the value of the firm.

ANALYTICAL APPROACHES FOR OBTAINING THE PROBABILITY DISTRIBUTION OF A WORTH MEASURE

Hillier (14) and Wagle (31) have been responsible for the development of an alternative exact analytic approach for measuring the worth of an individual project. The initial stages in the procedure are similar to those of the Hertz approach in that the essential structure of the problem must first be developed. Following this, the set of significant input factors for the investment decision must be identified and assessments of their probabilities in terms of parameters such as means, variances and patterns of intercorrelation must then be obtained. Given that the structure and project parameters have been specified, Hillier then makes the assumption that the probability of cash flows of various magnitudes occurring in a given year can be described by the normal distribution. With this assumption, it can be shown that the distribution of possible values of an investment's present worth will also be approximately normally distributed. This method is both a very flexible and simple one for obtaining the distribution of a project's NPV but less suitable for obtaining the distribution of the internal rate of return (IRR) criterion. However, although we do not recommend the use of the IRR distribution, we can obtain the IRR in the following manner. If the NPV distribution is normal and obtained with some discount rate r then the equation $P(\text{IRR} > r) = P(\text{NPV} > 0|\text{Discount rate} = r)$ (on the assumption that IRR $= r$ implies that the NPV $= 0$), can be used to give a point on the cumulative distribution of the IRR criterion. For example, if $r = 15\%$ and $P(\text{NPV} > 0)$ is 0.7 then $P(\text{IRR} > 15\%)$ is 0.7, or, put another way, the thirtieth percentile of the cumulative density function for IRR is 15 percent. Several points on the cumulative distribution can thus be obtained from the equation above by considering different values for the discount rate r in the NPV calculation. In this way, from the points obtained, the cumulative and probability density functions of the IRR criterion can be smoothed and thus approximated.

In situations where the distribution of IRR is required it can be seen that the analytical calculation is quite time-consuming, whereas the simulation model can give the IRR distribution directly. Further, if the NPV distribution is not normal, the equation above cannot be used to derive points on the cumulative distribution of the IRR function. Despite this difficulty, in situations when the assumptions or the analytic model hold approximately, it should give a quicker, cheaper and more accurate (at least as far as the tails of the distribution are concerned) measure than the equivalent simulation approach. Because of the sometimes costly and time-consuming nature of the simulation method, it is only likely to prove effective in a cost/benefit sense when the assumption of normally distributed cash flows is not realistic.

Analytical approaches have a built-in advantage in that they always involve some detailed model specification, and therefore a clearer set of assumptions about the underlying structure than alternative simulation approaches. As a result, such approaches can probably throw more light upon underlying cause-effect relationships because model output and predictions are, in part, a test of the reasonableness of the underlying assumptions. In addition, analytical approaches are well-suited for quick extension to situations in which we have to evaluate a series of risky interrelated investments, and wish to examine the worth of alternative project portfolio combinations as well as the characteristics and worth of individual projects.

The choice of approach is thus a complicated matter, which involves a number of issues. In particular, it is important to consider the nature of the investment decision, the expected shape of the probability distributions of the key input factors, and strategic factors such as the importance of the final decision (which will, in turn, indicate the potential cost/benefit picture for analysis in relation to factors such as time constraints).

A method which is often valuable to decision-makers in determining the choice between approaches is *sensitivity analysis*. Let us suppose, as an example, that we wanted to examine the appropriateness of the assumption of normality for each of the periodical cash flow distributions over the project's life in a situation where initial subjective assessments appear to indicate slightly skew distributions, i.e. departures from normality. We could, first of all, carry out a sensitivity analysis using normal distribution assumptions in one case, and the skew distribution assumptions in the other case. A comparison between the results of these analyses would then enable some conclusions to be drawn about the effect of skewness on the shape of the overall criterion distribution, NPV. Thus, we would have one possible empirical test of the robustness of the NPV criterion distribution to changes in assumptions about the underlying cash flow distributions.

Furthermore, whatever approach is used to derive the NPV distribution, a more comprehensive form of sensitivity analysis could be used to determine the sensitivity of the final results to changes in assessed values of each, some, or all of the key input factors. Indeed, there are an infinite number of possible sensitivity analyses, though hopefully some are more plausible than others.

Thus, it may be found, for example in R & D planning situations, that the effects of changes in the development costs are critical in terms of the value of the overall criterion function. If this is the case, greater effort must be expended on the estimation of such cost factors. In addition, the decision-maker's attention can be directed towards ways of reducing sources of variability in the whole range of costs, and perhaps highlight other critical factors, such as the sales volume likely to be generated from the commercial introduction of the results of the research effort.

Detailed Consideration of the Analytical Approach

The basic rationale of the Hillier type of analytical model (generally regarded as the most insightful analytical method) is to develop an approach for determining the best overall combination of projects from the group of proposed investments. The model uses as choice criteria the distribution of present value and the expected utility of present value in order to derive the best project portfolio.

Hillier's fundamental contribution to the literature is in the development and exposition of a model for describing the interrelated cash flows generated by a given set of investments. This model is then used for determining the parameters of the probability distribution of present value, and for a detailed exploration of the conditions under which the distribution of NPV is either exactly normal in form or approximately normal (in situations where the individual cash flow distributions differ from the normal form).

The analytical model presented here to derive the probability distributions of NPV is reproduced from Wagle's paper (31) with certain notational alterations.

Suppose first that an investment decision problem is characterized by m sources of cash flows $S_1, \ldots, S_m$ and let the random variable Y_{tk} denote the cash flow in year 't' from the kth source of cash flow S_k. Assume that Y_{tk} has a finite mean μ_{tk} and variance σ_{tk}^2.

Now let the net cash flow in year t be denoted by V_t.
Then

$$V_t = \sum_{k=1}^{m} Y_{tk}$$

and

$$E(V_t) = \sum_{k=1}^{m} \mu_{tk} = W_t$$

$$V(V_t) = \sum_{k=1}^{m} \sigma_{tk}^2 + 2 \sum_{k \neq j} \text{cov}(Y_{tk}, Y_{tj}) \, . \text{ (where } k = 1(1)m, j = 1(1)m)$$

If the project life is assumed to be n years,

then

$$(\text{NPV}_n(i)) = \sum_{t=0}^{n} \left[\frac{V_t}{(1+i)^t} \right]$$

Where (a) NPV_n denotes the net present value over a project life of n years,

(b) $100i\%$ denotes the rate of discount or cost of capital to the firm,

then

$$E(\text{NPV}_n(i)) = \sum_{t=0}^{n} \frac{W_t}{(1+i)^t} = W_n(i) \text{ (say)}$$

$$V(\text{NPV}_n(i)) = \sum_{t=0}^{n} \frac{V(V_t)}{(1+i)^{2t}} + 2 \sum_{t \neq t'} \frac{\text{cov}(v_t, v_t')}{(1+i)^{t+t'}}$$

$$= R_n^2(i) \text{ (say)}$$

Thus for fixed n the expressions above give the values of the mean and variance of NPV.

These expressions can be amended if n the project life is itself a random variable – a case which occurs frequently in practice. If n has some discrete probability distribution and P_n denotes the probability of the project life being n years, then

$$E(\text{NPV}(i)) = \sum_{n = N_1}^{N_2} P_n E(\text{NPV}_n(i))$$

$$= \sum_{n = N_1}^{N_2} P_n W_n(i)$$

Where the probability distribution for n is defined over the range $N_1 \leqslant n \leqslant N_2$ and

$$V(\text{NPV}(i)) = \sum_{n = N_1}^{N_2} P_n E(\text{NPV}_n{}^2(i)) - \left(\sum_{n = N_1}^{N_2} P_n E(\text{NPV}_n(i)) \right)^2$$

$$\sum_{n = N_1}^{N_2} P_n R_n{}^2(i) + \sum_{n = N_1}^{N_2} P_n \left(W_n(i) - E(W_n(i)) \right)^2$$

give the values for the mean and variance of the NPV criterion function.

In the derivation of the formula for the mean and variance of the net present value criterion we have omitted discussion of two critical problems:

(i) The conditions under which the distribution of net present value follows the normal distribution.

(ii) The formulae for the mean and variance of net present value require estimates of the means and variances of the various cash flows and of the covariances between them. It is extremely important to consider how to estimate these quantities and, in particular, the cash flow covariance.

We shall discuss each problem in turn.

(a) The Normality Problem

It should be noted that the mathematics involved in obtaining the mean and variance of NPV consists of summing a series of discounted net cash flow variables over the planning period. Because the cash flows are discounted the net present value is a weighted sum of random net cash flow variables, where the weights are the discounting factors. If the opportunity cost of capital is high it is possible that the distribution of NPV will be overinfluenced by the cash flow pattern in the early years and will, thus, tend to be somewhat skewed.

The assumption of normality can be justified if it is reasonable to assume that the cash flows for each year of the project's life follow the multivariate normal. Specifically, the working assumption is that the joint distribution of the V_t, the set of the annual cash flows, is the multivariate normal for all values of t. This conclusion follows from the result that the distribution of any linear combination of random variables is normal if their joint distribution is multivariate normal (14). This holds even if the linear combination is a weighted sum of cash flow variables.

In an investment decision situation, it is often not realistic to treat the distribution of the cash flow random variables as being exactly normal. This is because each of the annual net cash flow variables is generally the sum or difference of a number of single random variables such as sales, price, and cost or composite product random variables, e.g. revenue (sales × price), which may not themselves be normally distributed. In practical situations, therefore, we are faced with the problem of determining the conditions under which the distribution of a sum of non-normally distributed cash flow variables can be assumed to be approximately normally distributed. The central limit theorem in probability theory, is, in fact, very closely related to our practical problem. Hillier (14) discusses some of the most useful forms of the central limit theorem in the context of investment appraisal.

One version of the central-limit theorem allows us to state that if the annual cash flow variables V_1, V_2, ... etc. are independent, identically distributed random variables with finite mean and variance, then their sum is approximately normal. Thus, if the sequence of discounted cash flows can be assumed to be independent and have the same form of distribution, the distribution of NPV is approximately normal. However, the assumption of the independence of the cash flows is a restrictive one in project appraisal, and it is also very unlikely that the random cash flow variables will be identically distributed in practice. Therefore, this basic version of the central limit theorem (CLT) imposes a far stronger set of conditions on the investment appraisal problem than can be justified in practical terms. Nevertheless, some further work has shown that weaker sets of conditions for the application of the CLT can be found. They are noted below:

(i) If we keep the assumptions of independently distributed cash flow variables, it follows that if the discounted cash flows form an uniformly bounded non-degenerate sequence of mutually independent (but not identically distributed) random variables, then by the CLT, the NPV distribution is approximately normal provided that the number of years of the project's life is sufficiently large. Hillier notes that the non-degeneracy condition is quite restrictive to the problem, but that in practice the most restrictive condition is the assumption of the independence of the net cash flows in successive years over the planning horizon.

(ii) If we wish to extend the CLT to the situation of dependent cash flow variables, the CLT can be shown to be approximately valid for certain patterns of dependence between the variables. However, the case of dependent variables is far more tricky than the independent case. Hillier states that if we assume that the cash flows are *identically* distributed, then strong results are available for certain patterns of dependence between the cash flows. Weaker results are available if we assume that the cash flows are *non-identically* distributed, but only for more restricted patterns of dependence between the cash flows.

It appears that the most useful result to emerge in the dependent case is obtained under the following assumptions. If the discounted cash flows more than q years apart (where q is defined in relation to individual project characteristics) are independent and non-identically distributed, then under a condition which implies a certain pattern of uniformity and consistency in the cash flow covariances, the Hoeffding and Robbins (15) theorem can be used to show that the NPV distribution is asymptotically normal (i.e. is normal for fairly lengthy project lives).

Another useful result emerges if we are prepared to assume that the cash flow variables are identically distributed and that they form a stationary Markov dependent sequence. In this case Doob (5) provides a justification for CLT and thus the asymptotic normal distribution of NPV in this case.

It can be seen that the results just presented establish conditions (via the CLT), covering a range of possible practical situations, under which it can be assumed that the distribution of NPV is approximately normal. The relevant question to ask at this stage is 'How good is the approximation?'. The problem arises because we are unsure of the number of years of the project's life necessary to guarantee the rate of convergence of the NPV distribution to normality. If we assume independence between the cash flow variables, then Hillier states that the NPV distribution is normal for project lives greater than four or five years. However, under the assumption of dependence there is no guidance about the minimum value of project life except that it will be somewhat larger than in the 'independence' case.

Some limited experimental evidence has been reported concerning the reasonableness of the assumption of normality for the distribution of NPV.

Evidence on the normality of the NPV distribution

Bonini (1) reports his experience with Monte-Carlo simulations, which although not strictly comparable with analytical approaches, does lead to the conclusion that distributions of NPV are usually skewed, and sometimes bi-modal.

Hull (16), in an examination of five published case studies, points out that the distribution of NPV was approximately normal in three out of five cases, under a wide range of assumptions about input distributions. Under the same conditions, he found that in only one out of five cases was the IRR distribution approximately normal.

Thomas (29) in an earlier study, found evidence of the normality of the NPV distribution.

It seems clear, from such evidence, that firm conclusions about NPV normality cannot be drawn. However, it can be indicated that under certain conditions, such as when there are non-linearities in the cash flow patterns, or when such options as abandonment exist, the NPV distribution is unlikely to be of normal form.

Now, we turn to a consideration of the problem of estimating the covariances between cash flows in successive years.

(b) The Covariance Problem

We have seen from the derivation of the NPV distribution that it is necessary to make some assumptions about the extent to which the cash flows generated by a particular investment project are correlated over time. High correlation would be present in a situation in which a deviation of an actual cash flow, from that estimated in a given year, implies a comparable degree of inaccuracy in prospective cash flow estimates. Most practical investment problems can be regarded as having some form of correlation pattern between cash flows in successive years. One way of handling correlation patterns is to make some set of assumptions about their nature, but such assumptions should be both reasonable and adequate in terms of representing the nature of the process, and facilitating the procedures of calculation. Hillier suggests one set of assumptions about correlation patterns. It can be summarized as follows:

Again, if we assume that V_{tk} is the cash flow in period t derived from the kth source:

(i) Cash flows from the same source k are assumed to be first-order Markov-dependent, i.e. a cash flow in period $(t - 1)$ will influence a cash flow of that kind in period T where $T > t$ only inasmuch as this influence is carried over from period t.

(ii) The correlation pattern between cash flows of the same type in adjacent time periods is constant over time, i.e. independent of time (this is, in effect, a stationarity assumption).

(iii) We need to make assumptions about correlation patterns between cash flow originating from different sources. First, the correlation coefficient between cash flows from two different sources in the same time period is constant over time, i.e. independent of time. Second, the cash flow in a stated time period from a particular source is independent of the cash flows from other sources in previous time periods.

Further, if we let

(a) ρ_k be the correlation coefficient between the cash flows from each source S_k in successive time periods,

(b) ρ_{kl}^* be the correlation coefficient between the cash flows from sources S_k and S_l in the same time period,

It can be shown [14] for $t > t'$ that the correlation coefficient between Y_{tk} and $Y_{tl} = (\rho_{kl}^*) (\rho_l^{|t' - t|})$.

This formula requires the estimation of values for the variables ρ_k and ρ_{kl}^*. This assessment task will be considered in detail in Chapter 4, when we deal specifically with measurement problems.

There are other possible approaches for dealing with the correlation structure between cash flows arising in successive years of a project's life. For the moment we shall note that the problem could be treated using either the simulation approach, or by using certain concepts derived from statistical decision theory.

At this stage, it is useful to summarize the gains from the Hillier approach. Basically, for the single project, it provides a risk profile in terms of the probability distribution of present value. This risk profile can be used by managers to understand the impact of uncertainty on the individual project. Ultimately, as we have previously indicated, such projects must be reviewed in the context of the firm's portfolio of projects.

The Pros and Cons of the Hillier Approach

The major weaknesses of the Hillier model rest with the model's assumptions and the associated difficulties faced in using them in a practical appraisal context. Some of these weaknesses are listed below:

  (i) The Hillier model deals with sums of variables (cash flows). These cash flow variables are, however, not necessarily linear functions of the variables which determine the cash flow patterns. For example, revenue is typically generated as the product of price and quantity sold. Worse still, the variables which determine cash flow may themselves be interrelated and such intercorrelations, often of a complex type, may have to be assessed.
 (ii) There are a series of estimation problems with the model in establishing the appropriate subjective distributions for cash flow variances and for the intra- and inter-correlations in cash flow patterns.
(iii) The model produces a uni-modal, symmetric distribution of NPV, i.e. approximately normal – based upon the sufficient statistics of the mean NPV and the variance of NPV. Yet there is some evidence (see Bonini (1) and Thomas (29)) that skew and bi-modal distributions can occur.
(iv) It cannot handle abandonment decision situations without quite significant modifications and model restructuring.

The Hillier model does, however, possess a major strength, namely that it is quick to calculate and easy to use in many circumstances, provided that certain simplifying assumptions about cash flow and correlation patterns are made. Thus, it can provide a 'first-pass' attempt at the assessment of individual project-risk and the establishment of a project's risk class.

In addition, the Hillier model can easily be extended to handle portfolios of projects. This is a considerable advantage given that firms are more typically confronted with the problem of choosing that set of investment projects which in some well-defined sense maximizes the value of the firm, than with looking at each project as an individual entity and in a step-by-step individual project evaluation process.

In the case study which follows, we examine further the pros and cons of the Hillier approach.

EXAMPLE OF THE HILLIER APPROACH –
PROPERTY REDEVELOPMENT IN CARACAS CASE STUDY

To illustrate the use of the Hillier approach in practice, we present below a case history outlining its use in a property development context. This case history will emphasize the analytical approach, and present an approach based upon utility considerations incorporating risk aversion into the analysis. At the conclusion of the study, the results will be discussed and a critique will be given.

PROPERTY REDEVELOPMENT IN CARACAS:
AN INVESTMENT DECISION
(Written as at 1970)

INTRODUCTION

The Board of one of the major Venezuelan banking organizations was facing the problem of how best to re-utilize the considerable property value of its main office building in Caracas. The building was an extremely fine, fifteen-year-old block, architecturally splendid and occupying a magnificent site in the city centre. But, quite simply, the organization had grown too big for these offices and a much larger site was being developed a little way out from the centre which would provide the necessary extra space and better facilities for the modern style of banking with its greater range of financial services, extensive computerization, etc.

As an alternative to selling the existing property outright in its present condition, the bank could keep the building as an investment and redevelop it as shops, apartments, offices, hotel, or some seemingly optimal mixture of these uses. Apart from these various configurations of space utilization, there were various structural changes which could be made to the building. Two extra floors could be added which, together with further modification, would increase the choice of possible space utilization configurations. A major reconstruction could also provide a more efficient utilization of the floor space, and a plan devised in 1967 had already been approved by the planning authorities. A more recent scheme submitted in 1969 had not yet been approved. However, with certain members of the Board having considerable influence in the city, the possibility of the plans being turned down was described as inconceivable.

THE OPTIONS AVAILABLE

At this stage, the Board decided to enlist the help of a consultant, Mr R. B.

Gale, to assist in analysing and resolving the problem. His first act was to construct a list of the possible options open to the bank.

After considering systematically the possible space utilization configurations for each structural possibility, a set of apparent investment options was drawn up and is displayed in Appendix 1. In Appendix 2 the various costs involved in each of these investment options are listed. Indemnification refers to the cost of evicting present tenants. In an attempt to take into account the uncertainty in the estimates of construction costs in present value terms, and in order to facilitate subsequent calculations, these costs were assessed in terms of a Normal distribution function. The subjectively assessed means and variances are shown in Appendix 2. The mean was assessed as the fiftieth percentile (or median), i.e. that value at which it was thought there was an equal chance of the cost being above or below.

The variance (or squared standard deviation) was estimated indirectly by assessing first the fifth percentile and the ninety-fifth percentile of the distribution. These two percentiles were assessed by using the standard artificial device of drawing one ball at random from an urn with either 5 percent or 95 percent red balls and estimating the construction cost at which the decision-maker would be indifferent as between going ahead with the construction or receiving a prize equal to that cost if the ball drawn is red. The difference between the two costs estimated in this way is approximately equal to 3.3 times the standard deviation.

At the same time Mr Gale extracted from the Board their subjective probability estimate of 0.9 that the 1969 plans would go through the planning authorities unimpeded.

Appendix 3 lists the various categories of space utilization, which are then used in Appendix 4 to evaluate the expected rent revenues from each option. With the intention of granting leases for the full twenty-year planning horizon, the main uncertain factor in revenue estimation is the degree of occupancy over the period. The subjectively assessed probability distributions for revenues were again approximated by the Normal distribution function, with means given by the expected values for rent revenues from Appendix 4, and variances assessed at one tenth of these expected mean values for each alternative, being a measure of the uncertainty about the occupancy rates.

The terminal value of each investment option proved the most difficult to estimate. Clearly in twenty years time the value of the property will depend not only upon the general trend in land prices, but also on how a potential buyer in twenty years time would assess the revenue possibilities of the property. A city like Caracas changes its character rapidly and, with many of the other large financial and commercial organizations also planning new headquarters outside the centre, there were already the signs of the city shifting its centre of gravity. Even if a new building on the 1969 code were constructed, the market value of the property in twenty years time would clearly have to be based solely upon its redevelopment potential. The Board finally agreed upon a terminal value of 6.5 million bolivars, in present day terms, with a variance of 4.

THE BANK'S ATTITUDE TOWARDS NPV

A consideration persistently at the forefront of the Board's thinking is that of maintaining the company's image and customer goodwill. For this reason they would only be prepared to let the property out to prestige hoteliers and retailers. Hence in estimating the value of outright sale (Option 1), the need to find the right sort of buyer who would not pull it down immediately, but maintain it in first-class condition and use it for highly respectable purposes, had to be taken into account. As a consequence the subjective probability distribution of the sale value was found to have the rather high variance of 1 against the mean of 6. Furthermore, many members of the Board had expressed strong opposition to those options which involved demolishing and redeveloping the existing building. Their argument, perhaps owing more to sentiment than economic reality, was that the building symbolized the immortal and impregnable security of the bank and that they should avoid even the slightest undertones of transience.

As a starting point, however, net present value (NPV) was considered to be an appropriate criterion with which to evaluate these investment options. The sums of money involved in any of the options were not considered to impose any strain on the bank's resources. The cost of capital was taken to be about 10 percent, and the discount factor thus $1/(1 + 10/100)$ or 0.9091.

The NPV of rent revenues was easily obtained from the formula

$$R = 12r(1 - d^{20})/(1 - d)$$
$$= 113r$$

where R = NPV of rents over twenty years
  r = rent revenue per month
  d = discount factor (0.9091)

Since the sum of a number of independent Normal variables is itself distributed Normally, the NPV for each investment can be evaluated as a Normal distribution. Appendix 5 summarizes the mean and variance of the NPV for each investment option. In considering Option 17, the Board strongly favored the idea of holding an equity interest in the department store. 4m. bolivars was being contemplated, which they assessed as an independent investment, to give an NPV, distributed Normally with a mean and variance of 3m.

The Board looked to Mr. Gale for advice upon which of the seventeen options they should adopt. For each option the NPV, distributed Normally with specific means and variances, had been estimated and the problem was to determine the Board's attitude to risk and how they wished to trade off NPV mean against variance.

THE UTILITY EVALUATION

It was clear that some members of the Board evaluated risk as the probability of the NPV of the investment being less than zero. Clearly, in this case, the option

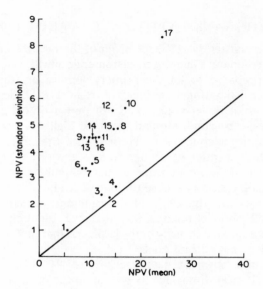

Figure 1   Mean and standard deviations of
the investment options

with smallest risk would be that with the highest value of the quantity NPV mean/NPV standard deviation.

Accordingly Mr. Gale plotted a graph (shown in Figure 1) of NPV mean against NPV standard deviation for the seventeen options. By considering the line from the origin to each of the seventeen points, the highest ratio of mean to standard deviation is achieved by Option 2, all other options having a higher slope and hence a lower ratio.

Other members of the Board were evidently less conservative in their attitude towards risk. Several expressed a preference for Option 17, with its high expected return, despite the greater risk. The decision-analyst realized, therefore, that it was necessary to evaluate more explicitly the Board's attitude to risk by constructing a corporate utility function for NPV.

A decision based upon expected utility would be a consistent one with respect to their overall preferences under uncertainty. A utility function over a range of NPV values could be obtained from responses to a set of artificial bets, similar to those used in the assessment of subjective probability. Since such a utility scale is arbitrary up to a linear transformation, the end points of the scale were conveniently established with an NPV return of 0 being given a utility of zero and an NPV return of 50, a utility of 1;

$$U(0) = 0$$
$$U(50) = 1$$

An intermediate utility can then be obtained as a certainty equivalent for a

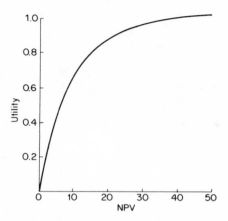

Figure 2   Utility curve for NPV

gamble on an NPV return of 50, with probability p, as opposed to an NPV return of 0, with probability $(1 - p)$. Probability is interpreted in the same sense as that used to assess the subjective probability distributions earlier, that is, comparison with a known number of red and black balls in a bag and the chance of drawing out a red one. This is essential to ensure consistency in the Expected Utility measure. Hence the 0.5 point on the utility scale was obtained by finding that particular investment for certain, with NPV equal to x, which was indifferent, from their point of view, to a gamble on receiving an investment with an NPV equal to 50, with a 0.5 chance, or receiving an investment with an NPV equal to zero with a 0.5 chance. Thus

$$U(x) = pU(50) + (1 - p)U(0)$$
$$= p$$

In this way enough points on the utility scale were obtained to interpolate a smooth curve, which is shown in Figure 2. Just as in the subjective probability assessments, the utility curve was an aggregate from all the individuals on the Board. The derivation of a consensus involved considerable introspection and questioning of the initial divergences in opinions and, unfortunately, the final consesus may perhaps have been over-influenced by those members of the Board with the more persuasive personalities.

The Expected Utility (*EU*) principle involves evaluating, for each invest-ment, the product of each possible NPV return with its associated probability. For investment $i(i = 1, 2, \ldots 17)$

$$EU_i = \int_{-\infty}^{+\infty} U(x)p_i(x) \, \mathrm{d}x$$

where $p_i(x)$ for each investment is a Normal density function with appropriate mean μ_i, and standard deviation σ_i.

110

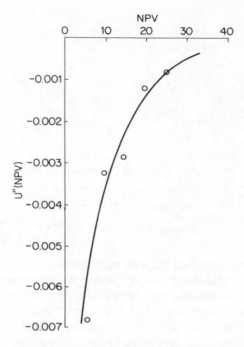

Figure 3 Second derivative of the utility
function

In order to avoid fitting a mathematical function to the utility curve and then evaluating the integral for each investment, advantage was taken of a well-known mathematical approximation

$$U(x) = U(\mu) + (x - \mu)U'(\mu) + \tfrac{1}{2}(x - \mu)^2 U''(\mu) \dots \tag{1}$$

where $U'(\mu)$ and $U''(\mu)$ represent first and second derivatives of the Utility function $U(x)$ evaluated at $x = \mu$. Hence taking the expectation of $U(x)$

$$E(U(x)) = U(\mu) + \tfrac{1}{2}\sigma^2 U''(\mu) + \text{(negligible terms)} \tag{2}$$

and therefore for investment i

$$EU_i = U(\mu_i) + \tfrac{1}{2}\sigma_i^2 U''(\mu_i) \tag{3}$$

$U(\mu_i)$ can be read off directly from the utility function plotted in Figure 2. In Appendix 6, second differences of $U(x)$ are evaluated by first evaluating $U'(x)$, the gradient of the utility function at intermediate points, and then $U''(x)$, the gradient of the gradient at specific points on x. A curve of $U''(x)$ is plotted in Figure 3, as an interpolation of points derived in Appendix 6.

Using this approximation, EU_i can be easily evaluated for all i. It is, in practice, only necessary to evaluate those investments which are contained in the 'efficient' subset of all investment options. The efficient subset excludes all dominated investments, and an investment is dominated if it has an NPV standard deviation roughly equal to another, but a significantly lower mean NPV.

As investment Option 2 did not turn out to have the maximum expected utility, the decision-analyst now had to advise the Board which approach was most valid. It was recognized that maximizing expected utility elucidated which investment option would be most consistent with the Board's own attitude to investment under uncertainty. It does nothing towards helping the Board to formulate what their attitude should be.

The method of using the ratio NPV (mean)/NPV (standard deviation) provided a very definite criterion, but one with the rather conservative basic interpretation of risk as the probability of a negative NPV.

Other, non-quantified, preferences of the Board, such as their desire to preserve the building and, through it, the Bank's image, if feasible, had moreover not been taken into account. Fortunately, such is the economic climate for commerce in Venezuela that, whilst the Government's taxation policies might be an important consideration in investment-planning in most other countries, taxation is blissfully negligible for the Venezuelans.

APPENDIX 1: THE SET OF APPARENT OPTIONS

1 Sell the property in its present condition.
2 Retain and use as offices.
3 Retain and use as offices with slight modifications.
4 Add two floors and use as offices and retail shops.
5 As 4, with slight modifications.
6 As 5, but with apartments.
7 As 5, but incorporate an hotel.
8 Construct new building (1967 plan) for offices and retail shops.
9 As 8, but incorporating an hotel.
10 As 8, but with department store.
11 As 8, but with apartments.
12 As 8, but with just offices and department store.
13 Construct new building (1968 plan) for offices and retail shop.
14 As 13, but use for hotel.
15 As 13, but use for offices and department store.
16 As 13, but with apartments.
17 Construct new building (1970 plan) but with considerable expansion and use it for department store.

112

APPENDIX 2: INVESTMENT COSTS*

Option	Facilities	Construction cost		Indemnification Cost	Total cost	
		Mean	Variance	Cost	Mean	Variance
1	−10.5			4.5	−6.0	1
2		1.55	0.1		1.55	0.1
3		4.53	0.8		4.53	0.8
4		6.90	2		6.9	2
5		8.85	7	4.5	13.35	7
6		8.20	6	4.5	12.7	6
7		8.35	6	4.5	12.85	6
8		14.80	17	4.5	19.3	17
9		13.70	15	4.5	18.2	15
10		16.45	25	4.5	20.95	25
11		13.72	15	4.5	18.22	15
12		16.00	24	4.5	20.5	24
13		13.87	15	4.5	18.37	15
14		13.79	15	4.5	18.29	15
15		14.70	17	4.5	19.2	17
16		13.69	15	4.5	18.19	15
17	10.3	25.80	64	4.5	40.6	64

*All units are million bolivars.

APPENDIX 3: SUMMARY OF FLOOR SPACE CATEGORIES

Code	Description
01	Class A office
02	Class B office
03	Class A office, new rentals
04	Class B office, new rentals
05	Class B office, existing rentals
A1	Class A apartment, 1970 plan
A2	Class A apartment, 1968 plan
A3	Class A apartment, existing building
H1	Class A hotel, 1970 plan
H2	Class A hotel, 1968 plan
H3	Class A hotel, existing building
D1	Class A department store, large
D2	Class A department store, medium
D3	Class A department store, small
R1	Class A retail, prime
R2	Class A retail, secondary
R3	Class A retail, mezzanine
R4	Class B retail, ground
R5	Class B retail, ground, existing rental
P	Parking space
U	Unusable space

APPENDIX 4: RENT REVENUES*

Space code	Rent† per square metre	Option							
		2	3	4	5	6	7	8	9
O1	16								
O2	14.5							11,380	
O3	11.5	4,674	4,898	3,798	4,053				
O4	10			4,674	5,412	5,412	5,412		
O5	10	514	514	514					
A1	17.5								
A2	16					2,981			
A3	13								
H1	14								13,063
H2	13						3,803		
H3	11.5								
D1	19								
D2	19								
D3	19								
R1	27							911	
R2	22.5							300	
R3	16								
R4	13	118	432	118	2,756	2,756	2,756	1,246	
R5	13	2,324	2,324	2,324					
P	4.8							4,310	4,402
U	0	232	232	232	232	232	232		
Total rent revenue/month		83,500	97,000	140,000	157,000	136,000	140,000	256,000	190,000

*Figures in table denote the appropriate space availability in square metres.
†Rent is expressed in bolivars per month.

(Table continued on next page)

114

RENT REVENUES (*contd*)

Space code	Rent per square metre	Option							
		10	11	12	13	14	15	16	17
O1	16								
O2	14.5		4,185	8,580	9,424		2,465	7,049	
O3	11.5								
O4	10								
O5	10								
A1	17.5								
A2	16		5,394					2,105	
A3	13								
H1	14					12,966			
H2	13								
H3	11.5								
D1	19						10,171		24,400
D2	19	14,018							
D3	19			6,390					
R1	27		720		1,176				
R2	22.5		240					1,246	
R3	16		1,014						
R4	13								
R5	13								
P	4.8	3,039	4,378	3,002	4,186	4,450	3,036	4,186	5,250
U	0								
Total rent revenue/month		285,000	210,000	276,000	200,000	202,000	250,000	202,000	495,000

APPENDIX 5: NPV MEAN AND VARIANCE

Option	Rent (mean) (a)	Cost (mean) (b)	Resale (mean) (c)	Equity (mean) (d)	Total NPV Mean	Total NPV Variance
1		−6.00			6.00	1
2	9.43	1.55	6.5		14.38	5
3	10.96	4.53	6.5		12.93	6
4	15.82	6.9	6.5		15.42	7.5
5	17.74	13.35	6.5		10.89	13
6	15.37	12.70	6.5		9.17	11.5
7	15.82	12.85	6.5		9.47	11.5
8	28.92	19.30	6.5		16.12	24
9	21.40	18.20	6.5		9.70	21
10	32.20	20.95	6.5		17.75	32
11	23.70	18.22	6.5		11.98	21
12	31.20	20.50	6.5		17.20	31
13	22.60	18.37	6.5		10.73	21
14	20.80	18.29	6.5		11.01	21
15	28.20	19.20	6.5		15.50	24
16	22.80	18.20	6.5		11.10	21
17	55.90	40.60	6.5	3	24.80	71

(1) All units are million bolivars.
(ii) Final variance: sum of variances for rent, cost, resale, and equity.
(iii) NPV is net present value at the discount rate used (see text).
(iv) Mean NPV is equal to (a) − (b) + (c) + (d)

APPENDIX 6: EVALUATION OF THE SECOND DIFFERENCES OF THE UTILITY FUNCTION

NPV	U(NPV)	U'(NPV)	U"(NPV)
0	0		
		0.080	
5	0.40		−0.0068
		0.046	
10	0.63		−0.0032
		0.030	
15	0.78		−0.0028
		0.016	
20	0.86		−0.0012
		0.010	
25	0.91		−0.0008
		0.004	
30	0.96		

ISSUES FOR DISCUSSION IN RELATION TO THE
CARACAS CASE

(a) Project Screening

It is possible to reduce the number of alternative options from seventeen to a smaller set by using a form of screening based upon principles of *stochastic dominance*. Thus, a simple form of stochastic dominance would allow us to argue that, for projects with the same mean values, we could eliminate those with higher variance. In a similar manner, for projects with the same variance, we could eliminate those with lower mean values.

The principle of screening is often called mean-variance (M/V) analysis in the finance literature and the approach is ascribed to Markowitz (23) and Tobin (30). The Markowitz–Tobin approach is generally applied to issues of portfolio analysis, i.e. in determining the choice of an optimal combination (portfolio) of projects out of the subset of efficient combinations (portfolios). The extension of the case to the portfolio situation will be developed later in this discussion.

For the moment, if we apply the dominance screening principle, we reduce the set of feasible options to the set (1, 2, 3, 8, 10, 17) from which the choice of the preferred option can be made.

(b) Selection of a Decision Criterion

The decision analytic approach for finding the optimal investment choice, outlined in the case, rests upon, firstly, the derivation of an appropriate corporate utility function for money and, secondly, determining the point of tangency between this utility curve and the efficient set. Note here that the utility function is assessed from the responsible decision-maker or decision-making group within the organization.

If we therefore use the derived utility function, and a decision criterion of the maximization of expected utility, option 17 would be chosen. The table below gives details.

Table 1: Derivation of Expected Utility Values for Efficient
Set Options

Option number	Expected utility		
1	$0.5 - \frac{1}{2} \times 0.005$	$=$	0.50
2	$0.76 - \frac{1}{2} \times 5 \times 0.0025$	$=$	0.75
3	$0.79 - \frac{1}{2} \times 7.5 \times 0.0021$	$=$	0.785
8	$0.8 - \frac{1}{2} \times 24 \times 0.002$	$=$	0.776
10	$0.83 - \frac{1}{2} \times 36 \times 0.0017$	$=$	0.80
17	$0.91 - \frac{1}{2} \times 71 \times 0.0008$	$=$	0.88

On the other hand, if we adopt a criterion of minimizing the chance of a return less than 10 percent (or equivalently an NPV less than 0), we would choose option 2.

In general, expected utility will suggest the option *consistent* with the company's overall attitude to risk. The choice of a minimum negative NPV criterion would generally be appropriate in circumstances where the company was *constrained* to provide a positive return on a particular investment. If this investment were, therefore, an unusually large venture, we would advocate this minimum loss criterion. However, we are told that the sums of money involved are well within the bank's resources and thus we could suggest that the less conservative expected utility criterion should be adopted.

It is worthwhile noting that such a corporate utility curve probably reflects a greater degree of risk than any individual member of the Board would adopt. The phenomenon of *risky shift* is a well-known group process, whereby a group of people as a whole may take a more risky attitude to decisions under uncertainty than they would individually.

This use of corporate utility functions in investment decision-making should, however, be questioned on theoretical grounds. To digress for a moment, in the theoretical context of capital budgeting under certainty conditions, firms are assumed to accept those projects whose NPVs are positive when discounted at that rate which reflects the firm's opportunity cost of capital. This decision rule follows from the assumption that firms act to maximize shareholder wealth since asset prices are determined in the 'certain' environment by their discounted present values.

Under uncertainty conditions, it can also be shown that the discount rate at which the 'market' adjusts the expected returns of a firm's shares is that opportunity cost rate which maximizes shareholder wealth. It is clear, therefore, that a maximization of shareholder wealth objective is paramount. Further, that M/V analysis can only work if shareholders and investors in the 'market' act in accordance with M/V principles. The weakness of the subjective expected utility approach in the capital budgeting context is that shareholders typically do not have quadratic utility functions and these are, in any case, unlikely to be in one-to-one correspondence with a utility function for money derived from a decision-making group or a single decision-maker. Such a subjective utility function is, therefore, not in general an investor's utility function and as such M/V analysis does not apply.*

In the portfolio section, we discuss how some of these defects can be overcome.

---

*Indeed, the so-called Fisher separation theorem states that the investment decision is independent of subjective individual preferences. As a consequence, optimal investment decisions are made by taking on projects until the marginal rate of return on investment equals the objective market rate (determined from a shareholder wealth goal). This could also be stated as a decision rule which accepts projects, whose NPV ≥ 0, when discounted at the firm's opportunity cost rate.

118

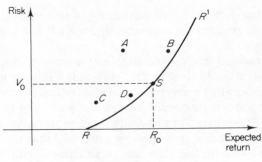

Figure 2

(c) Issues of Goodwill and Preservation of the Building

Project option 17 involves demolition of the building, and other attributes such as the desire to preserve the building, become relevant in developing a criterion for project choice. A later section in this chapter develops the topic of multi-attributed decision rules in greater detail. We could, however, handle the specific problem in relation to project 17 by asking the Board what sum of money they would be willing to pay in order to avoid the demolition of the building. For example, would it be one million bolivars? 2 million bolivars? etc. Such questioning is an example of the 'certainty equivalence' and 'risk premium' reasoning that is used in deriving utility functions from decision-makers (for example see Swalm (28), Hammond (9)).

(d) Technical Issues Associated with the Hillier Approach

The perceptive reader will notice that the analytical approach adopted in this case ignored correlation patterns both within and between annual cash flows. Such an assumption may be significant in terms of the interpretation of final output.

(e) The Portfolio Argument

Though the Caracas case involved seventeen possible development options for a single redevelopment project, we could, for the moment, regard them for illustrative purposes in relation to portfolio analysis, as seventeen *different* project combinations (portfolios) for the firm in question. Strictly they are portfolios of one project. Following the case scenario closely we note that by use of the mean-variance rule, we can determine a subset of efficient combinations (portfolios). The subset of such efficient investment combinations faced by the firm is illustrated (not to scale) by the curve RR^1 shown in Figure 2.

Note that all of the 'non-efficient' combinations lie to the left of RR^1 (where we note that R represents the rate of return on risk-less assets — however defined). Suppose that R_0 represents the minimum rate of return which investors require to receive from investment in the firm's shares (given the average return variance V_0 of all the firm's projects).

In applying mean-variance analysis it is clear that the higher the variability of investment returns, the larger will be the risk premium (average premium) demanded by investment in the firm's shares. This risk premium is determined by asset pricing in the stock market.

Now in Figure 2, if we assume that the firm only executes projects if, and only if, NPVs (discounted at R_0) are positive, then the portion SR^1 represents the relevant portion of the RR^1 curve for decision-making purposes. Generally speaking, a firm is confronted with projects of varying risk and the mean-variance model suggests that the equilibrium combination (R_0, V_0) might have been obtained with a portfolio of two projects, say B, having a higher expected return and risk than S, and C, having a lower expected return and a lower variance than S in Figure 2. Indeed, projects such as C (whose NPV is < 0 when discounted at R_0) may be perfectly acceptable for the firm to accept as part of a portfolio. This finding is intuitively reasonable — in effect, lower portfolio risk is being achieved through risk reduction involving combinations of negatively correlated investments (thus exploiting the advantages of covariance first suggested by Markowitz (23)).

Therefore, there are problems with the NPV decision rule when used in combination with mean-variance analysis such as the aforementioned possibility that negative NPV projects can be part of a portfolio. Recall that the minimum required rate of return R_0 reflects the average level of risk of all the firm's investments, and this creates problems when the firm is faced with evaluation of, and choice amongst investment opportunities of different risk levels. Clearly, these investment possibilities will have a major effect on the firm's average risk level, and ultimately also to the shareholders. Therefore, there must be a simultaneous determination of the optimal portfolio and the firm's minimum discount rate R_0 (the relevant opportunity cost rate).

Lintner's work (which assumes perfect markets and that there is no limit on the divisibility of investments) offers a way of resolving the issue of joint determination of the optimum portfolio and discount rate. In Figure 3, we show a scatter diagram which represents all attainable portfolios confronting investors in the stock market.

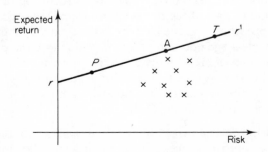

Figure 3

Lintner (20) argues that, in equilibrium, the slope of the line rr^1 determines the market value of risk. Further, the optimum portfolio of each investor is a combination of portfolio A plus bonds, e.g. a point such as P or T on the line rr^1 (which has slope $(R_A - r)/\sigma_A$ where R_A and σ_A are the mean and standard deviation of portfolio of A). Note that the line rr^1 (where r is the rate of return on riskless assets) with its associated slope defines the trade-off between risk and return for all investors. (This follows since borrowing and lending can take place along rr^1.) Thus, if the line rr^1 were drawn on Figure 2 then the point of tangency of rr^1 with the efficient set RR^1 represents the *optimum* portfolio of investments for the firm.

It is at this point that we must review the expected utility argument in the original Caracas case. Tangency between the efficient set RR^1 and the corporate utility function derived therein will not define the optimum portfolio since a firm's shareholders, generally, have different utility functions from those of the decision-making group or that of the 'single' decision-maker. That is, the utility function concept does not adequately represent total firm risk in the context of project selection. On the other hand, Lintner's approach relates the efficient set to the trade-off function for all investors between risk and return. Therefore, in reviewing the original Caracas case, and viewing the seventeen options as possible combinations, the straight-line Lintner approach is more useful and theoretically sound than the expected utility individual decision-maker approach.

We will discuss these issues during the course of this book, particularly when the relationship of risk analysis to the Capital Asset Pricing Model (CAPM) is taken up in Chapter 5. Readers are also referred to Levy and Sarnat (18) and Copeland and Weston (4).

STOCHASTIC DECISION-TREE ANALYSIS

The stochastic decision-tree approach was developed by Hespos and Strassmann (13) as a convenient method for representing and analyzing a series of decisions over time. It combines the logic of decision-tree analysis (see for example, Moore and Thomas (24), Raiffa (26), Thomas (29)) with the Monte-Carlo simulation approach adopted in risk analysis. It can, therefore, handle situations of sequential investment decision-making, (e.g. strategy decisions, abandonment decisions) by suitable structuring of the investment decision problem in terms of the decision-tree framework. Risk analysis, and other similar approaches, e.g. the Hillier model, treat the investment decision as if it were a single-stage decision problem, and ignore the possibility of the existence of a number of highly interrelated investment decisions occurring at different points in time over the time-span of the decision problem.

The essence of the stochastic decision-tree approach is summarized as follows by Hespos and Strassmann (13).

The stochastic decision-tree approach is similar to the conventional decision-tree approach, except that it also has the following features:

(a) All quantities and factors, including chance events, can be represented by continuous, empirical probability distributions.

(b) The information about the results from any, or all, possible combinations of decisions made at sequential points in time can be obtained in a probabilistic form.

(c) The probability distribution of possible results from any particular combination of decisions can be analyzed using the concepts of utility and risk.

The stages of the stochastic decision-tree procedure can, therefore, be summarized as follows:

Stage 1 Investment Decision Structuring

At this stage the investment decision team discuss the range of available alternative options, chance events which affect them, and possible valuation problems, as a prerequisite to structuring the problem in terms of a decision tree.

Such a structure might be the one given in Figure 4 for a market launch example. This structure shows that the company can choose initially to market a product nationally or regionally. If it decides to market regionally first, it can later go national or remain regional. It should be noted that once the decision to launch the new product has been made, then uncertain cash flow patterns can be associated with each branch (where chance event nodes are replaced by probability distributions) and represented by individual probability distributions.

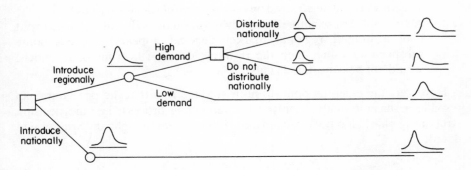

Figure 4 Stochastic decision tree for a market launch

Stage II The Evaluation Phase

In this phase, all possible combinations of decisions are evaluated in terms of probability distributions. Typically the decision tree is used as a model for a 'forwards-analysis' of the decision tree, and therefore each possible strategy path is evaluated in terms of a probability distribution for the NPV criterion. The decision focus is then concentrated upon this probabilistic output.

In more complicated and larger decision-tree structures than the one illustrated in Figure 4, it becomes much more difficult to obtain a complex enumeration of all strategy paths, quite apart from questions of the practicality, time and cost factors associated with such an enumeration. In those cases (and these are the *norms* in terms of practical applications) the following procedure is usually adopted. First, analyze the decision tree using the rollback principle (see Moore and Thomas (24)), and the expected value criterion following the standard decision-analysis approach. In this manner, the optimum strategy (or abandonment) for the investment decision is determined generally in terms of the EMV (expected monetary value) criterion. The 'pruned' tree based on the optimum strategy, which is now basically a probability tree, is then analyzed forwards and the NPV probability distribution and associated summary statistics are obtained for the optimum strategy.

Other simplifications are possible. For example, Hespos and Strassmann (13) suggested two possibilities as follows:

(i) A modified rollback principle might be used. Branches of the tree would be eliminated on the basis of *stochastic dominance* principles rather than the decision-analysis norm of expected value. For example, a branch would be eliminated if it had both a lower EMV and higher variance than an alternative branch. Such a *dominance* procedure might reduce the decision set, and allow more analytic effort to be expended upon an efficient set of decision paths.

(ii) A computational simplification, which would not affect the tree structure, could be effected by making sensible decision rules before the simulation. For example, if on any iteration the value of a chance event (say a limited regional market demand appears) exceeds some prespecified value, then the resulting decision (say national launch) would not be considered at all.

However, the essential point to note at Stage II is that the procedure can provide a sensible analysis only if the modelling process, i.e. the decision structuring phase, has been carried out with sufficient thought and attention to detail.

Pros and Cons of the Stochastic Decision-tree Approach

The strong advantage of the decision-tree framework is that the decision tree is a visual and easily understood means of representing the sequential, multi-stage logic of a decision problem. In any investment decision situation, there are a series of decisions to be made, and any action taken now must affect future decisions. The present strategy decision thus has a conditional impact upon future decisions and uncertainties.

The nature of the tree, and the structure agreed to by members of the investment team, implies that the statistical relationships between variables are defined and incorporated within the tree. Not only does this mean that correlation effects are explicitly modelled but, in addition, it also alerts the members of the team to the assessment of correlation effects, e.g. conditional probabilities which must be made *before* the optimum strategy can be determined.

The communication and logic framework provided by the decision tree is important and valuable and distills the essence of any problem. However, many problems are complex and the decision tree can quickly become a bushy mess. Thus, the decision tree can quickly lose many of its advantages solely because it becomes too large and cumbersome. This size factor means that many more uncertain quantities have to be assessed before any analysis can take place, and this alone will place great strains on the decision-making team. In addition, the computational demands can increase significantly and for some applications software may not be readily available.

Ironically, therefore, increasing size, which would normally lead to an argument for evaluation in terms of a more comprehensive analytic decision model, means that compromises about tree structure have to be made. Typically these involve ignoring some correlation patterns, and in particular, those involving time-series dependencies between variables in the tree. One effect of this is a reduction in the number of assessments which have to be made by the decision-making group.

It should not be forgotten, however, that the exercise of decision structuring and problem reduction is an important one for any decision-making group to undertake. Very often, relatively little effort is spent in understanding the decision problem and in creative thought about problem structure. In addition, few attempts are made to screen out unnecessary or obviously dominated options before analysis takes place. Therefore, the major advantages in favour of the stochastic decision tree approach arise from the logic of the decision tree structuring procedure.

STOCHASTIC DECISION-TREE EXAMPLES

Example 1: A Modified New Product Launch Example

The example presented here is based upon the decision-tree structure shown in Hespos and Strassmann's article. Certain simplifications are made for the purpose of illustration. First, it is assumed that the firm has just two initial options, namely either to introduce the new product on a regional basis or to go ahead immediately with a national launch. Second, chance events in the launch situation are assumed to be adequately represented by three-branch forks rather than many-branch forks, as would be required by the assumption of a continuous distribution. Third, it is assumed that the product has a three-year

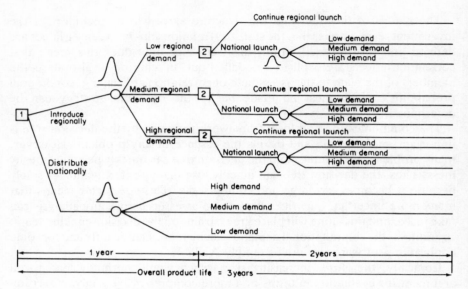

Figure 5 Decision-tree structure for product launch example

life, and if a regional launch is contemplated initially, then one year will be spent on regional marketing before a national launch decision.

The structure of the decision problem is shown in Figure 5. Note that in this figure no probability assessments or cash flow payoffs are given. In Figure 6, the probability assessments are given for the chance events and net present values figures for each decision-chance event path are assessed and calculated, assuming a risk-free rate (such as the yield on a Treasury bond of maturity equivalent to that of the project) of 5 percent after all taxes. (Note: it is further assumed for illustrative purposes that after three years, the product has no further useful life and no salvage value.)

The next figure, Figure 7, shows the first stage of a modified Hespos–Strassmann (H-S) type procedure. At this stage, we adopt the rollback principle of decision analysis using EMV (expected NPV) as a decision criterion in order to determine the optimal strategy path. The path is shown in the figure as the non-blocked-off path (i.e. the one with no barred gates (‖) on the tree).

Thus, the distribute nationally path is optimal because it has the highest EMV, 0.53 compared with 0.316 for the regional launch. Moreover, if we were to calculate the standard deviation (SD) of possible NPVs for the national launch strategy, we find it to be 0.74 compared to 0.62 for the regional launch strategy. This information probably reinforces the conclusion that we should launch nationally, since the coefficient of variation (SD/Mean) for the national distribution is smaller than for the regional distribution.

However, in order to show the overall rationale of the Hespos and Strassmann approach, let us derive the results for each of the following strategies:

(a) Introduce nationally from the outset.

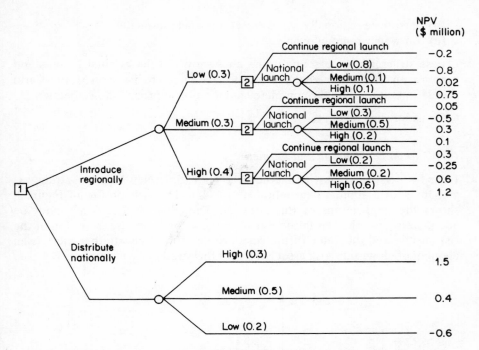

Figure 6 Decision-tree structure for product launch with assessments given

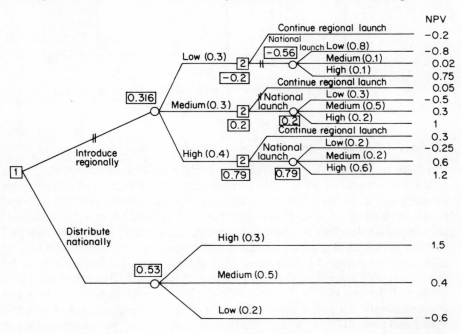

Figure 7 Rollback analysis of decision tree

126

(b) Introduce regionally at the outset, then act 'optimally'.
(c) Introduce regionally only.

(These strategies are essentially the ones shown in the original Hespos and Strassmann article, though the results derived there are based on Monte-Carlo simulation rather than the complete enumeration approach shown below.)

Consider each one in turn.

(a) National Distribution and Launch

It can be seen from Figure 8 that the mean NPV (or E(NPV)) for this strategy is $0.53m with a standard deviation of $0.74m. The risk profile in Figure 8 shows the implications of this strategy. Though a distribution cannot be adequately smoothed or faired out from these three points, the graph of the risk profile and the value of the standard deviation indicate that there is an element of 'downside' risk associated with this strategy.

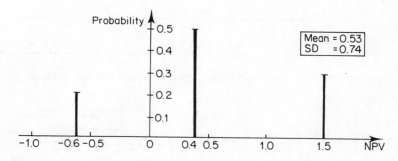

Figure 8 Risk profile of national launch strategy

(b) Regional Launch at the Outset, then 'Optimal Action'

It is here that the value of the rollback analysis becomes evident. For, if we follow the introduce regionally branch with an EMV = 0.316 (ignoring for the moment that it has been eliminated by comparison with the immediate national launch option) the tree analysis shows that if low regional demand is indicated, then regional distribution should be continued; further, if medium regional demand is indicated, then a national launch should be attempted and finally, if high regional demand is indicated, then again a national launch should be attempted. We know that the EMV of this strategy is $0.316m and the SD is $0.62m. The risk profile for this strategy is shown in Figure 9. The table presented with the graph shows each of the final outcomes together with the associated probabilities. Again, this distribution is fairly spread out and it can be seen that there is a 47 percent chance of NPV < 0.

	Strategy-event paths			Probability	NPV ($m)
Reg. launch	LOW reg. demand	Continue Reg. launch		0.3	−0.2
Reg. launch	MED Reg. demand	National launch	LOW demand	0.09	−0.5
Reg. launch	MED. reg demand	National launch	MED demand	0.15	+0.3
Reg. launch	MED. reg demand	National launch	HIGH demand	0.06	+1.0
Reg. launch	HIGH reg. demand	National launch	LOW demand	0.08	−0.25
Reg. launch	HIGH reg. demand	National launch	MED. demand	0.08	+0.6
Reg. launch	HIGH reg. demand	National launch	HIGH demand	0.24	1.2

Total probability =1.00

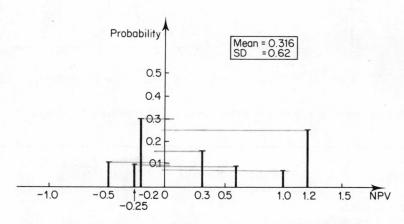

Figure 9 Risk profile for the regional launch/act optimally strategy

(c) Regional Distribution Only Strategy

This case is very straightforward. If we consider the initial decision tree, then the following probability distribution can easily be derived.

128

The risk profile for this strategy is shown in Figure 10.

Strategy-event paths	Probability	NPV
Reg. $\rightarrow$ High launch demand	0.4	0.3
Reg. $\rightarrow$ Med. launch demand	0.3	0.05
Reg. $\rightarrow$ Low launch demand	0.3	−0.2
Mean NPV = 0.075		SD = 0.021

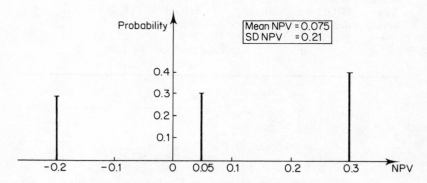

Figure 10 Risk Profile of Regional Distribution Only Strategy

Summary results for the three strategies are shown in the table below:

Strategy	Mean NPV	NPV SD	Coefficient of variation (SD/Mean)
National launch	0.53	0.74	1.4
Regional launch/Act optimally	0.316	0.62	1.99
Regional launch	0.075	0.21	2.8

Clearly the extended information provided here broadens the information base of the firm and its decision group. None of it would, however, probably change the decision to go for a national launch.

In Example 2, we extend this simple product launch example to show how an abandonment-type decision can easily be handled within the context of the stochastic decision-tree framework.

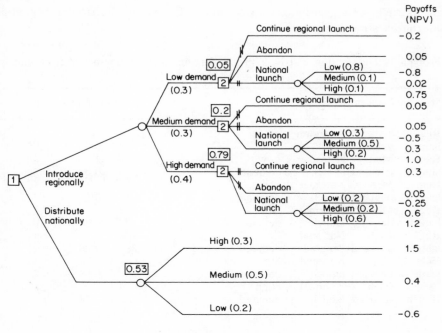

Figure 11

Example 2: New Product Launch Decision with Abandonment Strategies as Possible Options

Figure 11 shows the analysis of the new product problem with an additional abandonment possibility at the end of year 1 — the review point in relation to the regional launch strategy. It is assumed that the firm can recover an NPV of $50,000 at the end of year 1 by liquidating stocks, etc. and this value will be assumed to apply whatever might be the actual state of regional demand during the course of the first year. The effect of the introduction of the abandonment option is to raise the EMV of the regional/launch/'act optimally' strategy to $0.381m and to reduce the standard deviation to 0.57 without affecting the values for the immediate national launch strategy. In addition, some of the downside risk is removed because if low regional demand occurs in year 1, then the optimal act is to abandon with an NPV of 0.05 rather than the 'continue regional launch' option with an NPV of −0.2.

The risk profile for the abandonment case/regional launch/'act optimally' strategy is given in the following table and Figure 12. Note that the chance of the NPV being less than zero is now 0.17 or 17 percent compared to the 47 percent chance without the 'abandonment' option. Clearly, the stochastic decision-tree framework has considerable use when project amendment or even abandonment becomes a possibility, because it allows such strategic changes to be embedded within the tree as potential alternative strategy paths.

Probability Distribution and Risk Profile for the Regional Launch/'Act Optimally' Strategy

Strategy — event paths				Probability	NPV
Reg. launch	Low demand	Abandon		0.3	0.05
Reg. launch	Med. demand	National launch	Low demand	0.09	−0.5
Reg. launch	Med. demand	National launch	Med. demand	0.15	0.3
Reg. launch	Med. demand	National launch	High demand	0.06	1.0
Reg. launch	High demand	National demand	Low demand	0.08	−0.25
Reg. launch	High demand	National launch	Med. demand	0.08	0.6
Reg. launch	High demand	National launch	High demand	0.24	1.2
			Total probability =	1.0	

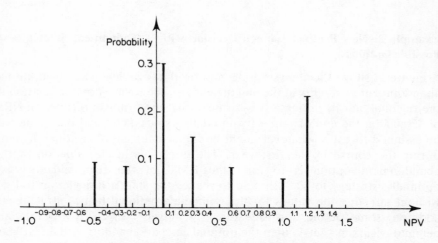

Figure 12 Risk profile for regional launch/'act optimally' strategy

In summary, examples 1 and 2 point out the value of the Hespos–Strassmann approach in the context of strategic financial decisions and abandonment decisions. A number of examples in the companion case volume give further applications of the Hespos–Strassmann approach.

CONCEPTS OF STOCHASTIC DOMINANCE

In many of the examples given in this book, particularly within the risk analysis chapter (Chapter 2) and the current chapter, we have seen the output of decision analyses presented in the form of probability distributions of a financial measure, typically *net present value*. Two issues emerge when a decision-making group is confronted with a series of projects evaluated in terms of probability distributions. These issues warrant further discussion:

(a) reduction or *screening* of the options into a feasible or efficient set: rules of stochastic dominance;
(b) deriving a choice criterion, e.g. expected utility for determining the 'most preferred' option within that feasible set.

Let us consider each of these in some detail.

(a) Screening for Risky Ventures: Dominance Approaches

The simplest approach for screening under uncertainty, which we saw for example in the Caracas case, consists of identifying the 'efficient' set of options. The efficient set excludes all 'dominated' options. An option is said to be dominated (in a mean-variance sense) in the set, if there exists either another option with the same mean but lower variance, or with the same variance but higher mean. This approach has been most evident in the literature on Portfolio Theory, for example, Markowitz (23).

This concept of dominance is founded in the principle of minimizing variance (a surrogate for risk) for risk-averse decision-makers, and can be summarized as follows for two alternatives X_1 and X_2 with means $E(X_1)$ and $E(X_2)$ and variances $V(X_1)$ and $V(X_2)$.

(1) Alternative 1 is preferred to Alternative 2 if
$E(X_1) \geq E(X_2)$ and $V(X_1) < V(X_2)$.
(2) Alternative 1 is preferred to Alternative 2 if
$V(X_1) \leq V(X_2)$ and $E(X_1) > E(X_2)$.

It can be shown that these rules hold if the probability distributions for the outcome of X_1 and X_2 are reasonably symmetrically (strictly normally distributed) distributed, and if the decision-makers' preferences for outcomes are of the quadratic form.

The mean-variance approach summarized above involves certain assumptions, and for screening purposes we have to question how robust these assumptions are in identifying the best subset. Less restrictive constraints on the form of implicit function can be dealt with using screening models developed from the concept of 'stochastic dominance'. Stochastic dominance is said to occur if the expected utility of an option is greater than that of another over a whole class of utility functions. The theory owes much of its development to Hadar and Russell (8), Hanoch and Levy (10), Porter and

Carey (25) and Whitmore (33). A recent survey article is that by Eilon and Tilley (7). The set of conditions derived from the stochastic dominance concept is given below.

First Degree Stochastic Dominance (FSD)

This makes very weak assumptions on the form of the utility function: only that $U(x)$ is finite, continuously differentiable, and strictly increasing over x. If $F_1(x)$, $F_2(x)$ are the distribution functions for two options, then if:

$$F_1(x) \leq F_2(x)$$

option 1 dominates option 2 (except, of course, in the case of equality over all x) in the sense of FSD.

Second Degree Stochastic Dominance (SSD)

This assumes a risk-averse (concave) utility function over x, in addition to the assumption of FSD. If

$$\int_{-\infty}^{z} (F_2(x) - F_1(x))\, dx \geq 0 \qquad \forall z$$

then option 1 dominates option 2 in the sense of SSD. This is more restrictive than FSD and can therefore, when appropriate, further screen an efficient set derived from FSD.

Third Degree Stochastic Dominance (TSD)

This test requires in addition to FSD, that $U'(x) > 0$, $U''(x) > 0$ and $U'''(x) > 0$ for all x. If

$$\int_{-\infty}^{y} \int_{-\infty}^{z} (F_2(x) - F_1(x))\, dx\, dz \geq 0 \qquad \forall y$$

then option 1 dominates in the sense of TSD. This can further screen an efficient set derived from SSD, but the assumptions of TSD do not have an intuitively obvious appeal.

To illustrate the application of stochastic dominance criteria more fully, a simple example is given below:

Example of 'Stochastic Dominance Rules'

It should be noted initially that the stochastic dominance approach examines the entire range of likely outcomes from an investment project, rather than concentrating upon parameters of the distribution of outcomes such as the expected value (mean) and the standard deviation (variance).

Therefore, the stochastic dominance approach may be employed as an additional refinement to the mean-variance type of analysis or as an alternative method. However, it is important to remember that, if the stochastic dominance approach is used as an additional analytic vehicle to mean-variance analysis, the rules of stochastic dominance may reduce the number of portfolios in the mean-variance efficient set. Equally, if the rules of stochastic dominance were applied before mean-variance rules, it would be possible to find that some portfolios not included in the mean-variance efficient set were members of the efficient set determined from the stochastic dominance rules. Generally, therefore, the efficient sets determined from both approaches will not normally be equivalent.

Now let us consider two portfolios X and Y (valued in NPV terms) both of which are members of the mean-variance efficient set (Markowitz (23)).

X			Y	
:---:	:---:		:---:	:---:
Probability distribution			*Probability distribution*	
X(NPV)	*Probability*		*Y(NPV)*	*Probability*
$m			$m	
$100 \leqslant X < 200$	0.1		$0 \leqslant Y < 100$	0.1
$200 \leqslant X < 300$	0.5		$100 \leqslant Y < 200$	0.2
$300 \leqslant X < 400$	0.2		$200 \leqslant Y < 300$	0.5
$400 \leqslant X < 500$	0.2		$300 \leqslant Y < 400$	0.2
Mean $E(X) = 300$			$E(Y) = 230$	
$V(X) = 8500$			$V(Y) = 7600$	

Figure 13 gives a visual representation of these two probability distributions in terms of histograms or probability density functions (pfds).

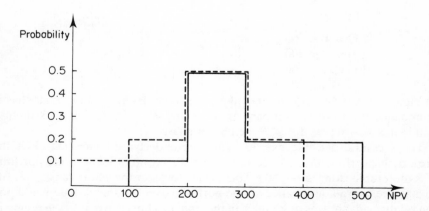

Figure 13 Pdfs for X and Y

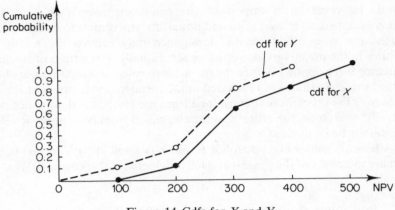

Figure 14 Cdfs for X and Y

An alternative representation in terms of cumulative density functions (cdfs) is shown in Figure 14. This figure shows quite clearly that portfolio X dominates Y in the sense of first-order stochastic dominance since the cdf for Y lies everywhere to the left of the cdf for X (i.e. $F(Y) \leq F(X)$ — first-orderStochastic Dominance Rule). In other words, for any value of NPV between 0 and 500 the probability of a better outcome than that value is greater with portfolio X than with portfolio Y.

Note that under mean-variance rules, both X and Y would be members of the portfolio efficient set although the first-order stochastic dominance rule eliminates portfolio Y from further consideration.

Now let us change our simple example slightly in order to show the application of second-order stochastic dominance rules. Basically, we need to ensure that the cdfs for X and Y intersect over the range of 0 to 500 so that the rule $F(Y) \leq F(X)$ is violated. Let us, therefore, assume the following distribution for Y and retain the initial assumptions about the distribution of X.

Y	Probability
$100 \leq Y < 200$	0.1
$200 \leq Y < 300$	0.3
$300 \leq Y < 400$	0.6

In Figure 15, the new cdfs for Y and X are shown. By second-order stochastic dominance we have to compare areas A and B. If Area $A > B$ then X dominates Y, whereas if $A < B$ then Y dominates X.

The second-order rule has the following underlying logic: first, Y is the preferable portfolio over lowish values of NPV say up to 350 whereas portfolio X is preferable from $350 \rightarrow 500$. Then, if we consider the whole range, i.e. 100 to 500, the overall dominance of one portfolio over another will depend upon the relative advantages of Y and X in that range. Thus, if Area A (the region in which X is preferred to Y (cross-hatched area)) exceeds Area B (the region to

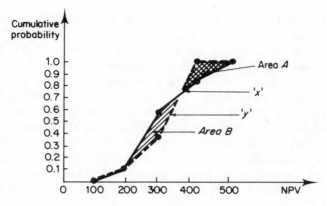

Figure 15 Revised cdfs for X and Y

which Y is preferred to X (shaded area)) and portfolios X and Y are equipreferable elsewhere, portfolio X should dominate portfolio Y in the sense of second-order dominance.

The perceptive reader will be aware that there could be situations in which, for example, the cdfs for portfolios X and Y intersected several times over the range of NPV values. In such more complex cases, a simple graphical treatment of second-order dominance would, of necessity, be replaced by formal integration as specified in the original definition of dominance given earlier.

In summary, therefore, we can say the following:

(i) First-order Stochastic Dominance states that any decision-maker who prefers more wealth to less wealth should never choose a portfolio whose cdf lies everywhere to the left of any other portfolio under consideration.

(ii) Second-order Stochastic Dominance is a logical extension of the first-order conditions. By assuming that the utility function is a positive function of wealth, and that the decision-maker is decreasingly risk-averse with increasing wealth, second-order dominance eliminates portfolios by comparing areas under the appropriate cumulative density functions.

(b) Choice of Most Preferred Option (Portfolio) Given a Feasible Set

We touched upon issues of portfolio (option) selection and the usefulness of utility functions in detail, both in the discussion of the Caracas case and in the discussion of investment policies in the risk analysis chapter. The purpose of this short section is to point out that with certain assumptions it may be possible to simplify this portfolio choice problem. The decision analytic route normally involves either the formulation of a stochastic dominance rule for choice, or the derivation of the decision-maker's utility function (recognizing that such a function may not be an adequate representation either of the corporate utility function or that of the shareholders in the firm), as a prelude to using expected utility as decision criterion.

If we follow the decision analytic route, and assume that both *constant risk aversion* and *independent events* hold, we can show that an important simplification for the portfolio selection problem is available to us. We can treat multiple projects separately, whereas in most situations in project evaluation, both the overall portfolio and all possible subset combinations must be evaluated and treated in detail (in *general*, the assumption of risk aversion requires that all possible combinations should be evaluated).

Therefore, individual project selection and portfolio selection coalesce under this set of assumptions. The extent to which this set of assumptions can be considered realistic is, however, a matter for examination in the actual problem situation.

For the record, we should note that the assumption of constant risk aversion means that the risk premium (the absolute value of the difference between the *certainty equivalent* and the EMV) depends only on the size of the difference between the outcomes and not on the absolute values of those outcomes. In mathematical terms, constant risk aversion implies a utility function, μ, for wealth, x, of exponential form. Specifically $\mu(x) = \alpha - \beta e^{-\mu x}$, where μ is a measure of risk aversion and α and β are constants.

ALTERNATIVE PROJECT WORTH APPROACHES BASED UPON MULTIPLE ATTRIBUTES

The Aztech (see Appendix to Chapter 2) and Caracas cases demonstrate clearly that attributes other than purely financial valuations often come into consideration in project worth evaluations. In the Aztech case technical and image factors were considered as having a bearing upon the ultimate decision. In the Caracas case the issues of goodwill and preservation of the existing building were considered as being relevant in relation to the choice of the preferred development option. When a single evaluation measure such as NPV is not considered to be sufficient for representing the outcomes of a decision problem we are forced to treat the evaluation problem in terms of the multiple attributes and criteria specified at the firm level. However, the choice amongst alternatives, characterized in terms of such attributes, can turn out to be a difficult problem. Several approaches are available (see MacCrimmon (21) and Keeney and Raiffa (17)), and here we concentrate mainly upon a discussion of those most commonly described as multi-attribute utility or MAU models.

For a moment let us return to the Aztech case. Two types of analysis were carried out in that situation. First, the purely financial analysis which used the Monte-Carlo risk analysis approach specified in Chapter 2 and produced output in terms of the mean and variance of financial criteria such as NPV. Second, a modified form of the Churchman–Ackoff model was used to handle the influence of multiple attributes. This second type of model will be the focus of attention in this section. In essence, this procedure obtains a score, S_i, for each project i in the following manner:

(i) the relevant set of attributes, 0_i, (mutually independent if possible) are developed ($\{0_i\}$, $i = 1(1)n$);

(ii) the set of possible projects (portfolios) P_j is also determined ($\{P_j\}$, $j = 1(1)k$);

(iii) a set of subjectively assessed scores S_{ji} (in the range 0: lowest to 1: highest value) are obtained for each project option against each relevant attribute;

(iv) relative weights, w_i, ($\{w_i\}$, $i = 1(1)n$, $\sum_i w_i = 1$) are assigned to each attribute;

(v) finally, a score for each project j, viz S_j, is obtained from the linear model $S_j = \sum_i S_{ji} w_i$.

The derived score S_j can then be used to rank the project options. The main value of this type of procedure lies in its intuitive appeal as a simple formalization of the decision situation. It should be noted that this procedure neither recognizes non-linear trade-offs that frequently exist among competing attributes, nor considers possible forms of interdependence between these attributes. It is sometimes argued (see for example Edwards (6)) that even if this linear scoring measure is not a totally adequate representation of preferences, it can still provide a sensible basis for handling the multiple-attribute problem (perhaps at the level of a 'first-order' ranking), because of the added measurement problems involved in relaxing the rather strong assumptions of a linear, additive form of scoring rule.

In order to demonstrate more realistic forms for the multiple attribute problem we present a simple example and follow through the underlying assessment assumptions.

Example

Suppose that the XYZ Company has to choose between three possible portfolios of new product development projects A, B, and C which have the following characteristics:

	A	B	C
Net Present Value ($m)	20	15	25
Time horizon (years)	8	5	12
Performance*	2	3	1

*Performance refers to marketing capability, quality and image. It is measured on a 3 point scale: 1, low through 3, high.

Assume also that there is no uncertainty about the value measures of the portfolios in relation to each of the three attributes (we shall relax this assumption later and treat the uncertainty case). Note also that a higher NPV is preferred to a lower one, a longer time horizon to a shorter one (because of the longer sales potential over the period of the product life cycle), and a higher to a lower performance capability.

Considering this decision situation the R & D manager might have in mind certain simplifying procedures by which it would be possible to discriminate between the portfolios *A*, *B*, and *C*. Such simplifying principles have been identified in terms of rules of *dominance*, *satisficing*, and *lexicographic* ordering. The essence of each of these principles can be explained as follows. *Dominance* means that one alternative is preferred to another if, and only if, it is at least as good as the other in value terms on all of the attributes, and clearly preferred in relation to at least one attribute. In the example given here not one of the portfolios A, *B*, and C exercises dominance over any of the other alternative portfolios.

The *satisficing* principle arises from the descriptive decision theoretic writings of such authorities as March and Simon (22) and Lindblom (19). Their argument is that decision-makers look for alternatives that have satisfactory values across a number of attributes. The decision-maker must, therefore, provide a set of satisfactory levels for each attribute. Following this, alternatives which are not satisfactory are discarded, and those which meet the specified satisficing levels are retained. In our example, suppose the decision-maker specifies satisficing levels as follows:

NPV: $15m or more;
time: eight years or more;
performance: level 2 or greater.

Therefore, portfolio *A* satisfies all three levels, whereas portfolios *B* and *C* fail on one attribute each. In this instance, *A* is preferred in terms of a satisficing criterion. It is important to note, however, that the determination of 'satisfactory' levels is a crucial and contentious issue, and that the procedure assumes independence amongst attributes, e.g. portfolio *C* has very good values on NPV and time and only fails on performance. Apparently this performance shortfall cannot be traded-off against the above-average levels on NPV and time.

Lexicographic procedures, on the other hand, require the decision-maker to provide an ordinal ranking of attributes. In this case, let us say that NPV is ranked first, performance second, and time horizon third. The decision-maker then compares each of the alternatives in terms of one attribute at a time, until a final choice is made. Using our example, in terms of NPV, alternative *C* is preferred to both *A* and *B*, therefore the choice would be for portfolio *C*. Notice that it was only necessary to compare *A*, *B*, and *C* in terms of the one attribute NPV for a choice to be determined. However, if, for the sake of argument, *C* and *A* were tied on the attribute NPV, then the decision-maker would move to look at the performance attribute and would choose *A* over *C*. The problems with this procedure are very similar to those with the satisficing principle, namely that the attributes are assumed independent and that 'trade-offs' cannot be made between poor values on one attribute and excellent values on other attributes.

Some decision-makers also appear to use combinations of these simplification rules. For example, dominance and satisficing can be used to reduce the number of alternatives to be considered before lexicographic ordering principles are used. However, such combination rules will not overcome the independence assumptions amongst attributes, and nor will matrix-type procedures of the Churchman–Ackoff type, which seek to provide a numerical weighting for each of the attributes prior to obtaining a project score.

It seems therefore that we must move towards procedures which allow for value trade-offs between attributes to be made. Let us use our original example to show how such procedures can be developed:

	A	B	C
NPV	20	15	25
Time	8	5	12
Performance	2	3	1

The essence of the form of trade-off procedure that we shall be advocating here was suggested by Raiffa (26). It requires that the multi-attributed outcomes for a given alternative be reduced to equivalent outcomes that differ only in terms of the levels of one attribute.

Suppose that we regard NPV as the attribute which we shall allow to vary, and that we also operate with fixed levels of time and performance. For example, let us fix time at the level of 5 years and performance at level 2. We need to question the decision-maker so that it is possible to come up with alternatives equivalent to A, B, and C, but with attributes other than NPV fixed at time = 5 years, performance = level 2.

The questioning process might be undertaken in the following manner:

(i) Consider alternative A which can be represented in triplet form (NPV, time, performance) as $A \sim (20, 8, 2)$ i.e. A is equivalent to the triplet $(20, 8, 2)$.

(ii) Assume that time is reduced to 5 years and performance maintained at level 2, what value of NPV (say, NPV*) would make the decision-maker indifferent between $A \sim (20, 8, 2)$ and the equivalent alternative (NPV*, 5, 2)?

Suppose that the decision-maker answers that the result of a reduction of the time horizon from 8 to 5 years, would involve a reduction of $3m in NPV with performance at level 2. This implies that A: $(20, 8, 2) \sim (20 - 3, 5, 2) \sim (17, 5, 2)$.

(iii) Now consider alternative B: $(15, 5, 3)$. Assume that performance level, e.g. quality, is reduced to level 2, what value of NPV would now make the decision-maker indifferent between B: $(15, 5, 3)$ and the equivalent alternative?

Suppose that the decision-maker answers that a reduction of NPV of $2m would be required if performance level were moved from 3 to 2, then $(15, 5, 3) \sim (15 - 2, 5, 2) \sim (13, 5, 2)$.

(iv) Finally we consider alternative $C \sim (25, 12, 1)$. In order to determine the equivalent outcomes (NPV**, 5, 2) the questions have to be answered in two stages. First, considering the change of time from 12 to 5 years and second, the change in performance from level 1 to level 2.

The decision-maker's answers might be:

(a) *Trade-off to time horizon of 5 years*
$(25, 12, 1) \sim (18, 5, 1)$
(i.e. a reduction in NPV of $7m results from the time horizon change, with performance maintained at level 1.)

(b) *Trade-off to performance level of 2 from position (18, 5, 1)*
$(18, 5, 1) \sim (21, 5, 2)$
(i.e. an increase in NPV of $3m results from performance level increase to a scale value of 2.)

(v) Finally we have:
$A \sim (17, 5, 2)$
$B \sim (13, 5, 2)$
$C \sim (21, 5, 2)$
Therefore, alternative project portfolio C is preferred since it has the largest value for the NPV attribute.

Two things are worth emphasizing about this trade-off procedure. First, we reduce the triplet in each case to an equivalent triplet with time and performance fixed. Second, we assume that there is no uncertainty whatsoever about the values of the attributes.

Let us now consider the impact of uncertainty on the multi-attributed procedure. Assume that there is uncertainty solely about present value and that it is of the following form for each of the alternatives:

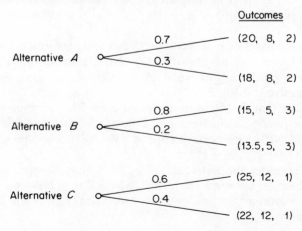

Outcomes

Alternative *A*
0.7 — (20, 8, 2)
0.3 — (18, 8, 2)

Alternative *B*
0.8 — (15, 5, 3)
0.2 — (13.5, 5, 3)

Alternative *C*
0.6 — (25, 12, 1)
0.4 — (22, 12, 1)

In decision tree terms this can be diagrammed as:

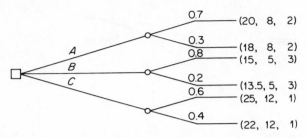

We now treat each of the outcome triplets in the decision tree separately and use the 'trade-off' questioning procedure just described to obtain the equivalent outcomes with base levels, now fixed at time = 8 years, performance = level 2.

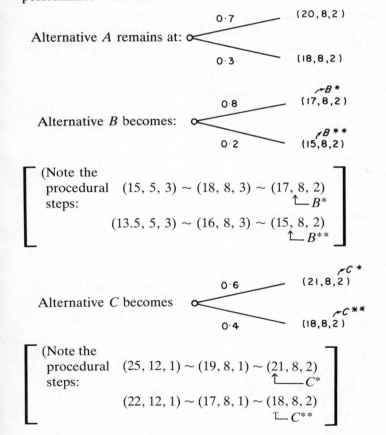

Alternative A remains at:

0·7 — (20, 8, 2)

0·3 — (18, 8, 2)

Alternative B becomes:

0·8 — B* (17, 8, 2)

0·2 — B** (15, 8, 2)

(Note the procedural steps:
$(15, 5, 3) \sim (18, 8, 3) \sim (17, 8, 2)$
$\uparrow\!\!\!\!- B^*$
$(13.5, 5, 3) \sim (16, 8, 3) \sim (15, 8, 2)$
$\uparrow\!\!\!\!- B^{**}$

Alternative C becomes

0·6 — C* (21, 8, 2)

0·4 — C** (18, 8, 2)

(Note the procedural steps:
$(25, 12, 1) \sim (19, 8, 1) \sim (21, 8, 2)$
$\uparrow\!\!\!\!- C^*$
$(22, 12, 1) \sim (17, 8, 1) \sim (18, 8, 2)$
$\uparrow\!\!\!\!- C^{**}$

The next step is to assess a preference (utility) function for NPV conditional upon a time level of 8 years and a performance scale level of 2. This means that

142

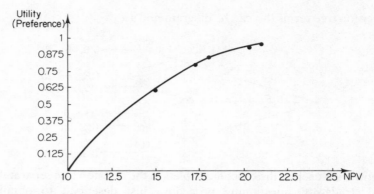

Figure 16 Utility function (conditional on time — 8 years, performance — 2)

the decision-maker must consider himself as having a time horizon of 8 years and a guaranteed performance level of 2 and must assess his attitude towards risk under this set of base conditions. Let us assume that the decision-maker can assign a preference curve (using standard procedures (see Chapter 3)) under these conditions and that its shape is given in Figure 16. With this curve we can derive utility values for each of the outcome triplets as follows.

$U(20, 8, 2) = 0.9$
$U(18, 8, 2) = 0.85$
$U(17, 8, 2) = 0.775$
$U(15, 8, 2) = 0.6$
$U(21, 8, 2) = 0.93$
$U(18, 8, 2) = 0.85$

Therefore, our decision diagram now looks as follows:

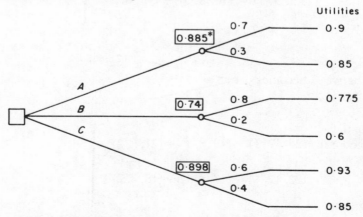

*Note: Expected Utility (A) = 0.7 × 0.9 + 0.3 × 0.85 = 0.885

Given this analysis, *C* would be the preferred option in terms of the expected utility criterion.

The perceptive reader will recognize that the combination of trade-off procedures with the uncertainty complication can quickly increase the complexity of the analysis. Serious questions about the ability of decision-makers to make the required trade-off assessments have been raised in the literature, and other MAU models have been suggested, e.g. additive (see Edwards (6)) and multiplicative (see Kenney and Raiffa (17)).

Let us illustrate the outline features of Edwards' (6) procedure in relation to the XYZ Company case, in which we required to evaluate projects *A*, *B*, and *C* in terms of the dimensions of NPV, time, and performance (assumed to be the relevant dimensions).

The members of the decision-making group would first *rank* the dimensions in order of importance. They would then rate these dimensions in importance, whilst preserving ratios. This would be done by first assigning the least important dimension, say **time**, an importance of 10. The next-least important dimension, say, **performance**, would then be rated relative to **time**, by asking the questions 'How much more important (if at all) is **performance** than **time**?' Operationally, a number is assigned, say 25, which reflects the relative importance ratio of performance to time. Similarly, NPV has to be compared both relative to time and performance, and the ratios checked for consistency. Suppose that, finally, a score of 50 is assigned to NPV.

The next step is to sum the importance weights, divide each by the sum and obtain relative weights which are thus 'normalized' to sum to 1. Therefore, NPV is assigned a weight of $50/(50 + 25 + 10) = 0.59$; **performance** is assigned a weight of $25/(50 + 25 + 10) = 0.29$, and **time** a weight of $10/(50 + 25 + 10) = 0.12$.

The final step is to 'measure' the location of each project (*A*, *B*, *C*) being evaluated on each dimension (NPV, time, performance). For each dimension, minimum and maximum plausible values are assessed. For NPV and time, they were assessed in terms of 99 percent credible intervals of probability distributions for those dimensions. Thus, NPV ranged from 0 to $40m, and **time** from 3 to 15 years. **Performance**, by definition, ranged from 1 to 3.

It is then necessary to draw value curves (strictly straight lines connecting minimum and maximum plausible values where 0 is defined as the minimum plausible value and 100 as the maximum plausible value), as shown in Figures 17, 18 and 19. (Note that the **linear** assumption is the most simple, and taken for illustrative purposes. Non-linear trade-offs require some additional trade-off assessments.)

Weighted value measures (utilities) are then calculated for projects using essentially a linear additive weighting similar to the Churchman–Ackoff procedure.

The tables below show the values derived for each of the end outcomes for three projects and also the resulting weighted value measures:

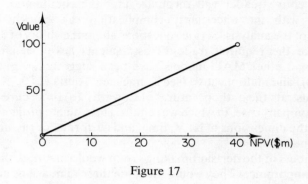

Figure 17

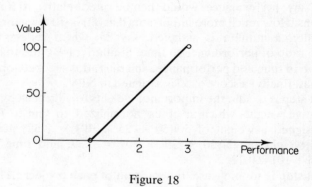

Figure 18

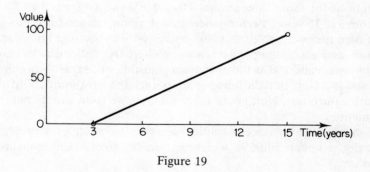

Figure 19

Values of end outcomes

Projects	weights	NPV (0.59)	Performance (0.29)	Time (0.12)
A		50	50	41.7
B		37.5	100	16.7
C		62.5	0	75.0

Weighted value measures

Projects	(Utility)
A	49.00
B	53.14
C	45.90

The projects would thus finally be ranked $B > A > C$.

Although this example is only illustrative, it does serve to point out that the procedure is simple and implementable, and avoids some of the difficult problems associated with more complex multi-attributed utility structures.

Some of these complicating issues will be treated in the Mucom case (and its commentary) in Chapter 6, and in addition, the reader can consult such references as Edwards (6), Keeney and Raiffa (17) and MacCrimmon (21). In particular, Keeney and Raiffa examine the range of mathematical forms for multi-attribute trade-off structures, and point out associated measurement and assessment procedures.

Before we attempt to summarize and draw lessons from the various approaches, it seems appropriate to offer an outline of the quickest and most simple approach to risk evaluation: sensitivity analysis in relation to the certainty model.

SENSITIVITY ANALYSIS AND THE CERTAINTY MODEL

Basically, the certainty model involves calculating the financial measure, say NPV, for an investment project on the basis of a single estimate for each cash flow source and thus a single value for each cash flow in each year of the project's life. Typically, the single cash values are described as being 'best' or 'most likely' estimates, and the resulting single value for NPV is thus akin to an 'average' value. However, it cannot be interpreted as the $E(NPV)$ or mean NPV, since each single cash flow might be represented by the modal or median value rather than the mean.

The sensitivity analysis is usually applied by using so-called optimistic or pessimistic values in place of the single-point 'best' values, and then testing their effects on NPV. Obviously, there are a myriad of possible sensitivity analyses available, and the design of sensible sensitivity 'runs' is a very important element with this procedure.

The potential advantages of the certainty model with sensitivity analysis back-up lie in relation to the simplicity, economy, and speed of the process. In addition, valuable effort can be expended on developing sensible and detailed cash flow models for annual cash flows while at the same time developing a sound understanding of accounting/cash flow relationships for modelling purposes. It has been argued that a simple model of the certainty type can be an important 'first-pass' element in a sensible project evaluation process by quickly highlighting projects which have high loss potential. This suggests that this simple model could, perhaps, be a very useful initial, rough screen in a project evaluation process, thus allowing effort in more complex modelling of uncertainty and multi-attributed issues to be concentrated upon reasonable projects and project combinations.

SUMMARY

The purpose of this chapter has been to examine alternative approaches for project evaluation, and also determine the advantages and disadvantages of each approach.

It should be noted that the approaches in both Chapter 2 and Chapter 3 attempt to estimate the risk associated with the single project in the context of the investment appraisal process. Clearly, from a firm's perspective, the risk of the total portfolio of investment projects is the focus of attention. The approaches for measuring risk of individual projects which are examined here are, however, an important step in the portfolio analysis of such projects. Portfolio issues are examined briefly here in relation to the Caracas case and further information on this topic will be given in Chapter 5. (For example, in relation to capital asset pricing, cost of capital problems.)

The first approach presented was the analytical model for the distribution of NPV, the so-called 'Hillier model'. This approach attempts to model correlation relationships between variables and also time-series autocorrelations between cash flows accruing in successive time periods. It treats the investment decision as if it were a single-stage decision, and provides output in the form of the mean and variance of the NPV measure. Its main advantage is, as seen in the Caracas situation, that once the various cash flow and probability assessments have been made, the calculation of the parameters of the NPV distribution can be performed very quickly. Further, the model can be generalized very easily to the portfolio as well as the single project case. The Hillier model can, therefore, provide a sensible, quick, and meaningful 'first-pass' measure of risk which is very robust if the underlying assumptions of the model (e.g. normality) hold.

The weaknesses of the Hillier approach are mainly a function of the model's underlying assumptions. The most crucial is the ability of the model (essentially an additive discounted aggregation of uncertain cash flows) to account for the realities of accounting relationships which make up the annual cash flows. Typically such relationships involve multiplicative (e.g. revenue = price × quantity) factors and non-linearities; the Hillier model requires additivity for the Central Limit Theorem results to hold.

The reader should try to contrast the Hillier approach with the Monte-Carlo approach given in Chapter 2. The Hillier model makes assumptions about distribution forms and correlation patterns whereas the risk analysis approach is distribution free, and allows the modelling of complex correlation patterns. The comparative weaknesses of risk simulation are the additional subjective assessments needed for the simulation model and the time involved in computation.

The stochastic decision-tree approach of Hespos and Strassmann (13) tries to incorporate the advantages of the decision-tree approach with the risk analysis simulation approach of Hertz. It is useful to remember that the essence of the decision tree is that, no matter how simple or complex the decision problem may be, it forces the decision-maker to define the problem clearly, consider all feasible alternatives, and clarify the nature of risks and uncertainties which he faces. This process of forcing the decision-maker to recognize, in visual terms, the structure of the problem in terms of a decision tree, can only contribute to the better understanding of multi-stage strategy and abandonment-type investment decision situations. Further, the tree structure specifies clearly which correlation patterns are modelled because the nature of the tree, i.e. the various conditional act-event paths, indicates the correlation structures considered relevant by the decision-making group and for which subjective assessment will be required. However, in most real-life investment decision situations, the decision-maker has quite a range of alternatives and uncertainties to consider. If he is not careful, the tree can quickly become a 'bushy mess' with an overemphasis on the need to take account of every possible eventuality. In such stochastic decision tree analyses, there must therefore be a trade-off between model complexity (e.g. looking for a simple way of handling time-series dependency) and computational and assessment efficiency.

Finally, we should not overlook the role of a deterministic certainty-type model used in conjunction with sensitivity analysis. It can provide a basis for a rough screening of projects into either 'further evaluation' or 'discard' categories and sensitize decision-makers to the impact of important uncertain variables.

In summary, the Hillier model gives a reasonable, quick measure of single-project riskiness which is robust, provided underlying distributions are not markedly skew. The simulation and, more generally, stochastic decision-tree approaches, are more flexible for modelling purposes and can handle multi-stage decision problems.

With any of these approaches, the final judgement may be based on a combination of attributes — including monetary analyses. We have demonstrated how these multi-attributed utility analyses can be handled and have indicated that the Mucom case (Chapter 6) gives a more detailed treatment of MAU situations.

148

In the next chapter, we concentrate upon the measurement and assessment problems commonly encountered with the approaches outlined in Chapters 2 and 3.

REFERENCES

1. Bonini, C. P., 'Risk Evaluation of Investment Projects'. *Omega*, **3**, No. 6, 1975, 735–750.
2. Carter, E. E., 'What are the Risks in Risk Analysis', *Harvard Business Review*, July–August **1972**, 72–82.
3. Chambers, D. J., 'The Joint Problem of Investment and Financing', *Operational Research Quarterly*, **22**, No. 3, September 1971, 267–295.
4. Copeland, T. E., and Weston, J. F., *Financial Theory and Corporate Policy*, Reading, Mass., Addison-Wesley, 1979.
5. Doob, J. L., *Stochastic Processes*, New York, John Wiley, 1953.
6. Edwards, W, 'How to Use Multi-Attributed Utility Measurements for Social Decision-Making', Report 76–3, Social Science Research Institute, SSRI, Univ. of Southern California, August 1976
7. Eilon, S., and Tilley, R., 'Stochastic Dominance for Ranking Ventures', *Omega*, **1975**.
8. Hadar, J., and Russell, W. R., 'Rules for Ordering Uncertain Prospects', *Amer. Econ. Review*, March 1969, Vol 49, pp. 25–34.
9. Hammond III, J. S., 'Better Decisions Through Preference Theory', *Harvard Business Review*, November/December **1967**, 123–141.
10. Hanoch, J., and Levy, H., 'The Efficiency Analysis of Choices Involving Risk', *Rev. Econ. Studies*, Vol 36, 1969, 335–346.
11. Hayes, R. H., 'Incorporating Risk Aversion into Risk Analysis', *Engineering Economist*, **20**, Winter 1975, 99–121.
12. Hertz, D. B., 'Risk Analysis in Capital Investment', HBR Classic, *Harvard Business Review*, Sept/Oct **1979**, 169–181.
13. Hespos, R. F., and Strassmann, P. A., 'Stochastic Decision Trees for the Analysis of Investment Decisions', *Man. Sci.*, **11**, No. 10, August 1965, B244–259.
14. Hillier, F. S., The Evaluation of Risky Interrelated Investments, Amsterdam, North-Holland Publishing Company, 1969.
15. Hoeffding, W., and Robbins, H., 'The Central Limit Theorem for Dependent Random Variables', *Duke Math. J.*, **15**, 1948, 773.
16. Hull, J. C., 'The Input to and Output from Risk Simulation Models', *European Journal of Operational Research*, **1**, 1977, 368–375.
17. Keeney, R. L., and Raiffa, H., *Decisions with Multiple Objectives: Preferences and Value Trade-offs*, New York, John Wiley, 1976.
18. Levy, H., and Sarnat, M., *Capital Investment and Financial Decisions,* Englewood Cliffs, N.J., Prentice-Hall, 1978.
19. Lindblom, C. E., 'The Science of Muddling Through', Reprinted in D. G. Castles *et al.*, *Decisions, Organisations and Society*, London, Penguin Books, 1976.
20. Lintner, J., 'The Valuation of Risk Assets and the Selection of Risky Investments in Stock Portfolios and Capital Budgets', *Review of Economics and Statistics*, **47**, Feb. 1968, 13–37.
21. MacCrimmon, K. R., 'An Overview of Multiple-Objective Decision-Making', in J. Cochrane and M. Zeleny (eds), *Multiple Criteria Decision-Making*, Univ. of So. California Press, 1973, 18–46.
22. March, J. G., and Simon, H. A., *Organisations*, New York, John Wiley, 1958.
23. Markowitz, H. M., *Portfolio Selection: The Efficient Diversification of Investments*, New York, John Wiley, 1959.

24. Moore, P. G., and Thomas, H., *The Anatomy of Decisions*, London, Penguin Books, 1976.
25. Porter, R. B., and Carey, K., 'Stochastic Dominance as a Risk Analysis Criterion', *Decision Sciences*, Vol 5, 1974, 10–21.
26. Raiffa, H., *Decision Analysis*, Reading, Mass., Addison-Wesley, 1968.
27. Rappaport, A., 'Sensitivity Analysis for Decision-Making', *Accounting Review*, **XLII**, No. 3, July, 1967, 441–56.
28. Swalm, R. O., 'Utility Theory: Insights Into Risk-Taking', *Harvard Business Review*, **44**, 123–136, 1968.
29. Thomas, H., 'The Assessment of Project Worth with Applications to Research and Development', in J. N. Wolfe (ed.), *Cost-Benefit and Cost-Effectiveness*, London, Allen and Unwin, 1973, 88–117.
30. Tobin, J., 'Liquidity Preference as Behaviour Towards Risk', *Review of Economic Studies*, **25**, February, 1958, 65–86.
31. Wagle, B. V., 'A Statistical Analysis of Risk in Capital Investment Projects', *Ops. Res. Quart.*, **18**, 1967, 13–33.
32. Weingartner, H. M., 'Some New Views on the Payback Period and Capital Budgeting Decisions', *Management Science*, **15**, August 1969, 594–607.
33. Whitmore, G. A., 'Third-Degree Stochastic Dominance', *Amer. Econ. Rev.*, June **1970**, Vol 60, 457–459.

Chapter 4

Measurement Problems Associated with Risk Analysis Approaches

INTRODUCTION

The measurement problems encountered in implementing risk and decision analysis approaches (refer to the schematic diagrams Figures 1, 2 and 3 of Chapter 2) need to be clearly understood. This is important because the analysis itself depends heavily upon such things as the decision-maker's ability to structure the problem, and to provide meaningful assessments of such things as chance events and value measures for each of the possible outcomes in the decision problem.

As we have seen, decision analysis can be regarded as an umbrella term both for an approach to logical and consistent decision-making and as a set of decision techniques and aids. Above all, it provides a guide for taking decisions in an environment of risk and uncertainty. In carrying out such an analysis, certain stages can be identified. The stages are *problem structuring*, assessing the *uncertainties and values* of the possible outcomes, and *determining the best strategy*. Therefore, decision analysis attempts to deduce which of the decision-maker's alternatives is best according to his stated preferences.

In this chapter we concentrate upon the measurement aspects of decision and risk analysis and indicate those measurement methods which seem to be most useful in operational terms. We follow the stages of the decision process taxonomy identified earlier, and treat the approaches and problems in structuring, assessment, and strategic choice in subsequent sections.

Decision Structuring

The essential question to be discussed in this section is: 'How should a decision-maker *decompose* the decision problem? In other words, how can the decision-maker model reality and complexity as far as possible without hindering the ability to see "the wood for the trees"?' There is no simple answer to this problem, but some guidelines can be provided. There appear to be two separate tasks that the decision-maker must perform. First, the process of developing an understanding of the problem and of formulating and defining its structure. Second, the process of selecting the structural model and generating a fuller understanding of the problem variables and their

150

correlation patterns. This structuring phase is, therefore, creative in nature, and once a problem has been understood it involves breaking or decomposing that problem into its constituent parts. The underlying assumption is that, provided the problem decomposition is appropriate and meaningful, the process ultimately results in better judgements and decisions.

Some of the elements in this phase are listed below:

(i) The generation of any available prior information about the decision problem.
(ii) The characterization, by flow charts or some other graphical or verbal approaches, of a conceptual mapping of the problem. Such a mapping will indicate:

    (a) the bounds on the decision problem;
    (b) the generation of the relevant problem variables;
    (c) the identification of the set of possible alternatives;
    (d) the definition of the criteria, goals, or value dimensions — the answers to questions such as: 'What are the firm's growth directions?' 'What are its goals?' (e.g. shareholder wealth maximization, long-term cash generation, etc.) are the required inputs.

The mapping might be presented in the form of a crude or rough decision tree, which can then provide a preliminary 'model' and a basis for further debate about such issues as underlying assumptions.

(iii) The creation of a working conceptualization or structural model of the problem which will serve as a basis for subsequent problem analysis and further debate. For example, the working decision tree would indicate the relevant alternatives, the problem variables and their interrelationships, resulting correlation effects, and the possible impacts of uncertainty.
(iv) The development of a model for measuring the value of outcomes. Typically in financial decision problems, this involves an understanding of cash flow models and relationships.
(v) An understanding of the impact of time and time preference (e.g. discounting) on the problem.
(vi) A screening process in which forms of sensitivity analysis and matrix models can be used to identify redundant problem variables and alternatives, which may not be worthy of further detailed consideration. This screening process thus reviews the basic structural model, and indicates the most sensible revisions to its form before any further analysis is carried out.

Some further comments about these steps follow:

Information

There are strong indications from the cognitive and behavioral decision theory literature that decision-makers have limited information-processing and assumption-integration capacity. Moreover, evidence suggests that decision-makers tend to adapt slowly, selectively, and in a step-by-step fashion to new information. However, it seems sensible that decision-makers should be provided with any available prior information about a given decision problem, and also be offered the opportunity to consider the effects of such information on the definition of the problem.

Whilst it has been established that many decision-makers adopt rules of thumb when considering and perceiving information, their perceptions, albeit biased, provide a useful launching point for initial discussion of the elements of the problem by the decision-making group. From this point, the decision-making group can subsequently undertake a first-stage attempt at 'mapping' the problem.

Decision Mapping

This can be characterized as the pilot stage of the process in which a basic conceptual structure and framework of assumptions for the problem is developed, and subjected to limited forms of testing. Perhaps the main responsibility of the decision-making group is to provide a sharp and precise specification of the nature of the decision problem. Therefore, in such an endeavor, we need to develop an understanding of the character of the decision problem. Is it of the *strategic* growth type (e.g. expansion of product ranges or plant investment) or does it involve *abandonment* possibilities (e.g. withdrawing from a particular product range or indeed from a particular overseas territory)? Further we need to establish the nature of the resource allocation problem, the responsibilities of the decision-making group and the issue of whose values, preferences, and goals are to be articulated by the decision-making group. For example, are such goals and values specified by the firm as an entity and indicated as such to the decision-making group? Such questions must be addressed and answered initially in order that sensible constraints and boundaries are specified for the problem. Once this has been achieved, the identification of alternatives, decision variables, and problem elements can more meaningfully be carried out. Though such decomposition is much more an art than a science, we recommend that a preliminary mapping in terms of a decision tree can help decision-makers to concentrate upon the essentials of the problem and reduce initial confusion. In this manner, some alternatives can be articulated, and the subsequent discussion and brainstorming amongst members of the group can enable this set to be widened or more clearly focussed. This mapping skill is probably an experiential one and ultimately decision-makers 'learn by doing', by gaining practical experience with the skill of decision-tree diagramming and other matrix-type techniques. Decomposition ultimately involves:

(i) The process of generating alternatives and focussing on the overall problem framework. A decision tree is extremely useful here because it forces consideration of issues such as the problem's time horizon perspective, and the kinds of alternatives, issues (e.g. the treatment of inflation), and factors (decision and chance variables) that are considered to be important. We believe that initial meetings of the decision-making group should have an agenda consisting of unstructured discussion of prior information about the problem, its assumptions, and managers' concepts of problem structure and relevant issues. That is, it should provide a wide-ranging forum for debate before any decision framework is mapped out.

We recommend that a subsequent attempt at drawing a rough decision tree will enable those managers to speculate about the nature of the possible strategy/chance event configurations over the time horizon of the problem, and possibly eliminate *clearly* dominated options or unimportant decision variables.

Simon (38) has referred to this stage of the decision process as the *intelligence and design phase*. During this phase, the important managerial skills are creativity, assumption testing, insight into decision problem definition, search for decision opportunities, and construction of all the possible routes by which the specific decision problem can be attacked. These pre-decision phases are crucially important prerequisites to the choice phase in which the selection of the 'best' alternative available is made.

In an earlier article (Bunn and Thomas (6)) it is 'indicated that at least 60% of the time spent in analysing a complex investment decision was taken up with this pre-decision phase'. Indeed, the decision tree was seen as a useful vehicle for communication and discussion about problem structure.

(ii) Developing an understanding of the relationships amongst decision variables, probably by describing them in a mathematical form. For example, in a financial decision context we have functional cash flow relationships for annual or periodic cash flows. Similarly, correlational relationships exist amongst the decision variables, and also help to describe the time-series patterns of periodic cash flows (i.e. the stream of cash flows often has some identifiable pattern involving correlations between cash flows in different periods of a project's life).

(a) Examples of the functional cash flow relationships are

$$CF_t = [S_t(P_t - VC_t) - FC_t - D_t][1 - T] + D_t - \Delta WC_t$$

where CF_t = cash flow in year t;
$\quad\quad\quad S_t$ = sales in year t;
$\quad\quad\quad P_t$ = price in year t;
$\quad\quad\quad VC_t$ = variable costs in year t;
$\quad\quad\quad FC_t$ = fixed costs in year t;

154

D_t = depreciation in year t;
T = corporation tax rate;
ΔWC_t = change in working capital (could be positive or negative).

Note that cash flow is a complex function of underlying variables, and involves product terms (e.g. revenue = sales × price) and other non-linear relationships.

(b) Examples of correlations between problem variables are easy to hypothesize. It would be a prediction of economic theory that in most circumstances prices would be related to quantities sold and also to the costs of manufacture, administration, and sales. The crucial issues are the form of such correlations, and the methods available for obtaining satisfactory estimates of their magnitude.

(c) The time-series pattern of cash flows is very difficult to identify, and the process generating such a series of cash flow streams is both important and elusive. Simple assumptions about the time-series pattern can be made *ex-ante*, as for example in the case of the Hillier model, but the important issue is to provide a practical basis and justification for such assumptions.

(iii) The construction of an acceptable working decision tree or model of the problem in which specific allowance is made for the impacts of correlation through the assessment of conditional probability distributions. This provides the basis for modelling and perhaps further data collection, if required, in order to develop deeper problem understanding.

At this stage the decision tree provides the overall problem framework and also indicates which forecasts and inputs are necessary for the problem analysis. Examples of these inputs are cash flow projection models, probability assessments for uncertain variables and measures of effectiveness for outcomes specified in terms of organizational decision goals. The decision tree and these sub-models together form an overall flow diagram and logic structure for the project.

Those readers who refer to the Oil and Gas Exploration Case in the Appendix to Chapter 2 will be able to look at the conceptualization of the process of modelling. Sub-models, in flow diagram terms, are developed there for, *inter alia,* the estimation of hydrocarbon potential.

Time Horizon Issues

The selection of a planning horizon, i.e. the period of economic life of the investment, is an extremely important issue because uncertainty about project life often has a significant effect on the standard deviation of NPV.

Once the time horizon problem is resolved, it is usual to decompose the decision problem into sub-periods (usually annual periods), and for the purpose of analytical convenience, treat the outcomes of the decision period by period. In adopting such a procedure, it is not necessary to assume that the time horizon is fixed. It may well be that the project's economic life is a highly uncertain variable, and this factor could be handled in analytic terms by assessing a probability distribution for project life.

It should be noted that time has an effect on the investment decision process in at least two other ways. First, changing inflation rates in different time periods make future assessment of cash flows complicated. Second, managers have a time preference for cash flows, meaning that positive cash flow generation is preferred as early as possible. This is treated through discounting such cash flows by the firm's opportunity cost for capital (in principle an important factor to determine). This opportunity cost rate will vary between firms as a result of project mix, capital structure and economic performance.

Screening

Screening procedures could be distinguished as those which attempt to reduce the set of options and those which attempt to simplify the structure of the decision model. In conceptual terms it might appear that these are two distinct stages in a rational decision analysis framework. The options are first reduced to a minimum and the final decision model is then simplified to the most realistic structure. However, options or alternatives cannot be adequately 'screened' without a simple decision model, and furthermore, in 'screening' the structure of that model, extraneous options would fall out anyway as additional complications. There is, therefore, a simultaneity in screening options and structural assumptions and this should always be recognized.

Some decision analysts agree that an initial prior analysis of the rough decision tree as well as the use of sensitivity analysis to test and question assumptions, can help to 'screen out' both in terms of structural reduction and refinement of the set of alternative options. Bunn and Thomas (6) used this particular procedure in the pre-decisional phase of a strategic decision problem.

We turn now to a detailed consideration of the assessment phases of the decision process, i.e. the development of sensible measures for inputs in the decision model. Such measures include probability assessments, treatment of correlation patterns, and assessments of values for outcomes.

First, we treat the problem of assessments for chance events.

MEASURING UNCERTAINTY

The Process of Probability Assessment

The process of making assessments of uncertain events involves three distinct parts, which together form a logical structure. Initially, the individual assessor

156

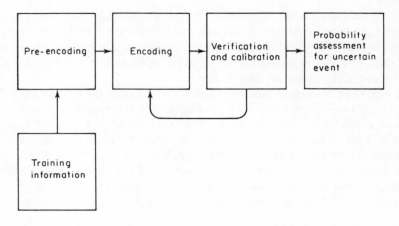

Figure 1 The process of probability assessment

must have some experience of, and training in, the available methods for assessing probabilities. This phase is sometimes referred to as the *pre-encoding* phase. The second phase of *encoding* relates to the actual quantification of the decision-maker's judgement in probabilistic terms. The appropriate methods are those which the assessor finds that he can understand, use, and is comfortable with. In addition, a third phase of *verification and calibration* is needed in which the responses obtained in the encoding phase are checked for internal consistency and amended, if inconsistency manifests itself. The overall process is depicted schematically in Figure 1.

In this section, attention is focussed primarily on the *encoding* phase, in which an appropriate assessment method is chosen and applied. A recent working paper by Thomas (43) discusses the issue of training in assessment, and argues that such training provides necessary experience with probabilistic concepts, whatever assessment approach is used. In addition, a literature survey on measurement methods has been given by Hampton, Moore, and Thomas (16).

As probability assessment is one of the important measurement tasks to be undertaken in the decision analysis approach, it is therefore assumed that the analyst and decision-maker have discussed the decision problem and the set of underlying assumptions, and have reached the point at which a realistic decision tree has been constructed. At the same time, a crude sensitivity analysis of the tree will also have been performed. This will have identified the important features of the problem and, in particular, the areas in which uncertainty plays a crucial part. The aim is then to proceed to a careful assessment of the probabilities for the uncertain events on the decision tree.

We will first treat methods for assessing discrete event probabilities, and

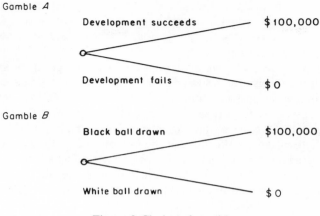

Figure 2 Choice of gambles

then, following a discussion on judgemental biases, we consider methods for asssessing continuous probabilities.

The Equivalent Urn (EQU) Method: Discrete Probabilities

This method is described in terms of the following example. Suppose the probability of the successful development of a new product by 1985 is required. The assessor is offered the choice between gamble A or gamble B, shown in Figure 2 in terms of probability trees. Under gamble B, one ball is drawn from the urn at the end of 1985, the urn containing 900 black balls and 100 white balls.

If the assessor chooses A, the assessment is repeated, but with more black balls (and correspondingly fewer white balls) in gamble B. If he chooses B, it is repeated until the proportion of black balls in gamble B is such that he is indifferent between the two gambles. The required probability is then taken as the final proportion of black balls in B. At no time in this process is it necessary to ask a more difficult question than 'do you prefer this gamble, or that one, or can't you say?'. Numerical measurement of an individual's degrees of belief can thus be obtained simply by asking questions of preference.

In the foregoing discussion an urn with colored balls was used to vary the probabilities. Such a decision aid (or standard device) as the urn is intended to help the manager in probability assessment tasks. However, although many executives have made use of such standard devices, not all have felt totally at ease using them. The main objection seems to be the close analogy drawn between business and gambling.

Furthermore, for a complex problem with many probabilities to be estimated, they find that the discipline imposed is tiring — they get stale and hence are not so certain that later assessments are realistic. Therefore, although these methods are quick and easy to use, they are probably best used as initial training aids. Care must be exercised to ensure that the assessor does not react unfavorably to the standard device, and as a consequence produce ill-considered judgements.

Other standard devices have been popular. A pie diagram, or spinner, is a favorite with the Decision Analysis Group at the Stanford Research Institute. A circle is divided into two sectors and the relative sizes of the sectors can be adjusted. A spinner randomly selects one of the two sectors. Thus, the larger a sector, the greater its chance of being chosen. The same bets as those shown in the earlier figures can be offered, but the outcomes for bet B are determined not only by drawing a ball from an urn, but by noting which sector is chosen. The relative sizes of the sectors are adjusted until the indifference point is reached; the sector sizes then represent the probabilities of the event being assessed and its complement.

The prerequisite of a standard device is that it should have easily perceived probabilistic implications, otherwise it will introduce bias. Phillips and Thomas (35) report some preliminary investigations which suggest that assessments using the urn device are 0.02 to 0.07 larger than the probabilities from the SRI spinner.

We should, at this point, note quite explicitly that the indirect estimation of probabilities from gambling preferences makes strong behavioral assumptions. Quite often, it is assumed that the individual is behaving so as to maximize expected monetary value. Thus, returning to the development gamble presented here, a statement by the decision-maker of his certainty equivalent (CE) for gamble A (i.e. his minimum selling price for that gamble) allows the probability of development success to be imputed as the CE/$100,000.

However, in order to have any confidence in this imputed value as a predictive probability, we should need to determine whether the decision-maker's preference function is in fact of linear form over the relevant range of assets. If trouble is to be taken in measuring the individual's utility curve in the first place, there is no reason why the payoffs should not be appropriately mapped into utility values in order to obtain consistent subjective probabilities. If a Von Neumann–Morgernstern utility function is derived using standard devices to articulate the probabilities presented in the artificial gambles, then the subsequent use of this function in the derivation of subjective probabilities should give valid estimates provided that the individual acts in a coherent and consistent manner. Unfortunately, this may not be the case. Phillips (33) has pointed out that Slovic (39), in some experimental work, observed that individuals react and behave differently in gambling situations. Some people pay more attention to the chance of winning, others to the chance of losing, whilst a further group seems to look mainly at the size of the payoffs.

In summary, we believe that standard devices should primarily be used as training aids for the probability assessment process. Thus, managers can be alerted to the nature of probability, but are not asked to treat business decisions as forms of gambling.

Potential Biases in the Probability Assessment Process

At least two forms of bias should be noted: *task bias*, which is characteristic of the assessment method itself, and *conceptual bias* which is idiosyncratic and thus individually based. *Task bias* could be caused by the standard device having misunderstood probabilistic implications, or because it structures thinking in some systematic way. Thus, it is possible that characteristics of the method may impede the assessment of the individual's fundamental beliefs. The more fundamental *conceptual bias* represents a faulty or weak cognitive structure, and will relate to the decision-maker's inability to process information and deduce the causal implications of the various inductive hypotheses.

Tversky and Kahneman (44, 45), in a series of important articles, have attempted to provide a characterization of some types of conceptual bias. They isolate three types of systematic bias in the formulation of probabilistic judgement: *representativeness*, *availability*, and *adjustment*

Representativeness

Individuals, apparently, formulate probabilistic judgement by means of a representativeness heuristic. Thus, if x is considered to be highly representative of a set A, then it is given a high probability of belonging to A. However, this approach to the judgement of likelihood leads to serious bias, because many of the factors important in the assessment of likelihood play no role in such judgements of similarity. One factor is the prior probability or base rate frequency. For example, if given a neutral description of a person and if then asked to estimate the probability of that person being a lawyer or an engineer, subjects were found to answer 0.5, regardless of prior information on the relative numbers of lawyers and engineers in the population. Similarly, the representativeness heuristic does not take any account of sample size. Thus, the manifestation of the so-called gamblers' fallacy (a well-known phenomenon in the probabilistic literature) can be ascribed to the belief that randomness is expected to be represented even in very small samples. Tversky and Kahneman believe this reveals a lingering belief in what they call 'the law of small numbers', according to which even small samples are highly representative of the population from which they are drawn.

Availability

Reliance on the availability heuristic introduces bias through the inadequacy of the cognitive process in conceptualizing all of the relevant information. There is a memory retrievability problem which can cause a bias such as, for example, the assessment of the probability of a road accident increasing dramatically after witnessing such an event, or having a relative or friend involved in one. The limitations of the memory search process cause people to judge that more words begin with 'r', than contain 'r' as the third digit. In reality, the converse is true. Conceptual limitations of availability and scenario formulation encourage subjects to believe, for example, that many more committees can be constructed of size 2 from an overall set of 10 than of size 8 — yet the number of committees is exactly the same in the two cases.

Adjustment and Anchoring

In most situations it has been found that individuals formulate their general belief structure by starting from some obvious reference point and then making adjustments for special features. Typically, however, the adjustment is not sufficient and a bias towards these initial values is described as *anchoring*. For example, when subjects were asked to estimate within five seconds the product $8 \times 7 \times 6 \ldots \times 1$ they gave a much higher answer than those asked the product $1 \times 2 \times 3 \ldots \times 8$. We will treat the influence of the anchoring heuristic in a situation specific context through our later treatment of the CDF fractile estimation method for continuous probability distributions.

In general it would be valid to say that there is now an enormous and ever increasing amount of published experimental work investigating how individuals deviate from axioms of rationality and rationalist perspectives in formulating their probabilistic judgement. A further well-known example is the *conservatism bias* (Phillips, Hays, and Edwards (34)), i.e. individuals have generally been found to be 'conservative' in information processing because they underestimate the overall diagnosticity of observed evidence.

Much of the evidence, however, from this behavioral decision theory literature is piecemeal and largely based on laboratory evidence. Indeed, apart from Tversky and Kahneman's contribution, there have been few attempts at deriving an overall theory. For example, what determines particular bias sources? How can we reduce biases in assessments and alert assessors to the pitfalls? This cognitive engineering task has largely still to be undertaken though the researchers at Decision Research in Eugene, Oregon, appear to be putting considerable effort into this research field (see, Hogarth (20), Kahneman, Slovic and Tversky (23)).

We turn now to a consideration of probabilistic assessment of continuous probability distributions.

Continuous Distribution Assessments Using the Continuous Distribution (CDF) Fractile Method

Where, for example, a decision tree involves the probabilities of several different levels of demand it is more realistic to assess the complete distribution by the fractile method and then read off the required probabilities, than to proceed by the EQU method just described for each separate probability required.

The CDF method in which the range, median, and quartiles are assessed, has found by far the greatest favor in the experiments that have been carried out so far. The method has been described by Howard Raiffa (36) and, as usually carried out, consists of a number of steps:

(a) The assessor is asked to choose a value for the unknown quantity x (e.g. sales in the next month) such that he thinks it equally likely the true value will fall below or above it. (Call this value x_{50}.)

(b) The assessor is now asked to consider only those values above x_{50} and again asked to repeat the process of judgementally sub-dividing the range above x_{50} into two equally likely parts. (Call this dividing point x_{75}.)

(c) The procedure in (b) is now repeated for values below x_{50} and a value x_{25} hence obtained.

(d) The procedure is repeated again for each of the four intervals now available, so that in all, seven assessed values of x are obtained.

(e) Finally, a graph of the cumulative percentage probability (25, 50, 75, etc.) is plotted against x and a smooth curve drawn by eye through the plotted points. Any required probabilities are now read off the graph.

An example of this approach is given by Keeney and Raiffa (25) concerning the proposed development of facilities at the Mexico City airport (see also (10)). The procedure outlined above was carried out, the quantity to be estimated being the average number of people who would be subjected annually to noise levels of 90 CNR (Composite Noise Rating) or above in 1985. The one major difference was that the first step in the assessment procedure was to estimate x_{100} as 1,200,000 and x_0 as 700,000 (i.e. the absolute bounds for the variable x). Figure 3 shows part of the results obtained. As illustrated, the probability of the true figure being between any two adjacent fractile points should be the same, namely 0.125. To check the consistency of the assessments, the assessor can be asked if in fact his judgemental probability of falling into any of the eight such ranges of impact is the same. If not, the assessor would adjust his various estimates until no more such discrepancies could be found.

An alternative to Raiffa's procedure has been proposed by Barclay and Peterson (3). Although not the only possible alternative, its rationale is nevertheless explained here.

Suppose the problem is to estimate the population of the United States. The person might assess initially that it is most unlikely that the population is either less than 90 million or more than 300 million. A scale is now marked from 90 to 300 and two cardboard pointers placed on the scale. The person adjusts the position of the points so that he can consider the three alternative ranges equally likely: that is, the true value of the variable would fall above both pointers, between them, or below them. The object of trisecting the range, rather than bisecting it, is to overcome a tendency for assessors to give too

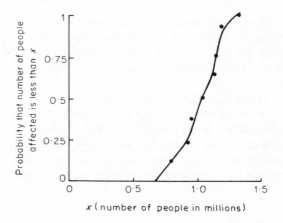

Figure 3 Cumulative density function for aircraft
noise nuisance above 90 CNR

narrow a range in their assessments. The four points now available can be plotted and a smooth curve drawn freehand through them.

Of course, the slope of the CDF obtained by methods such as those just described will vary according to the information available, and the technical skill of the assessor in being able to handle such information. Gustafson (14) has reported on some experiments in hospitals in estimating the length of stay for operations for various medical problems. The assessment was made by different groups of assessors such as medical students, interns, and consultants. Whilst the distribution of 'actual time minus assessed time' had a mean of approximately zero for all three groups of assessors, the variability of this quantity as measured by the standard deviation showed considerable differences, the consultants having a smaller standard deviation than the interns, whose standard deviation was smaller than that of the medical students.

Similar results have been found in assessments made of the time necessary to repair electrical failures in a large UK plant, where the more skilled and experienced assessors showed a much tighter estimation of the true figure.

Other Evidence on Procedures for Continuous
Probability Assessment

Whereas the family of CDF fractile methods appears the most convenient way to estimate continuous distributions, other suggestions have been made. For example, the method of relative heights (see Moore and Thomas (30)) has been suggested as an approach for obtaining a direct assessment of the probability density function (pdf). Indeed, Kabus (22), in a recent article in the *Harvard*

Business Review, indicates how forecasting teams in Morgan Guaranty Bank have been using such direct assessments of histograms to predict, for example, future (say, 90 days ahead) interest rates and bond rates.

The drawback to procedures involving the direct estimation of a probability histogram over a set of pre-specified intervals on the probability range lies in the fact that, unlike the CDF method, the responses are not immediately in the form of a probability metric, and subsequent interpolation and smoothing must be undertaken in order to obtain the pdf.

An example below illustrates this procedure. Suppose that you are an automobile dealer trying to determine how many cars you should stock for sale next month, given that you order stock for the next month's potential sales now. You feel that the most likely value is four cars. A typical form of dialogue between the analyst and car dealer now follows:

Analyst: I will mark the most likely value on the graph (Figure 4) with a height of eight units.

Dealer: O.K. I understand that.

Analyst: Now can you can find a value below four cars a month that you feel is half as likely to occur as four?

Dealer: Well, I would say that two cars is half as likely as four.

Analyst: Right, I will mark the value of two cars as four units on the graph. Now, can you give me a value above four cars a month that is again half as likely as four?

Dealer: Yes, I'd say five.

Analyst: O.K. then, I'll mark the value for five as four units on the graph. Can you now give me a value which is a quarter as likely as the four-car value?

Dealer: That's difficult, maybe one car if we do poorly or seven cars if we do well. Can you put the question another way?

Analyst: Well, is it also four times as likely for you to sell four cars as seven cars next month?

Dealer: Yes, that's also about right.

Analyst: Right, those points will be marked with two units. Finally, what are your minimum and maximum possible sales levels next month?

Dealer: I guess zero and ten.

Analyst: Let's enter all the relative heights in Figure 4 and see how we can derive the probabilities by drawing a smooth curve through the various points and 'normalize' the data to form a pdf.

Table 1 shows how the procedure can be inverted by interpolating relative heights for all possible levels of car sales after drawing a graph of the value, and then scaling them by the total of all the relative heights to form probabilities that sum to unity. The probabilities form a slightly asymmetric set with the longer tail to the right (as shown by the probability scale and associated pdf in Figure 4).

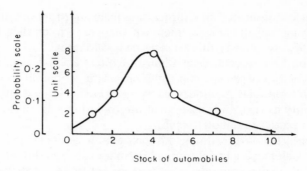

Figure 4 Relative heights and pdf for automobile stock
situation

Table 1 Relative heights calculation

Cars (1)	Relative heights plotted (2)	Relative heights smoothed (3)	Probabilities (3)/Σ(3) (4)
0	—	0.7	0.02
1	2	2	0.06
2	4	4	0.12
3	—	7.4	0.22
4	8	8	0.24
5	4	4	0.12
6	—	2.7	0.08
7	2	2	0.06
8	—	1.7	0.05
9	—	0.6	0.02
10	—	0.3	0.01
	totals	Σ(3) = 33.4	1

Possible Biases with the CDF Fractile Method

Alpert and Raiffa (1), in a report on the training of probability assessors, indicate the existence of 'tightness' and 'anchoring' biases. The 'tightness' effect means that naive assessors (i.e. those not expert in the area of the assessment) have difficulty in assessing the variability of their probability distributions; usually, the tails of the distribution are too tight. This phenomenon, however, does not appear to exist with experienced assessors. For example, Winkler and Murphy (47) report that weather forecasters are sound in their judgement of variability.

The 'anchoring' effect occurs in the method of questioning, and may also be given as an explanation for the tightness of the resulting distributions. In the CDF method, the assessor is asked, after specifying the 0.01 and 0.99 fractiles (i.e. the range of the variable), to determine the 0.50 fractile (or median) of the distribution. In other words, the questioning forces the assessor to anchor on an 'average' measure of the distribution (ignoring for the moment whether the assessor can distinguish between mean, median, and mode). In general, the assessor's adjustment process about this 'anchor' is not sufficient to reflect the variability in the underlying variable. One factor which may also reinforce such anchoring biases is the importance generally placed upon self-consistency within the decision-maker's set of assessments. In a straightforward assessment method, it is easy for the subject to be pseudo-consistent precisely because he can perceive what he should believe in order to be consistent with his previous response. In this way, his responses become firmly anchored from the starting point. This led to the development of approaches such as the tertile assessment method of Barclay and Peterson (3) (i.e. assessing tertiles which split the range into three equally probable intervals) precisely because of their potential tendency to reduce the anchoring effect.

A number of writers have also reported the existence of a tendency for assessors to estimate symmetrical probability distributions, and to shy away from asymmetry. Whether this is because the normal distribution is widely known and understood is a matter for speculation. Cognitive psychologists have also argued that symmetry *is* much easier for an individual to visualize and report than asymmetry. This may also have some influence on the lack of understanding of differences between the mean, the median, and the mode as a measure of central tendency of a distribution.

Other biases have been noted but this is not an attempt at a detailed review. The strength of the expanding literature in behavioral decision theory is the concentration on understanding how an individual confronts and assesses the impact of uncertainty. By so doing, we can help the decision-maker to better understand the process of probability assessment.

We believe that the following guidelines are useful:

(i) We encourage assessors to develop a 'thinking structure' for conceptualizing the probability assessment for an uncertain variable. We have
found that many assessors find mapping devices such as logic trees or
probability trees useful in their assessment task. The example below
(Figure 5) shows that such a tree can be used to assess the chance that
the Dow–Jones Index will increase by say 100 points over the next three
months — i.e. the assessor's logic is that changes in the Dow–Jones are
dependent upon the price index level, the rate of strikes, and the
incidence of wage claims. By considering such scenarios he can better
structure the assessment task. That is, instead of making the direct
assessment of a 100-point change in the index, the assessor breaks up
the assessment into a series of much more meaningful sub-assessments.
For example, given a scenario of a 10 percent rise in CPI, high strike and
wage rates, the assessment of a rise in the index is then made.

166

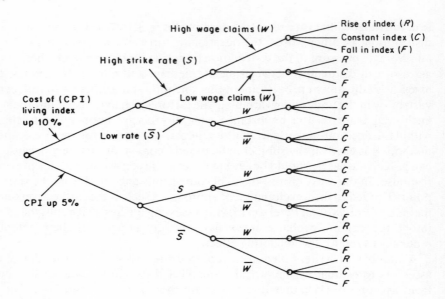

High wage claims (W)
Rise of index (R)
Constant index (C)
Fall in index (F)

High strike rate (S)

Cost of (CPI)
living index
up 10%

Low wage claims (W̄)

Low rate (S̄)

CPI up 5%

Figure 5 A probability tree diagram as a 'thinking' structure

It should be noted that engineers use a form of logic tree, called a fault tree, in order to understand the nature of such complex systems as nuclear reactors. Such a tree could then be used to assess, say, the chances of reactor failure.

(ii) We believe that training programs can help an assessor to build up a body of experience with probability assessment techniques, and at the same time alert him to some of the potential cognitive biases, e.g. anchoring. However, we do not believe that such biases can be either eliminated or necessarily reduced by such an approach. Only through a more extensive understanding of cognitive processes can we develop a cognitive engineering phase in which improvement of methods will be a by-product.

(iii) Given the existing set of approaches we believe that an assessor should feel comfortable with the method, the responses, and the assessment task he faces. This can be achieved by training the assessor to understand the nature of the assessment methods and basic statistical concepts. Such training would provide the assessor with a far broader awareness base.

The development of computer software (e.g. Schlaifer (37)) has proved to be useful with some assessors, in that the analyst's role is modelled by means of an interactive computer program in which assessors respond to pre-programmed questions about their probability assessments.

Group Assessments

The discussion so far has been concentrated on the individual assessor. Frequently, however, a group assessment has to be made. In these circumstances the Delphi technique is suggested as a useful vehicle for obtaining probability estimates. In the Delphi technique, a panel of experts is interrogated by a sequence of questionnaires in which the summarized responses to one questionnaire are used to produce the next questionnaire. The rationale is that as a result of several rounds of the procedure, most of the assumptions and information about the problem should have been exchanged amongst the participants. Eventually, it is argued, the process leads to an acceptable group consensus. This technique also attempts to eliminate the bandwagon effect of majority opinion.

Whilst the Delphi method provides one approach for handling the problem of consensus in terms of group probability, it is clear that it is only partially successful. One of the main problems is that it sometimes produces an artificial 'average' form of consensus. Winkler (46) has tried to tackle this problem by suggesting that the final consensus should be a weighted average of each relevant decision-maker's evaluation. This is a reasonable procedure, but it leaves open the question of how the weights are determined. Winkler suggests four approaches: equal weights, self-weighting, subjective weighting by a third party, or weighting based on past experience. The last suggestion seems to have the greater merit, yet it requires information on the assessor's historical assessment performance. It should be clear that historical assessment performance data is not always available, particularly as many decision situations are unique, one-off cases.

The Analyst–Manager Interaction

In our earlier discussion on the process of probability assessment, attention was concentrated on the encoding phase. This passes over one vital point in relation to the pre-encoding phase, namely training and experience in available assessment methods, which has a considerable bearing on the assessment task. Training is important both for the assessor, who may or may not be the manager responsible for the overall decision, and the decision analyst. The assessor needs to be aware of probability concepts and have some experience, at any rate on a pilot basis, of the most useful methods for probability encoding. For this purpose, an introductory lecture on probability concepts, followed by a number of sessions of a tutorial nature on the use of assessment methods and computer routines, such as those of Schlaifer (37) is a useful and instructive format. Such training can also indicate to the assessor the types of behavioral biases which psychologists have identified as occurring in probability assessment tasks.

Some assessors comment that they sometimes find it difficult to concentrate attention on the decision situation and the assessment tasks which confront them. Psychologists such as Kogan and Wallach (26) and Slovic and Lichtenstein (40) have demonstrated that individuals react to different dimensions of the decision-making task. For example, the latter found that the perceived attractiveness of a posed wager differs between individuals, mainly because they find differing characteristics of the situation more important than others, e.g. some concentrate on the win or lose probabilities, whilst others look mainly at the financial outcomes of win or loss.

This tendency for the assessor to lose concentration with the assessment task leads naturally to a consideration of the role which the analyst can play in probability assessment. The analyst needs experimental training because he must create the type of communication atmosphere in the interview situation which will ensure that the assessor understands his assessment task, and feels sufficiently involved and motivated to carry it through consistently to a logical conclusion. For example, some analysts, because of inexperience with the interactive interview section, may be too willing to accept without question the first probability judgement which the assessor gives them. Also, when interviewing executives in their role as expert assessors, inexperienced analysts often feel intimidated by the pressure of time in such a context, and find it difficult to confront the assessor with the necessary consistency checks and questions about his initial probability judgements.

Analysts, therefore, can usefully benefit from training in interviewing, and also from a thorough grounding in the details of decision analysis techniques. Experienced analysts, however, may exhibit another source of bias, namely an overeager response to the probability judgements of the assessor. To these, they mentally fit a distribution (e.g. beta, normal, log-normal) which may not be a true reflection of the assessor's degrees of belief about that uncertain event. For example, in capital investment decision problems, there is a wide literature (see Hillier (19)) about useful analytical models for measuring the worth of capital projects. Some models constrain the uncertain quantities to be of a particular analytical form (e.g. beta or normal) and a hard-pressed analyst may try to fit the assessor's judgements to one or another of these forms even though the fit may be, at best, a shaky approximation.

Sometimes assessors prefer the analyst to take on a more limited role in the assessment task. Once assessors feel confident with probability concepts, they often prefer to make the assessments on their own and perhaps only then to discuss them with the analyst. Indeed, in some current studies carried out within the Post Office Corporation (see Burville and Thomas (7)) most assessors have, after training, preferred using Schlaifer's interactive assessment computer programs, which have built-in consistency checks on an on-line terminal. Even skeptical non-quantitative executives have found such interactive devices to be of great use to them.

These findings suggest that the behavioral implications of probability assessment need to be carefully considered in designing the assessment procedure for use by a particular individual or group.

Conclusions on Probability Assessment

Before concluding the section on probability assessment, it is of value to examine notions of consistency and coherence by which the effectiveness of the various available assessment methods can be tested.

Whatever the technique used to assess the prior probabilities, the derived probabilities must be non-negative and sum to unity. If they are, then the probabilities are said to be consistent or coherent. The coherence axiom is fundamental to the existence of a rational subjective probability measure. Briefly, it states that an individual's subjective probabilities should be sensible in so far as it would be impossible to construct a set of bets to continually make money from the individual. D. V. Lindley (27) defends the coherence axiom in the following manner.

Suppose an incoherent person said A is less likely than B, B is less likely than C and then instead of concluding that A is less likely than C, concludes that C is less likely than A. Suppose now you offer him a prize if A occurs, but not otherwise. Keeping the prize fixed, he would prefer to base the receipt of the prize on B rather than A. Indeed, he would pay you a sum of money (or part of the prize) to substitute B for A. You accept the money and replace A by B. The argument can now be repeated so that you receive a further sum of money from him by replacing B with C. Having gained two sums of money, you now offer to replace C by A and the person would accept, since he regards C as less likely than A. A third sum of money now passes and the incoherent person is back to the initial situation where the prize depended on A. The sole difference is that he has already given you three sums of money. The cycle can be repeated if he holds to his uncertainty relations, and the incoherent person provides you with a perpetual money-making machine. This demonstrates that incoherence is unacceptable.

The purpose of the final stage in subjective probability assessment is accordingly to confront the individual with any incoherence in his assessments so that he can reassess them, possibly by making the same set of probability assessments in an alternative manner. This final procedure is commonly referred to as consistency checking. Any sensible assessment procedure should give self-consistent results, although some of the methods which do not involve an explicit articulation of probabilities will require a larger number of feedback iterations to achieve a satisfactory level of self-consistency.

In the direct percentile method for assessing a subjective probability distribution, the assessor is asked to give probabilities for percentiles intermediate to those chosen in the original assessment procedure. Achieving self-consistency in these cases is equivalent to obtaining responses which allow a reasonably smooth subjective probability distribution to be drawn. In the more indirect methods, based upon imputing probabilities from betting behavior, the subject has to be shown whether or not his responses lead to the possible construction of any kind of perpetual money-making machine.

Some interactive computer programs have been developed (e.g. the MANECON suite (used in the previously mentioned Post Office Study) by R. Schlaifer at Harvard, and those of the Stanford Research Institute) to aid this final stage of confronting the assessor with his inconsistencies. Training and practice in the technique of assessing probabilities will help to reduce inconsistencies in assessments. Self-consistency by itself does not, of course, guarantee the validity of a subjective probability measure. The measure could still contain biases due to other factors, such as the provision of incorrect input data to the assessor.

Even when an individual assessor has been taken through consistency checks to ensure self-consistency, and in addition, other possible behavioral biases have been eliminated as far as possible, the consensus problem may remain if individual assessors have to agree on a group view. We feel that more understanding of the behavioral factors which operate in group discussion should materially assist in the resolution of the problem of choosing a suitable method for obtaining a decision from an executive group.

ASSESSMENT OF CORRELATION EFFECTS

Introduction

In many of the early risk analysis applications, insufficient attention was paid to the existence of correlations between variables which determine project cash flows. Undoubtedly, one of the major reasons for this was the fact that ignoring the existence of correlation would simplify model development and result in a structure that could be handled and analyzed quickly and efficiently. It was also widely believed that correlation patterns were difficult to identify and even more difficult to measure. At the same time, many analysts recognized that overlooking correlations in project variables would probably lead to a misleading risk analysis and, worse still, it would allow incorrect conclusions to be drawn on the basis of the results of the analysis.

Important findings about the difficulties in identification and measurement of correlation patterns have also been reported by cognitive psychologists, who have looked at the role of man as an intuitive statistician. Researchers (see Chapman and Chapman (9)) have, for example, identified the existence of a phenomenon which they describe as 'illusory correlation'. In those experiments, subjects clearly overestimated the frequency of co-occurrence of natural associates (such as suspiciousness and peculiar eyes). This phenomenon suggests that individuals have difficulty in assessing the extent to which variables are correlated. Tversky and Kahneman (45) point out that the availability heuristic provides a natural explanation for the illusory-correlation effect. The judgement of how frequently two events co-occur could be based on the strength of the associative bond between them. When the association is strong, one is likely to conclude that the events have been frequently paired.

Consequently, strong associates will be judged to have occurred together frequently. Indeed, this correlation would apparently hold even if contradictory data were presented to subjects.

It is important to realize that there are also problems in assessing correlation patterns in risk analysis, when assessors may be confronted with the problem of assessing conditional probability distributions. Studies of choice among gambles, and of judgements of probability, indicate that people tend to have great difficulty in assessing the probabilities of conjunctive (e.g. 5 heads on 5 tosses of a coin, the joint probability of independent events) and disjunctive (e.g. at least one head on 5 coin tosses) events. Tversky and Kahneman argue that these biases can be explained in terms of the anchoring heuristic. Their argument is that the stated probability of the elementary event (e.g. head at any one stage) provides a natural starting-point for the estimation of the probabilities of both conjunctive and disjunctive events. Since adjustment from this starting-point is typically insufficient, the final estimates remain too close to the probabilities of the elementary events in both cases. Note that the overall probability of a conjunctive event is lower than the probability of each elementary event, whereas the overall probability of a disjunctive event is higher than the probability of each elementary event. Therefore, Tversky and Kahneman argue, as a consequence of anchoring, the overall probability will be overestimated in conjunctive problems and underestimated in disjunctive problems.

The same researchers further indicate how such biases in the estimation of compound events (often of the conditional character) are particularly significant in a planning context. They give examples of conjunctive and disjunctive structures that are of relevance to our study of risk and decision analysis applications. For example, a conjunctive-type structure exists in new product planning. In a new product development, the product will be a success if each of a series of events occur such as good test markets, a low cost product, high sales, etc. The general tendency to overestimate the probability of conjunctive events would lead to unwarranted optimism about the likely success of a new project development.

An example of the underestimation of the probabilities of disjunctive structures occurs in risk evaluation. Suppose it were necessary to estimate the overall failure of a complex system such as a nuclear reactor. Such a complex system will fail if any of its key components fails. It is argued that because of anchoring, individuals will tend to underestimate the overall failure of nuclear systems.

Perhaps the main conclusion to be drawn from man's failures as an intuitive statistician and, in particular, in assessing correlational phenomena, is that assessors should be alerted in training to the existence of possible judgemental biases (such as the use of a small number of cues and the anchoring and availability heuristics) and be provided with all information relevant to the assessment prior to the process of assessment.

We now examine possible approaches (and assessment implications) in risk analysis for handling correlation patterns in project variables.

ASSESSING FORMS OF DEPENDENCE

The issue of assessing the correlation patterns between variables has not really received adequate attention from the proponents of risk analysis approaches. In Chapters 2 and 3 we examined the array of risk analysis approaches and their rationale. That review should have made clear that the problem of assessing dependencies between variables depends upon the approach adopted. In what follows, we shall categorize the assessment approaches in terms of either the *risk simulation* (the Hertz, Hespos–Strassmann models) type or the *risk analysis* type (e.g. Hillier and other analytical approaches, which make, for example, specific distributional assumptions).

Let us consider, first, risk simulation approaches. This also requires us to examine sampling procedures for such simulations. We could assume the following forms of dependency in risk simulation:

   (i) no dependence — project variables are mutually independent;
  (ii) total dependence;
 (iii) partial dependence.

The *no dependence* assumption is the one which leads to independent sampling of the uncertain variables in the analysis. Very often, analysts argue that the *no dependence* assumption is appropriate because it is difficult enough to obtain data in the form of independent probability distributions, even from experienced assessors, without considering the added complexity of conditional probabilities. The *no dependence* assumption is also convenient because it simplifies model structure and some analysts justify it further (and really this is a manifestation of the cognitive phenomenon of ignoring uncertainty and correlation effects) by arguing that any underlying interrelationships amongst variables are implicitly taken into account in the values attributed to the variables by the assessors.

We believe that the *no dependence* assumption is only reasonable when that state is, in reality, the status quo. The effect of assuming *no dependence* in a simulation when in reality there is some dependence, can be seen in the output from such an analysis. Whilst the expected values of the criterion, say NPV, are reasonably accurate, the assumption of no dependence leads to a significant degree of overestimation of the NPV standard deviation. Since one of the main proposed advantages of risk analysis is in the presentation of the variability of the functional worth measure (intuitively risk is often expressed in terms of the SD), it is clear that non-allowance for correlation patterns can lead to serious weaknesses in practice and invalidate the risk simulation and assessment process.

The second case presented here is again probably a special and rather limited one. Total dependence can be defined in a number of ways. Perhaps the strongest possible version could be the assumption of perfect positive or negative correlation between pairs of variables x and y. It can be shown that this assumption means that the marginal distributions of x and y must have the same mathematical form. This is not necessarily very useful because, for example, the distribution of x may be symmetrical (e.g. of normal distribution form) whilst the distribution of y may be asymmetrical (e.g. of log-normal or beta form, with appropriate parametrization). We therefore need to adopt a definition of total dependence which would define positive dependence, such that if x were at its median value, then so would y be at its median value. This leads, in general, to the proposition that x and y are totally positively dependent if, when x takes a value at the Pth percentile, then y would also be at its Pth percentile value. Such a definition would allow x and y to take on different distribution forms and the process of sampling values for a simulation process would be quite a simple task. It would take the form of sampling a value from the distribution of x (the fractile would be identified) and then sampling the same fractile value from the distribution of y.

Patterns of total dependence rarely occur in practice. The more common form is some type of partial correlation between variables x and y. Hertz in the original paper (17) on risk analysis suggested a method of handling such forms of dependence in the context of risk simulation. Basically, the assessment requirements for this method are that we must obtain the marginal distribution for the independent variable, and then a series of conditional subjective probability distributions for the dependent variable. Each one of this series of conditional distributions would be dependent upon a particular value (or range) of the independent variable. The sampling procedure for risk simulation which would take account of such dependence relationships is called *conditional sampling*. That is, on each simulation run, a value would be sampled for the independent variable and this in turn would determine which of the series of conditional distributions would then be utilized for subsequent sampling.

It can be seen that our original suggestion (i.e. Hertz's) suffers from a major drawback — namely, that it is extremely difficult to design procedures in order to obtain meaningful assessments for the large number of conditional probability distributions required for the analysis. In most risk simulations of investment projects, there are a significant number of chance event variables for which unconditional subjective assessments must be made using procedures such as the CDF fractile method already described. Once patterns of partial dependence are treated within the framework of the analysis, the cognitive burden faced by the assessor in specifying the set of conditional probability distributions often becomes too great for most assessors. It is unrealistic to assume, therefore, that most conditional assessments obtained will be reasonable enough for practical use.

It appears, therefore, that the only sensible direction in which to move is towards more limited forms of conditional sampling in which patterns of dependence are specified in a simpler form. For example, Eilon and Fowkes

174

(13) have put forward an idea called discriminant sampling. They observe that managers prefer to consider relationships in terms, not of probability distributions, but of the range of values which one variable might assume, given the values of other related variables. Their assessment requirements are that subjective probability distributions be obtained for the independent variables, and then permissible ranges for dependent variables be obtained, given the possible values for the related variables. Let us repeat their example here.

Suppose we have two variables, x and y, where x may assume values in the range 0 to 100, and y may be between 20 and 80. Management may then state that if x is below 60, then y will probably be less than 40, but that if x is above 60, then y should be in the range 40–80.

In this case, their sampling procedure would first generate a value for x obtained by sampling from the assessed marginal distribution for x. Now, if this value x is below 60, a value of y is then generated over the range 20–40 (specified by some assumed probability density function). Similarly, if the sampled value for x is between 60 and 100, then the generating process for y (of some assumed probabilistic form) is designed to ensure that its value is between 40 and 80. In general, however, their discriminant sampling schemes are more complicated than this. The essence of their idea to restrict the range of values of the dependent variable according to the sampled value of the independent variable is a logical and sensible development. Their results indicate that efficient estimates of the standard deviation of the criterion measure NPV can be obtained from discriminant sampling, and these tend to be very close to those obtained from conditional sampling.

Other writers, such as Hull (21) have attempted to look for simpler sets of assessments and sampling procedures. Hull's suggestion is that marginal distributions for two correlated variables x and y are first obtained using accepted procedures for probability assessments. Then the assessor is asked to suppose that x is fixed at some value x^* (not the 0.50 fractile) and subsequently to assess the median y_{50} or 0.50 fractile for the distribution of y given that $x = x^*$. Thus, the single assessment required of the assessor is the median estimate for y, given x fixed at some other value x^*. Hull argues that, once this is obtained, both a set of conditional distributions for y and a correlational measure of dependence between x and y can be derived. A form of conditional sampling is then applied and results obtained which give efficient estimates of the standard deviation of the NPV measure.

In seeking to model correlation patterns using structural simplifications (either by assumptions about problem or technique structure) the work of Eilon and Fowkes, and Hull, is extremely useful. Following along similar lines, we would like to extend the argument, and suggest that the problem of framing correlation structures between variables is most crucial at the stage of decision structuring. It is at this point that trade-offs can, and must, be made between model complexity and problem reality. Thus after introspection and informal sensitivity analysis, certain patterns of correlation may be recognized as important. If the model's structure is sufficiently realistic, then attention can be concentrated upon these crucial dependence patterns. We also feel that the procedures expressed by the above authors need to be developed even further. For example, getting the assessor, as in Hull's procedure, to give a 0.50 fractile or median may be difficult. As has been mentioned previously, it is unclear whether many assessors understand the difference between the mean, median, and mode. As a result, any measure of central tendency may be given for the 0.50 fractile and this will cause bias if the underlying distribution is asymmetrical. Further, *multi-variate correlations* (i.e. situations where a particular variable is dependent on several other variables) may need to be handled in addition to *time-series patterns of correlation* (i.e. a particular variable in one time period may have a relationship with values of that variable in previous time periods).

We turn now to assessments needed for the analytic-type approaches, i.e. the risk analysis type characterized, in particular, by Hillier and Wagle.

Let us recapitulate for a moment and remember that the Hillier model assumes that for a simple project:

(i) The correlation between cash flows from two different sources x and y, r_{xy} is the same for all time periods, i.e. r_{xy} is constant over time.

(ii) For a given cash flow source y, corr $(y_t, y_{t*}) = \rho^{t* - t}$ for $t* > t$. This implies that cash flows from a single source have a time-series autocorrelation pattern of a first-order type. Thus, the correlation between period t and period $(t + 1)$ is ρ and this is the same for all time periods.

(iii) In a specified time period, suppose one cash flow source x has a relationship with another source y. It is not affected by and is independent of values of y in earlier time periods. With this assumption, the correlation between different cash flow sources in different periods can be written as follows:

$$\text{corr } (x_t, y_{t*}) = \text{corr } (x_t, y_t) \, \text{corr } (x_t, x_{t*})$$
$$= r_{xy}.\rho^{t* - t} (\text{for } t* > t)$$

We therefore require to estimate and assess values for the r_{xy} (correlations between different sources in the same time period) and ρ (the autocorrelation coefficient). Further, if we are also evaluating investment portfolios we will need to assess the covariances between projects.

In considering approaches for the measurement of correlations, we need, therefore, to differentiate between procedures for assessing *within period* correlations and *between period* autocorrelations for the single project. The distinction is very important because researchers (e.g. Brown (5)) have found that assessors have cognitive problems in assessing uncertain quantities over time and particularly when the time horizon becomes long.

If there is historical information within the firm on the relationship between x and y in a reasonable number of samples, then a historical estimate of the correlation between them may be obtained using standard statistical procedures. If there is no adequate data base, the *within period* correlation assessment can be handled using Hull's procedure, generalized from the earlier suggestions of Hillier and Wagle. In essence, the decision-maker provides an assessment in answer to the question: 'what is the median estimate for y_{50} given x = a fixed value x^*?' y_{50} is, therefore, the median of the distribution $f(y/x = x^*)$.

Since $\phi(y)$, the unconditional distribution of y, is given by the relationship

$$\phi(y) = \int_x f(y/x).g(x)\, dx$$

where $g(x)$ is the pdf of x, we should be able to derive r_{xy}, the correlation between x and y, by making assumptions about the form of $\phi(y)$ and $g(x)$. Indeed, Hillier and Wagle both show for the assumption of normal distributions for the x and y values (i.e. $\phi(y) \sim N(\mu_y, \sigma_y^2)$ and $g(x) \sim N(\mu_x, \sigma_x^2)$ that

$$f(y/x = x^*) \sim N\left(\mu_y + r_{xy}.\frac{\sigma_y}{\sigma_x}(x^* - \mu_x),\ \sigma_y^2(1 - r_{xy}^2)\right)$$

Thus, since y_{50} is the median of $f(y/x = x^*)$

$$y_{50} = \mu_y + r_{xy}.\frac{\sigma_y}{\sigma_x}(x^* - \mu_x)$$

and

$$r_{xy} = \frac{(y_{50} - \mu_y).\sigma_x}{(x^* - \mu_x).\sigma_y}$$

Since every quantity on the right-hand side has already been assessed, a value of r_{xy} can be obtained.

Hull shows that the formula given above can be generalized when $\phi(y)$ and $g(x)$ are not of normal form — provided that the distributions of x and y can be transformed to normality. Clearly, the value of this approach is that it limits the number of assessments that the assessor has to make. The reader is, however, left to judge whether, given the cognitive evidence on man as an intuitive statistician, the decision-maker can understand the assessment task and provide a meaningful response.

If we move now to the issue of the assessment of between-period project correlations, both Bussey and Stevens (8) and Bonini (4) have made separate contributions which rest upon the same underlying idea, namely to treat a series of estimates as a time series, and use this series to estimate the appropriate correlations. Though they differ in their methods of generating the cash flow series, the approach which appeals to us (and which is in the flavor of the structuring arguments we have already emphasized) namely, Bonini's, requires first that decision-makers' create *scenarios* of what might happen to cash flows over a project's life. These scenarios can be translated into a tree-type logic of the stochastic decision-tree type and cash flows C_t can be generated for different probabilistic manifestations of the project's life. Suppose ultimately we generate 5 to 10 scenarios, we can then calculate an estimate for the first-order autocorrelation coefficient ρ from the formula

$$\rho = \frac{\sum\limits_{t} (C_t - \overline{C_t})(C_{t-1} - \overline{C_{t-1}})}{\sum\limits_{t} (C_t - \overline{C_t})^2}$$

(where $\overline{C_t}$ denotes the mean of the C_t)

This process can be extended to handle cross-correlations between projects but we will not develop that point here.

The reader will by now have deduced that the process of obtaining adequate assessments for correlation patterns is quite complicated and the subject of many possible sources of bias. The generation of cash flow scenarios (and indeed of annual cash flow models) may be difficult (and also important in the context of portfolio planning as witness the approaches adopted in portfolio planning by organizations such as the Boston Consulting Group). However, we believe that it will become an increasingly fruitful approach for understanding the nature of correlations within single periods (through cash flow modelling) and between periods (through the generation of a range of project scenarios rather than the entire set of probabilities). We expect also that more general approaches will be developed for handling any number of intercorrelated project variables, each of which might have a different form of autocorrelation pattern associated with it, e.g. greater use of distributions such as the multi-variate normal distribution for cash flow variables.

We would like to say, finally, that we do not recommend the use of approaches which suggest that an assessor can be asked to provide direct assessments of correlation coefficients. Such assessments are not at all precise, and in such situations it may be better to examine the influence of correlation patterns by evaluating certain associative scenarios, and applying a form of sensitivity testing to those scenarios.

ASSESSMENT OF UTILITY

Introduction

We assume here that a financial model has been developed to provide value measures for outcomes. We would stress, however, that the processes of cash flow modelling (for example, the identification of accounting determinants of cash flows; the project's time horizon and the relationships within and between cash flows over time) are critically important, and considerable efforts should always be made to obtain a sensible problem structure. Guidelines given earlier should enable readers to move in the right direction in handling their own modelling effort.

178

Our interest in this section is in the elicitation of the decision-maker's preferences for outcomes in a meaningful form. In much of the discussion, we shall be suggesting how to implement the concept of utility, particularly in the sense that it measures the decision-maker's attitudes to risky outcomes in decision problems. In general decision-making situations, preferences of decision-makers for outcomes can be of two types.

(a) *Direct Preference*. An example is given by the statement 'I prefer outcome X to outcome Y'.
(b) *Attitude to Risk*. An example is given by the statement 'I prefer to play safe and take the outcome which gives me a guaranteed $1,000 rather than a strategy which gives me a 20 percent chance of losing $5,000 and an 80 percent chance of gaining $4,000.

Typically, most important commercial decisions involve preference patterns which are a complicated mix of types A and B. Any theory of choice behavior must explain both direct preferences and attitudes to risk, and utility has been found to be the most acceptable current theory of choice behavior.

A utility function does no more than associate a relevant set of numbers with a set of outcomes. The principles of decision analysis will still apply. Instead of using expected monetary value as the criterion of choice between alternative actions, we now replace money with utility and use the expected utility value criterion (EUV) for the choice between alternative actions. Moreover, the role of utility is the same whether the outcomes are monetary or non-monetary; single variable or multi-variable; quantifiable or non-quantifiable. When the outcomes of a decision can be described in terms of one variable, then the utility function is said to be uni-dimensional, or a function of a single attribute. An investor, for example, invokes a single attribute utility function when choosing between alternative options offering chances of different short-run gains. If, on the other hand, the consequences of a decision have a number of attributes, the utility function is described as multi-attributed. Typical examples, in a cost/benefit analysis situation, are attributes such as time saved, money saved, and convenience.

Summarizing the discussion so far, a utility function is 'a function defined on the outcomes' with the following properties:

(i) each possible outcome is defined by a single number;
(ii) the outcomes are ranked in preference order by these numbers;
(iii) the optimal decision strategy is to maximize expected utility.

A utility function does not, however, provide absolute value judgements. Outcomes are valued relative to each other and, if the scale of measurement U of a utility function is linearly changed to a new scale V using the formula

$$V(X) = rU(X) + s \text{ for all outcomes } X$$
$$(r \text{ and } s \text{ are constants with } r > 0)$$

Table 2 Probabilities and Outcomes

Contract K		Contract L	
Probability	Outcome	Probability	Outcome
0.6	+$80,000	0.5	+$50,000
0.1	+$10,000	0.3	+$30,000
0.3	−$30,000	0.2	−$10,000

then V is essentially the same function as U, and will always lead to the same optimal decision being made. The units used on the scale are commonly referred to as *utiles*.

Measuring Utility for Money

The following example illustrates the implementation of the utility concept in practice. The owner of Small Biz Ltd is deciding whether or not to undertake one of two contracts, K and L, that have been offered to him. He cannot undertake both, and to simplify the illustration, suppose that each contract can lead to only three possible outcomes. The probabilities and payoffs are shown in Table 2. If both contracts are refused, it is assumed that the EMV will be zero.

Under an EMV approach, the appropriate calculations are as follows:

$$EMV(K) = 0.6 \times 80,000 + 0.1 \times 10,000 + 0.3 \times (-30,000) = 40,000$$
$$EMV(L) = 0.5 \times 50,000 + 0.3 \times 30,000 + 0.2 \times (-10,000) = 32,000$$

On this basis, contract K should be accepted. However, since contract K shows a 30 percent chance of making a fairly large loss of $30,000 whereas contract L has only a 20 percent chance of a much smaller loss, utility concepts may be relevant. The owner of Small Biz might, for example, be unwilling to consider making such a large loss as $30,000 and would tend to opt out of contract K. This would depend upon a number of factors such as his asset position and cash flow situation. This suggests that an analysis using expected utility values (EUV) would be appropriate for the problem.

Consider next how this might be done. There are, in decreasing order, seven possible outcomes: +$80,000, +$50,000, +$30,000, +$10,000, $0, −$10,000, −$30,000. ($0 corresponds to taking neither contract.) Because the scale of a utility function is discretionary the analyst defines

$$U(+\$80,000) = 100 \text{ and } U(-\$30,000) = 0$$

and asks a sequence of questions to determine the utility of the other outcomes. Three possible methods to do this are described, each involving a form of the standard gamble approach.

Method 1 (illustrative determination of $U(+\$50,000)$)

Analyst: Which would you prefer:
    (a) gaining $50,000 for certain;
    (b) having a 75 percent chance of gaining $80,000 and a 25 percent chance of losing $30,000?
Owner: (b) is too risky; I'd prefer to take (a).
Analyst: Suppose I changed (b) so that you had a 95 percent chance of gaining $80,000 and a 5 percent chance of losing $30,000, which would you prefer then?
Owner: (*after some hesitation*) I'd prefer (b) then.
Analyst: What if I made (b) an 85 percent chance of gaining $80,000 and a 15 percent chance of losing $30,000?
    etc.

Eventually the decision-maker will be indifferent between (a) and (b). Suppose this happens when he has a 90 percent chance of gaining $80,000 and a 10 percent chance of losing $30,000. This enables us to write:

$$U(+\$50,000) = 0.9U(+\$80,000) + 0.1U(-\$30,000)$$
$$= 0.9 \times 100 + 0.1 \times 0 = 90$$

The procedure can be repeated for the other four outcome values.
    Method 2 varies the certain event, keeping the lottery fixed.

Method 2

Analyst: Which would you prefer:
    (a) gaining $40,000 for certain; or
    (b) a 70 percent chance of gaining $80,000 with a 30 percent chance of losing $30,000?
Owner: I'd prefer the $40,000 for certain.
Analyst: What if I reduced the certain gain in (a) to $10,000?
Owner: Well, then I'd prefer (b).
Analyst: What if I made the certain gain $25,000?
    etc.

The certain gain continues to be varied until the decision-maker is indifferent between (a) and (b). One point on the utility curve is then known and the percentage chances used in (b) can be changed to determine further points.
    Both Methods 1 and 2 have a big disadvantage in that the decision-maker may find it difficult to think in terms of the probabilities being used by the analyst. Indeed, many people cannot directly visualize the difference between, say, the probabilities 0.8 and 0.9. Both are just 'pretty likely'. For

this reason Method 3 has been devised using only the conceptually simple 50:50 gambles.

Method 3

The question and answer sequence using Method 3 can be abbreviated as follows:

Analyst: What certain outcome would you consider equivalent to a 50:50 gamble on outcomes +$80,000 and −$30,000?
Owner: +$10,000.
Analyst: What certain outcome would you consider equivalent to a 50:50 gamble on outcomes +$10,000 and +$80,000?
Owner: +$25,000.
Analyst: Which certain outcome would you consider equivalent to a 50:50 gamble on outcomes −$30,000 and +$10,000?
etc.

In this way the interval between the best and worst outcomes is bisected repeatedly. Soon the questioner will have enough information to plot the decision-maker's utility function. If, as before, the analyst sets:

$$U(+\$80,000) = 100 \qquad U(-\$30,000) = 0$$

then, from the first two questions above

$$U(+\$80,000) = 50$$
$$U(+\$25,000) = 75 \text{ etc.}$$

Analysis with Utilities

Taking the problem outlined at the outset of the section 'Measurement Utility for Money', suppose that Method 1 has been used to assess the various utilities with the following results:

$U(+\$80,000) = 100$ $U(\$0) = 30$
$U(+\$50,000) = 90$ $U(-\$10,000) = 20$
$U(+\$30,000) = 80$ $U(-\$30,000) = 0$
$U(+\$10,000) = 50$

These values have been plotted in Figure 6 and a freehand curve drawn to illustrate the decision-maker's utility curve.

182

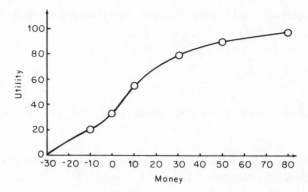

Figure 6 Decision-maker's utility curve

The EMV analysis used earlier can now be repeated, only using utility values instead of the monetary payoffs. The appropriate calculations are:

EUV (contract K) $= 0.6 \times 100 + 0.1 \times 50 + 0.3 \times 0 = 65$
EUV (contract L) $= 0.5 \times 90 + 0.3 \times 80 + 0.2 \times 20 = 73$
EUV (neither K nor L) $= 30$

Thus the utility analysis leads to acceptance of contract L rather than contract K as with the EMV approach.

Some basic points about the utility concept can be noted immediately. First, there is no such thing as *the* utility function for money, either for an individual or for a company. A utility function gives an assessor's relative preferences for money, that is the assessor's preferences scaled relative to two arbitarily chosen reference points. It is only meaningful to compare intervals of utility with one another. Thus, one interval of utility may be expressed as being twice that of another interval; but it is not correct to say that one amount of money has twice the utility of some other amount of money.

Secondly, utility assessments may change over time. A utility function assessed today at Chrysler would probably look rather different from one assessed in 1970. If you go home tonight to discover you have inherited a fortune, tomorrow's utility function may well reflect tomorrow's greater willingness to take monetary risks.

Thirdly, every utility function should be identified with a horizon date. In other words, you are assessing today what you think money will be worth to you at some future defined date and usually also in relation to a number of projected projects defined over that time horizon.

The Psychology of Preference

It is useful and important to examine some of the evidence on the cognitive processes underlying the formulation of preferences. This parallels our examination of such processes in the formulation of belief and subjective probability, and leads us to ask whether preference judgements obey the fundamental normative principles of decision analysis.

Though Kahneman and Tversky (24) are by no means the only researchers to have presented evidence on this topic (for example, Slovic, Lichtenstein, Fischoff and others at Oregon have developed many cognitive insights) their recent paper on Prospect Theory presents evidence of systematic variations by assessors from choices predicted by expected utility theory. They describe two phenomena which they call the *certainty effect* and the *reference effect*. These seem to occur very frequently when assessors are confronted with choice situations of the type illustrated in the Small Biz example, stated earlier. The *certainty effect* means that the decision-maker's attitude to risk is affected by whether the outcomes have positive or negative consequences. Apparently, decision-makers are risk-averse for positive outcomes and risk-seeking for negative outcomes. It should be noted that these risk attitudes are incompatible with any convex or concave utility function.

The *reference effect*, on the other hand, means that attributes, e.g. money, are most often perceived and evaluated relative to some reference point — the status quo. This means, for example, that when the utility function for money is assessed in terms of assets or wealth, the resultant curve is usually concave in shape (see Hammond (15)). When the function is assessed in terms of gains or losses (as in our example) S-shaped curves centred on the status quo are generally obtained. Swalm (42) in a *Harvard Business Review* article provides many examples of such shapes.

Whilst the certainty and reference effects provide useful insights, other researchers have argued, for example, that both the magnitudes of the probabilities, and the magnitudes of consequences, are important to decision-makers in confronting financial choices. Some have also sought to explain deviations from expected utility by arguing that the real consequence to the decision-maker is not necessarily clear to the observer. Meyer (29a,b) makes the point that if the range of a businessman's utility function for assets includes bankruptcy, then his utility function will be risk-averse for normal business risks but very risk-seeking near to bankruptcy. In other words, if the *real consequence* to the businessman is bankruptcy then it is not important to him whether he goes down the road to liquidation for $1m or for $100m. There is, therefore, a totally artificial scale for large negative consequences.

Much of the field is currently in a state of flux with some researchers developing alternative axiomatic and normative structures to amend expected utility. Others have suggested that by better defining the consequences in terms of multiple attributes, more useful utility functions can be obtained. On the other hand, cognitive psychologists are trying to develop a better understanding of the decision processes used by the decision-maker in the elicitation of preferences. The approaches used by them are either of the prospect theory, or the 'process tracing' (simulation of decision processes) type.

Our belief is that approaches for the improved assessment of risk attitudes will be developed. Currently however, it is important that when executives are being trained they should be alerted to the possible sources of biases which may confront them when dealing with practical assessments. Further, it seems clear that when handling utility assessment, it is necessary to elicit the base or reference point for the assessor. If the assessor feels more comfortable assessing his utility function in terms of gains and losses from a reference point, i.e. changes in net assets, then the assessor should be allowed to do so. The conventional decision analytic argument of assessing a utility function over final asset positions (end-outcomes) because decision-makers are too sensitive to small changes around the reference point is also defensible. The lesson is perhaps that we should design assessment procedures in order to provide the decision-maker with meaningful and useful assessment instruments.

Utility Functions of Executives

A number of studies have been carried out to measure the utility functions of executives. All used variations of the standard gamble methods described in the section 'Measuring Utility for Money' and some are presented here to give an insight into the results obtained and the practical problems encountered.

The first study concerned presented oil executives with a series of hypothetical drilling opportunities and asked them whether they would accept or reject each one. Most of the oil executives readily accepted the general concepts of decision trees but they were wildcatters in the sense that they would accept some apparently unfair gambles, although differing on how great the possible rewards had to be before they would do this. There was only moderate success at introducing the oil men to the formal concept of utility because they seemed to distrust the idea of using formal graphs to replace judgement. This highlighted the need for more effort to be devoted towards demonstrating the value and practicability of such an approach.

The next set of studies asked executives from one company a common set of questions, using an averaging procedure to obtain a corporate utility function. One of these studies attempted to determine the utility function of sixteen executives from a large chemical company, both as private individuals and as business executives. Another study, possibly the largest ever attempted, used 100 executives with different backgrounds, from a number of companies, and produced a variety of different utility plots. All the studies showed that different executives have utility functions of varying shapes and that obtaining a utility function is a particularly tricky task. In practical terms, there are three basic shapes for utility functions: risk-averse, risk-neutral (EMV) and risk-seeking. They are graphed in general form in Figure 7. In general, most executives seem to be slightly risk-averse, and also find it difficult to conceive of utility for negative cash flows, perhaps because of an adverse emotional reaction to tight financial situations.

Another difficulty which emerged with the use of standard gamble methods was that many managers found it hard to distinguish, on the one hand, between events with probabilities such as 0.2, 0.1, and 0.05 and, on the other hand, between events with probabilities such as 0.8, 0.9, and 0.95. To them, these

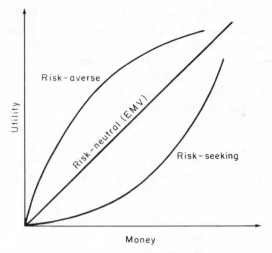

Figure 7 Specimen utility functions

were simply classifiable as very unlikely and very likely events respectively. This means that the utility function will be inadequately determined at the upper and lower ends of the range. Some analysts have attempted to overcome this by using Method 3 with only 50:50 gambles — but on a variety of outcomes instead of just the best and the worst. This makes the problem conceptually a great deal more simple for the decision-maker, but it can have disadvantages. The oil executives, for example, could reply, 'but we never get drilling opportunities with odds as good as 50:50'. On the other hand, the reaction on occasion was 'but we never accept investments unless the odds are much better than 50:50'.

Ideally, in deriving utility functions, executives should always be presented with the kinds of decisions they are used to in real life, posing questions phrased in familiar language of the decision-maker's own environment. Preliminary studies should be undertaken to determine what these are, and how small differences in probability can be made meaningful to the executive. Only then are the procedures likely to be successful in that situation.

Group Utility

So far, we have assumed the existence of one decision-maker with a single utility function. In many practical situations this is unrealistic; often it is necessary for groups of people, or even the whole firm, to choose between alternative outcomes. There are a number of possible voting procedures for accomplishing agreement between group members, and bargaining procedures can be devised where individuals 'give way' on the evaluations of some outcomes in return for their own evaluations being accepted. There is, however, no reason to suppose, *a priori*, that there exists any voting or bargaining process which will result in a single unique group utility enabling the group, whatever the decision procedures it adopts, to act as a whole 'rationally' and maximize the expectation of a single consensus utility function.

The measurement of group utility is clearly an important practical problem, particularly because utility evaluations of individuals cannot be simply aggregated to obtain a group utility — it being a relative and not an absolute measure. As an illustration of a possible procedure, consider the formulation of a risk policy for making capital investment decisions in a corporation. One general procedure (see Spetzler (41)) is as follows:

(a) Present a number of executives in the company with a series of hypothetical investment decisions and, from their answers, plot utility functions (one for each executive) using the methods of the section 'Measuring Utility for Money'.
(b) Agree with the help of further questioning on a functional form to fit the utility plots (the same functional form, but with different parameters being used for each executive).
(c) Reinterview, allowing each executive to spend a great deal of time on a few questions, and determine each executive's parameters for the functional form from the results.
(d) Present the results to top management, attempting to form in discussion with them the best parameters for a corporate risk policy.

Basically, step (d) argues that a group utility is best obtained by a consensus process of 'thrashing out' the inconsistencies of individual decision-makers at the level of the top decision-making group. In most cases, it is found that, at all levels of investment, the final corporate utility function is far less conservative than the average for the individual executives interviewed. (This can be regarded as a particular example of the 'risky shift phenomenon', i.e. a willingness to be more risky in group situations, which has been well documented by psychologists.)

The main identifiable advantages accruing from a study like the one discussed above are, first, that it is educational in the sense that executives are forced to consider their individual risk attitudes; second, that the premature rejection of risky projects by middle management is avoided; and finally, that it allows the development within the corporation of a way of communicating risk by means of utility evaluations, and of identifying a rational form of corporate risk policy which can be compared to the organization's perceived goals, e.g. the maximization of shareholder wealth.

There appears to be little doubt that the only realistic and practical approach for obtaining a group utility structure is for the group to meet, and approach a group utility view through a consensus process. The method of conducting such a meeting is, however, of crucial importance in order to ensure that the final view which emerges is that of the group.

Though the entire discussion has been centered around the assessment of single-attributed utility, we have already discussed one or two approaches in Chapter 3 for assessing multi-attributed utility functions. Indeed, that discussion and the MUCOM case, as included in the case-study chapter, should provide the reader with much basic background. Further reference should be made to the excellent book by Keeney and Raiffa (25).

SCREENING POLICY OPTIONS

A thorough decision analysis of even a relatively small set of decision options can be extremely complex and time-consuming. It is important in practice, therefore, to undertake the maximum amount of preliminary screening in order to reduce the initially envisaged set of options to a minimum set worthy of more detailed evaluation. Conceptually, as we have stated previously in this chapter, it might appear that there are two distinct stages in any decision analysis, i.e. the options are screened into a minimum number and the decision model is then pruned or screened into the simplest form. However, there is a simultaneity in screening options and structural assumptions. This is because options cannot always be screened without some form of model structure and equally, in simplifying the model, additional options might fall out as part of this model screening process.

It is perhaps useful to examine and present some of the available screening models. A fairly common type of multi-attribute screening model in the literature of decision mapping is a simple extension of the class of procedures known as matrix procedures. For example, in the goals/achievement matrix of, for example, Hill (18) the matrix consists of a set of subjectively assessed scores for each option (defining the rows of the matrix) against each relevant dimension (defining the columns). On assigning relative weights to each dimension, the weighted score can then be computed for each option. In formal terms, if S_{ij} denotes the score of option i on the jth attribute and w_j the relative weight given to attribute j, then the score S_j, where

$$S_j = \Sigma_j S_{ij} w_j$$

is used to rank the options. This is often known as the Churchman–Ackoff procedure and it has been used for example in the Aztech case (see Appendix to Chapter 2).

The main value of the Churchman–Ackoff procedure is in its intuitive appeal as a simple formalization. As a decision model, however, it does assume that the attributes are considered to be independent, and that preferences are adequately represented by the implicitly linear scoring measure. It is often argued, however, (see Edwards (11) that even if these assumptions are too strong to provide a valid ranking of all the options, they may still be sufficiently robust for screening out the top subset.

Reviewing the Churchman–Ackoff (C–A) part of the Aztech case, we note that in this instance, the financial risk analysis was carried out first, and hence the C–A score embeds the financial analysis. This does not necessarily have to be the case. For example, if we were to use C–A as a preliminary screen, we could rely upon the decision-maker's judgement of financial value rather than any formal analysis. Further, if we were to attach equal weights to each of the four decision-makers in aggregating the project scores, we could obtain an overall project ranking which could serve as the basis for a project screening process (incidentally projects (2, 10, 7) would rank as the three worst).

Obviously C–A is but one of a range of screening devices which could be used to rank these projects. Simpler screening models, especially checklists, (see Mottley and Newman (32), Dean (11)) are used by many R & D managers. However, C–A has many defects, e.g. its lack of attention to uncertainty and risk (though risk could be treated as one of the attributes, but that would beg the question of its definition).

In summary, therefore, an ideal screening procedure would represent a balance of being relatively simple and speedy, sufficiently robust and intuitively appealing. In addition, the importance of the screening process as a preliminary familiarization device before an expected utility analysis should not be overlooked.

We should also point out that screening for risky ventures has received considerable attention in the literature of capital budgeting and financial investment analysis, but in all cases, in terms of a single financial outcome attribute. Screening under uncertainty has apparently not been extended to the multi-attributed domain and incorporated in matrix approaches.

We have already discussed some of the issues relevant to screening under uncertainty in our earlier treatment of stochastic dominance in Chapter 3. Perhaps the simplest option in screening under uncertainty is the most common one, namely, equating risk with the variance of the outcome in which the screening process involves identifying the 'efficient' set of options (Markowitz (28)).

Finally, it is worth mentioning that the development of sensible screening procedures can be seen as having wider usage than solely being aimed at facilitating the practical aspects of decision analysis. Baecher, Gros, and McKusker (2), for example, argue that since major policy decisions are essentially political, the role of decision analysis should be to present a final subset of good options for political evaluation. If this is the case, then the entire decision analysis is effectively directed towards a screening procedure.

TRAINING ASPECTS OF DECISION AND RISK ANALYSIS

One of the main questions that has arisen from the reporting both of applications of decision analysis and of the biases inherent in human judgement under uncertainty, is 'how do we train decision-makers in order that they better use and apply decision analysis?'.

Some of the issues which are important in designing training programs for an organization follow. First, we have to be clear about the role and purpose of training, and to recognize that it is likely to be specific to situations and organizations. For example, do we wish to develop particular skills and expertise, e.g. probability assessment skills? Second, we need to understand fully which skills and attitudes must be transmitted in training decision-makers. Third, we must relate training needs to the characteristics of the organizational decision-making process being studied, e.g. is the decision more strategic than tactical? Fourth, how do we sensibly provide feedback and performance evaluation for those decision-makers undergoing training? What are the effects of task characteristics such as the response mode, and of the availability/absence of management information systems on decision-making judgements.

The evidence on existing training programs for decision analysis suggests the following hypotheses.

(i) Problem definition as a conscious discipline requires more effort in the decision-making process. Specific skills development in problem structuring is an absolute necessity.

(ii) The formulation of alternative courses of action is very often a more important consideration for managers than their subsequent comparison.

(iii) Getting decision analysis performed well in practice may be limited both by the lack of well-trained practitioners, and by the limited understanding of the 'people' problems of implementation. There is, therefore, a crucial need for expert training.

(iv) Judgemental biases in assessing beliefs and values cannot simply be reduced by alerting people to them. For example, the use of a small-scale operational problem to provide practice in assessment and feedback on 'biases' can help decision-makers understand the nature of the process. However, bias is generally judged in terms of a standard of the commonly accepted normative theory. We do not know, for example, whether the biases may be due to differences in assessment methods, or to individual differences in decision-makers, e.g. personality traits, etc. Therefore, there is a need to understand how each form of bias may arise and research must be directed towards this in the future. Until this research has proven fruitful, it is not helpful to suggest simplistic procedures for debiasing judgemental assessments — rather we should try to understand and improve the heuristics decision-makers use.

(v) Judgemental assessments of probability and utility tend to be more difficult in 'one-off', unique decision situations. Decision-makers tend to be much more comfortable in decision situations with a background of past decision-making history, data gathering, and generation of forecasts. It is argued that previous experience of such decision-making situations is an asset.

(vi) Assessors find difficulty in assessing and structuring problems with a long-term horizon, e.g. pharmaceutical research and development. The important issue is how we train decision-makers to confront future events more effectively.

(vii) Computer programs and decision support systems can often help decision-makers. For example, many assessors have found the Schlaifer MANECON programs for probability and utility assessment effective in providing a kind of simulation of the analyst/manager interaction, and in improving the quality of the subsequent judgements and assessments.

The current state of the art in financial modelling computer packages is such that most could be used by a reasonably well-trained manager. First, there are packages which allow for projections of pro-forma balances and profit/loss statements to be made. They only require simple accounting relationships to be specified by the manager. Second, there are packages for risk analysis of the Monte-Carlo type which are typically general purpose programs, but require the manager to model the problem structure and identify the relevant variables. A sub-program would have to be written to highlight the problem's structure and once this is achieved, the sub-program can be used with the modules in the general risk analysis program.

Much effort needs to be expended in alerting the decision-maker to the potential of such interactive programs and packages. Many simple programs are not used because the on-line terminal is viewed with fear by many managers, often because they are too embarrassed to admit that generally they cannot understand it or use it.

In summary, we believe training development in the organizational context is extremely important for the implementation of decision and risk analysis. Current research efforts will clearly provide guidelines for program development and should improve the ability of decision-makers. Yet we can never be absolutely sure that training improves decision-making because it is extremely difficult to do hindsight research and examine *outcomes* of the process in real-life decision analyses. More often, we justify improvements effected through training in terms of a 'better' and more rational decision process.

SUMMARY AND CONCLUSIONS

During the course of this chapter we have examined many, but not all, of the problems encountered in approaches for:

   (i) decision structuring;
  (ii) subjective probability assessment;
 (iii) the assessment of correlation patterns;
 (iv) the assessment of risk attitudes;
  (v) the screening of projects and policy options;
 (vi) the training of decision-makers.

Our main conclusion is that, since most decision and risk analyses require subjective judgements about uncertainty, belief, and value, we have to base many of our measurements on the judgement of the decision-maker or the decision-making group. Yet research by cognitive psychologists has clearly demonstrated that such judgements are somewhat shaky and often biased, and this suggests that analysts must not blindly accept judgemental data. We believe that the normative underpinnings of analytic procedures are being questioned by cognitive research, and the lesson for the decision analyst is that he must detect the major sources of error and bias in the judgemental process and devise training programs of a more effective character. Such programs should alert decision-makers to assessment problems, and try to help them to resolve any inconsistencies. However, we do not believe that it is time yet to reject applied decision and risk analyses (see, for example (31)). Instead, we would argue that sensible adaptations to the decision analysis paradigm are required to resolve some of the measurement problems. Furthermore, insightful cognitive engineering inputs should be incorporated in training programs in an attempt to develop the decision technology and make it increasingly applicable. It is certainly premature, given our knowledge of many successful applications, to reject an approach purely on the grounds of biases in judgemental assessments. Firstly, we firmly believe that research will constantly improve the conduct of the assessment process. Secondly, many decision-makers find that decision and risk analysis is a logical vehicle for structuring, understanding, analyzing, and communicating about their decision problems.

REFERENCES

1. Alpert, M., and Raiffa, H., 'A progress report on the training of probability assessors', unpublished Working Paper, Harvard Business School, 1969.
2. Baecher, G. B., Gros, J. C., and McCusker, K., 'Methodologies for Facilities Siting Decisions', in *Formal Methods in Policy Formulation*, Bunn, D. W., and Thomas, H. (eds.) Basel, Birkhauser-Verlag, 1978, 34–83.
3. Barclay, S., and Peterson, C. R., 'Two Methods for Assessing Probability Distributions', Working Paper, Decisions and Designs Inc., Washington, 1973.
4. Bonini, C. P., 'Risk Evaluation of Investment Projects', *Omega*, 3, No. 6, 1975, 735–50.
5. Brown, R. V., 'Do Managers Find Decision Theory Useful', *Harvard Business Review*, May/June **1970**, 78–84.
6. Bunn, D. W., and Thomas, H., 'Decision Analysis and Strategic Policy Formulation', *Long Range Planning*, **10**, December 1977, 23–30.
7. Burville, P. J. and Thomas, H., Strategy Planning: *A Public Sector Application*, London, Croom-Helm, (forthcoming).
8. Bussey, L. E., and Stevens, G. T., Jr., 'Formulating Correlated Cash Flow Streams', *Engineering Economist*, **18**, 1972, No. 1, 1–30.
9. Chapman, L. J., and Chapman, J. P., *Abnormal Psychology*, 1969, **74**, 74.
10. de Neufville, R., and Keeney, R. L., 'Systems Evaluation Through Decision Analysis: The Case of Mexico City Airport', in Kaufman, G. M., and Thomas, H., *Modern Decision Analysis*, London, Penguin Books, 1977, 387–416.
11. Dean, B. V., *Evaluating, Selecting and Controlling R & D Projects*, Research Study, American Management Association, New York, 1968.

192

12. Edwards, W., 'How to Use Multi-Attributed Utility Measurements for Social Decision-Making', *Report 76–3, Social Science Research Institute*, SSRI, Univ. of Southern California, August 1976.
13. Eilon, S., and Fowkes, T. R., 'Sampling Procedures for Risk Simulation', *Operational Research Quarterly*, **24**, No. 2, 1973, 241–252.
14. Gustafson, D., 'Behavioral Decision Theory in Medical Care', Working Paper, Depart. of Industrial Engineering, University of Wisconsin, 1971.
15. Hammond, J. S., III, 'Better Decisions Through Preference Theory', *Harvard Business Review*, November/December **1967**, 123–141.
16. Hampton, J. M., Moore, P. G., and Thomas, H., 'Subjective Probability and its Measurement', *Journal of the Royal Statistical Society*, A, **136**, 1973, 21–42.
17. Hertz, D. B., 'Risk Analysis in Capital Investment', *Harvard Business Review Classic, Harvard Business Review*, September **1979**, 169–181.
18. Hill, M., *Planning For Multiple Objectives*, Monograph 5, Reg. Sci. Res. Institute, Philadelphia, PA, 1973.
19. Hillier, F. S., *Evaluation of Risky Interrelated Capital Investments*, Amsterdam, North-Holland Publishing Company, 1965.
20. Hogarth, R. H., *Judgement and Choice,* Chichester, John Wiley and Sons, 1980.
21. Hull, J. C., 'Dealing with Dependence in Risk Simulations', *Operational Research Quarterly*, **28**, No. 1, 1977, 201–213.
22. Kabus, I., 'You Can Bank on Uncertainty', *Harvard Business Review*, May/June **1976**, 95.
23. Kahneman, D., Slovic, P., and Tversky, A., (eds.) *Judgement Under Uncertainty: Heuristics and Biases*, Cambridge, Cambridge University Press, 1982.
24. Kahneman, D., and Tversky, A., 'Prospect Theory: An Analysis of Decision Under Risk', *Econometrica*, February **1979**, 263–293.
25. Keeney, R. L., and Raiffa, H., *Decisions With Multiple Objectives*, New York, John Wiley, 1976.
26. Kogan, N., and Wallach, M. A., *Risk Taking: A Study in Cognition and Personality*, New York; Holt, Rinehart and Winston, 1965.
27. Lindley, D. V., *Making Decisions*, London and New York, John Wiley, 1968.
28. Markowitz, H., *Portfolio Selection*, New York, John Wiley, 1959.
29a. Meyer, R. F., 'On the Relationship among the utility of assets, the utility of Consumption, and investment strategy in an uncertain but time-invariant world', *Proc. 5th Inter. Conf. on O.R.:* OR69 (ed. J. R. Lawrence), London, Tavistock, 1970.
29b. Meyer, R. F., 'Preferences Over Time', in Keeney, R. L., and Raiffa, H., *Decisions with Multiple Objectives*, London, Wiley, 1976, Chapter 9.
30. Moore, P. G., and Thomas, H., *Anatomy of Decisions*, London, Penguin Books, 1976.
31. Moore, P. G., Thomas, H., Bunn, D. W., and Hampton, J. M., *Case Studies in Decision Analysis*, London, Penguin Books, 1977.
32. Mottley, C. M., and Newman, R. D., 'The Selection of Projects for Industrial Research', *Operations Research*, **1959**, 740–751.
33. Phillips, L. D., 'The Psychology of Measuring Probability', Working Paper, London Business School, Decision Analysis Unit, 1973.
34. Phillips, L. D., Hays, W. L., and Edwards, W., 'Conservatism in Complex Probabilistic Inference', IEEE Human Factors in Electronics, 1966.
35. Phillips, L. D., and Thomas, H., 'Assessing Probability and Utility', Working Paper, London Business School, Decision Analysis Unit. Presented at the Royal Economic Society Conference on Decision Theory, Lancaster, 1973.
36. Raiffa, H., *Decision Analysis: Introductory Lectures on Choices Under Uncertainty*, Reading, Mass., Addison-Wesley, 1968.

37. Schlaifer, R. O., *Computer Programs for Elementary Decision Analysis*, Cambridge, Division of Research, Harvard, 1971.
38. Simon, H. A., *The New Science of Management Decision*, (Rev. Edn) Englewood Cliffs, New Jersey, Prentice-Hall, 1977.
39. Slovic, P., 'The Relative Influence of Probabilities and Payoffs on the Perceived Risk of a Gamble', *Psychonomic Science*, **9**, 1967.
40. Slovic, P., and Lichtenstein, S., 'Relative Importance of Probabilities and Payoffs in Risk Taking', *Journal of Exp. Psych.*, **78**, 1968, 1–18.
41. Spetzler, C., 'The Development of a Risk Policy for Capital Investment Decisions', IEEE, *Transactions on Systems Science and Cybernetics*, Vol. SSC-4, 1968, 279–300.
42. Swalm, R. O., 'Utility Theory: Insights into Risk Taking', *Harvard Business Review*, **44**, Nov/Dec 1966, 123–136.
43. Thomas, H., 'Training and Applied Decision Analysis', Working Paper, 1979. Presented at AIDS National Meeting, New Orleans.
44. Tversky, A., 'Assessing Uncertainty', *Journal of Royal Stat. Soc.*, B. **36**, 1974, 148–159.
45. Tversky, A., and Kahneman, D., 'Judgement Under Uncertainty: Heuristics and Biases', *Science*, **185**, 1974, 1124–1131. (Reprinted in Kaufman, G. M., and Thomas, H., *Modern Decision Analysis*, London, Penguin Books, 1977).
46. Winkler, R. L., 'Consensus of Subjective Probability Estimates', *Man. Sci B*, **15**, No. 2, 1970, 61–76.
47. Winkler, R. L., and Murphy, A. H., 'Subjective Probability Forecasting in the Real World', 4th Research Conference on Subjective Probability and Utility, Rome, 1973.

Chapter 5

Risk Analysis and its Relationship to Finance

INTRODUCTION

The purpose of this chapter is to summarize the various approaches to risk analysis and relate them to modern theories of finance, particularly the capital asset pricing model. The underlying aim is, therefore, to understand the usefulness of risk analysis in the management of the resource allocation process.

In Chapter 1 we emphasized that managerial judgement about risk must, ultimately, involve a judgement about the riskiness of the overall portfolio of the firm's activities, and therefore about the relationship any individual investment project has to the firm's total risk. Further, we argued that if the objective of the firm is to maximize shareholder wealth, then managers entrusted with shareholders' funds should not invest them in capital projects unless the expected returns exceed those available to shareholders in the capital market.

In Chapters 2–4, we then examined the full implications of approaches for risk assessment, either of individual projects, or of combinations of projects (known hereafter as the *total risk* approach, i.e. the notion that the relevant risk of a project should be measured by the variance of its rate of return). We now wish to consider how such risk information might be used in investment decision-making where the accepted goal of management (as stated above) is to maximize shareholders' wealth, and thus the value of the firm.

As we have not presented a summary of the capital asset pricing model (CAPM), except for references to Lintner in Chapter 3, we shall briefly examine its rationale, assumptions, and implications for financial decision-making under risk. Our aim is to present the basis of the CAPM approach, namely, that the important consideration is the examination of a project's *systematic risk*, and that knowledge of this fact is sufficient for making investment decisions.

We shall then contrast the systematic or market risk approach of the CAPM with the total or firm risk approach for the evaluation of risky investments, which has been the subject of the earlier chapters. Some of the questions we shall seek to answer are: can the two approaches be reconciled? Are there circumstances in which features from each can be used to make a final judgement? What is the role of risk positioning and assessment in the understanding of the risky environment faced by the firm?

While following the argument here, we urge readers to review some of the schematic flow diagrams of risk analysis processes presented in the first chapter. These should provide a further rationale for our search for a meaningful, operationally sensible procedure for risk judgement in the context of investment decisions.

THE CAPITAL ASSET PRICING MODEL (CAPM)

In Chapter 3 of this book we briefly discussed aspects of portfolio analysis and gave a basic introduction to the concept of the security market line, i.e. the trade-off between expected return and risk, put forward by Lintner (6b) and Sharpe (10). Our purpose here is to summarize the CAPM in a nutshell by listing in outline its assumptions, framework, and implications. The aim is not to give a comprehensive treatment, but to provide a concise statement of the CAPM approach.

The underlying market equilibrium model on which the CAPM is based can be stated in terms of the following equation.

$$E(R_j) = R_F + \beta_j[E(R_M) - R_F] \tag{1}$$

wherein the following factors can be identified:

$E(R_j)$ = expected return on an investment (asset);
$E(R_M)$ = expected return on a market index of investments (e.g. the Dow–Jones or Financial Times 500 Indices);
β_j = measure of systematic, non-diversifiable risk, i.e. the regression coefficient of R_j on R_M;
R_F = a risk-free interest rate (usually to be found from prevailing interest rates on government or gilt-edged securities).

Put simply, the equation above indicates that the expected return on a given investment (asset) is the sum of two terms: a risk-free rate, and a term which represents a required risk premium.

Further, the theory indicates that the risk premium should be calculated from the formula $\beta_j((E(R_M) - R_F)$ and this means that the risk premium is the market's risk premium $(E(R_M) - R_F)$ weighted by the index of volatility, or systematic risk, β_j, of the given investment. This quantity, β_j, is often called the beta-coefficient and measures the sensitivity of the investment's returns to market returns. For example, a beta value of 0 would indicate no correlation between investment j and the market, whereas a beta of 1 would imply that the investment would have a risk exactly equivalent to the market risk. A beta value greater than 1 would, on the other hand, imply an aggressive type of investment which has more risk than a market portfolio. In other words, beta takes account for a given investment, of factors such as the overall economy and industrial structure, which reflect risk sources that have not been diversified away.

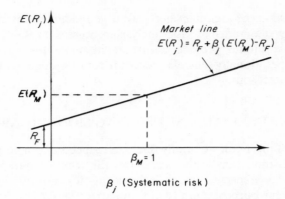

Figure 1 Graphical description of the basic model

One of the key assumptions of the CAPM is that perfect efficient capital markets exist, and that investors have homogeneous expectations. The evidence which has emerged from both the University of Chicago (Fama (1)) and other sources has provided no consistent evidence of market inefficiency. Therefore, the market appears to be neither unduly optimistic nor pessimistic, and does not seem to exhibit any generalizable sources of bias. The general mathematical relationship of the CAPM given in equation (1) can be graphed as shown in Figure 1.

It is further argued that for a well-diversified portfolio of investments (say of twenty or more randomly selected investments), the total risk of the portfolio is reduced to the point where only systematic risk remains. Therefore, the only important source of risk for a particular investment is the sensitivity of its returns to those of the market portfolio — the so-called 'beta' risk, or in other words, the undiversifiable risk that has not been eliminated by an efficient diversification process. Thus, for a particular investment, 'beta' is a sufficient measure for its risk and, more specifically, it can be shown that 'risk premiums' are proportional to 'beta' risk. (This differs from the total risk view which argues that the risk of the project is its marginal contribution to firm risk, as measured by the covariance of the project's return with that of the firm's portfolio.)

One of the other advantages of the model described by equation (1) is that the only factor which needs to be estimated is the beta-coefficient. Every other factor has a market-determined value and can be obtained relatively easily from existing data sources.

How then does the CAPM relate to capital investment decision-making? It is agreed that the stated aim of management is to maximize the firm's value, as measured by a maximization of shareholder wealth objective. Further, assets are priced in such share markets by discounting cash flows at a risk-adjusted rate, which reflects both the market's risk premium and the investment's volatility relative to the market. Therefore, for capital project appraisal, an individual project's expected cash flows should first be discounted by the required risk-adjusted rate of return determined from the CAPM. Any project which then increases the value of the firm, i.e. has an NPV > 0 when discounted at the required risk-adjusted rate (which equals the opportunity cost of capital) should be accepted.

In the following section, we will look more closely at the CAPM and capital project appraisal (see also, Franks and Broyles (5), Mullins (7), Myers and Turnbull (8), and Weston (12)).

THE CAPM AND PROJECT APPRAISAL

If we return for a moment to the graphical depiction of the model in Figure 1, we can translate the logic of the CAPM for project appraisal into visual terms. Recall for a moment that equation (1) gives us a formula for the expected return of a project or investment in terms of the risk-free rate, and the market's risk premium weighted by the beta coefficient. If we can determine, in reality, that the expected return for investment j exceeds the sum of the risk-free rate and the beta-weighted market premium, then we should clearly accept the jth investment. In graphical terms, this means that projects with expected return-systematic risk characteristics which ensure that they lie above and to the left of the market line, must be acceptable to the firm.

Let us now compare this criterion with the test-discount rate or hurdle-rate approach which is sometimes used in corporate finance to determine acceptable projects. There is, apparently, a commonly held view that the application of a single cut-off or hurdle rate (reflecting the firm's weighted average risk) for all investment projects will lead to correct and sensible capital investment decisions. Let us examine this in graphical terms. Figure 2 shows the now familiar *market line* and also a hurdle rate, R_o, which is the minimum 'average' return for any investment.

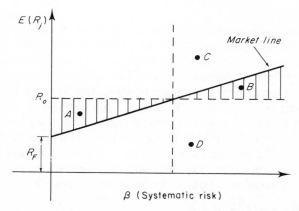

Figure 2 The CAPM and the hurdle-rate method compared

In terms of Figure 2, the CAPM and hurdle-rate procedures would imply different accept/reject decisions for four typical projects A, B, C, and D. We list the decisions in order below:

(a) *Hurdle-rate criterion* — accept project j if $E(R_j) > R_o$, if not, reject.

    A — reject;
    B — accept;
    C — accept;
    D — reject.

(b) *Market-line criterion* — accept all projects which lie above the market line.

    A — accept;
    B — reject;
    C — accept;
    D — reject.

It can be seen that both approaches give the same decisions for projects C and D, but disagree on A and B. A is a low-risk project whose rate of return exceeds that of the market, but such a project would be rejected in terms of the cut-off rate because it has a rate of return smaller than that of the hurdle rate. B is a higher return but higher risk project which does not meet market requirements, yet exceeds the hurdle rate R_o. A possible conclusion from this simple example is that hurdle-rate procedures will provide investment decisions in which higher risk projects may be favored.

The general point is that conflicting results are most often obtained, and this occurs even if we restrict hurdle rates to particular investment risk classes. In the example which follows, we try to illustrate how the CAPM can be used in relation to capital investment appraisal.

Example

The XYZ Company is considering four additional investment projects which will yield vastly different expected returns under the different economic conditions of growth, stagnation, and decline. It is further assumed that each project will cost roughly the same amount, i.e. $100,000.

The Finance Department has further estimated likely market returns under the same economic scenarios, and has projected a weighted average cost of capital of 15 percent as a possible average hurdle rate. It was assumed that a reasonable risk-free rate would be 6 percent. How should the firm appraise its investment possibilities using the market-line and hurdle-rate approaches?

Let us consider the market-line approach first. In order to evaluate each of the four projects we must use our basic equation (1) which is restated here:

$$E(R_j) = R_F + \beta_j(E(R_M) - R_F) \tag{1}$$

where from standard linear regression

$$\beta_j = \frac{\text{cov}(R_j, R_M)}{V(R_M)} = \frac{E((R_j - E(R_j))(R_M - E(R_M)))}{V(R_M)}$$

where $\text{cov}(R_j, R_M) = E((R_j - E(R_j))(R_M - E(R_M)))$ is the covariance between investment returns and market returns and $V(R_M)$ is the variance of market returns.

The basic project information and the steps involved in project appraisal using CAPM criteria are outlined in succeeding paragraphs.

Basic Project Information

Economic conditions	Prob. of such conditions	Market returns	Projects (and returns, %) 1	2	3	4
	(P)	(R_M)				
Growth	0.3	+20%	+30	+50	+40	+15
Stagnation	0.6	+10%	+20	0	+10	+10
Decline	0.1	−5%	−20	−50	−10	0

Step 1. Calculate $E(R_M)$: expected market return
   $V(R_M)$: variance of that return

$E(R_M) = 0.3 \times 20 + 0.6 \times 10 + 0.1 \times -5$
$ = 6 + 6 - 0.5$
$ = 11.5\%$

$V(R_M) = E(R_M - E(R_M))^2$
$ = [0.3 \times (8.5)^2 + 0.6 \times (-1.5)^2 + 0.1 \times (-16.5)^2]$
$ = 50.225$ (Standard deviation of $R_M = 7.1\%$)

Step 2. Calculate $E(R_j)$: expected return for project j
   and $\text{cov}(R_j, R_M)$: co-movement or covariance between project j and the market

Project 1 (Return: R_1)

Economic conditions	P	$R_1(\%)$	Derived Calculations
Growth	0.3	30	$E(R_1) = 19\%$
Stagnation	0.6	20 >	$\text{cov}(R_1, R_M) = 91.5$
Decline	0.1	−20	

$$\beta_1 = \frac{\text{cov}(R_1, R_M)}{V(R_M)} = \frac{91.5}{50.25}$$
$$= 1.8$$

Project 2(Return: R_2)

Economic conditions	P	$R_2(\%)$	Derived Calculations
Growth	0.3	50	$E(R_1) = 10\%$
Stagnation	0.6	0	$> \mathrm{cov}(R_1, R_M) = 210$
Decline	0.1	−50	

$$\beta_2 = \frac{210}{50.25}$$

$$= 4.2$$

Project 3 (Return: R_3)

Economic conditions	P	$R_3(\%)$	Derived Calculations
Growth	0.3	40	$E(R_3) = 17\%$
Stagnation	0.6	10	$> \mathrm{cov}(R_3, R_M) = 109.5$
Decline	0.1	−10	

$$\beta_3 = \frac{109.5}{50.25}$$

$$= 2.2$$

Project 4 (Return: R_4)

Economic conditions	P	$R_4(\%)$	Derived Calculations
Growth	0.3	15	$E(R_4) = 10.5\ \%$
Stagnation	0.6	10	$> \mathrm{cov}(R_4, R_M) = 29.25$
Decline	0.1	0	

$$\beta_4 = \frac{29.25}{50.25}$$

$$= 00.58$$

Step 3. Calculation of required rate of return from capital asset pricing model (where required return = $R_F + \beta_j(E(R_M) − R_F)$)
Note: We know $E(R_M) = 11.5\%$
$$R_F \quad = 6\% \text{ (assumption)}$$
Required returns now follow

Project 1: Required return = 6% + 1.8 × 5.5% = 15.9%
Project 2: Required return = 6% + 4.2 × 5.5% = 29.1%
Project 3: Required return = 6% + 2.2 × 5.5% = 18.1%
Project 4: Required return = 6% + 0.58 × 5.5% = 9.2%

Step 4. We now wish to compare the required returns from Step 3 with project expected returns.

Project 1 $E(R_1) = 19\%$;   Required rate = 15.9%;
        Excess return = +3.1%
Project 2 $E(R_2) = 10\%$;   Required rate = 29.1%;
        Excess return = −19.1%

Project 3 $E(R_3) = 17\%$;   Required rate $= 18.1\%$;
     Excess return $= -1.1\%$
Project 4 $E(R_4) = 10.5\%$; Required rate $= 9.2\%$;
     Excess return $= +1.3\%$

Therefore, Projects 1 and 4 should be accepted and 2 and 3 rejected using CAPM criteria.

Note, we could compare these results with the accept/reject decision using an assumed hurdle rate of 15 percent. Under this cut-off criterion, Projects 1 and 3 would be accepted and 2 and 4 rejected, indicating yet again that such a criterion may favor the high return projects.

The drawback of a constant cut-off rate is that it clearly does not take account of risk as effectively or directly as the CAPM approach. Indeed, it could be argued that each of the four projects belongs to a different risk class and that, therefore, there should be a different hurdle rate for each risk class. The weighted average cost-of-capital approach therefore needs some procedure for screening projects into risk classes and also determining hurdle rates for each of these classes. Even if all this were done, however, it would not be clear how the accept/reject decisions offered by the cut-off procedures would connect satisfactorily with a valuation objective of maximizing the overall value of the firm.

In concluding this section we should note that the CAPM approach for project appraisal implies that the required rate of return for a particular investment project does not only depend upon the policy of the company contemplating that investment possibility. Since investment projects should be evaluated solely in terms of their systematic risk, the market will expect and require a return from that project which would be at least as good as for any other firm in the same industry confronting such a project. Some firms, because of internal reasons of capital structure, efficiency or cash flow potential, may derive greater benefit from a given project once accepted, but at the decision stage, acceptance or rejection should only be made in terms of the market's required rate of return. This may be calculated for the relevant industry if acceptable firm beta information is not available. Foster (4, Chapter 8) gives a list of sources from which estimates of firm and industry betas can be readily obtained.

IMPORTANT ASSUMPTIONS IN THE CAPM

Before attempting to draw together the total risk approaches to capital investment decision-making and the CAPM approaches, it is perhaps useful to review the nature and character of the assumptions underlying the CAPM. It might also be of value to indicate areas in which such assumptions may be sources of weakness in terms of operational, practical decision-making.

The CAPM states that the risk inherent in an individual investment can be diversified into two components: systematic risk or beta (the non-diversifiable risk) and the diversifiable risk (often called the unsystematic risk). In other words, in *efficient markets* investors can eliminate the unsystematic component through a sensible diversification process and need concentrate only on the beta factor.

Most of the problems associated with the CAPM in practical decision-making revolve around the efficient markets set of assumptions and the existence of market imperfections in practice. For example, although we have not specified every assumption in detail (for a more complete treatment see Brigham (1), Copeland and Weston (2), Van Horne (11), Sharpe (10) and Lintner (6a, 6b)) the following seem important. First, the assumptions of homogeneous expectations on the part of investors. Second, that information is freely available to all participants in markets. Third, that there are no transactions costs in markets. Fourth, that borrowing and lending can be effected at an identical rate of interest. Fifth, that there are no costs associated by a firm when it faces bankruptcy or insolvency.

As an example, bankruptcy is a very costly process in the real world. Typically, the economic value of a bankrupt firm's assets declines far below market value, and very often significant transactions costs are incurred in the bankruptcy process. In such potential insolvency situations, it is important, therefore, for a firm to look at a broad 'total risk' set of guidelines for investment decision-making. Concentration solely on systematic risk elements whilst at the same time ignoring the firm's 'total risk' picture may lead to unwelcome outcomes.

THE CAPM AND THE TOTAL RISK APPROACH: AN OPERATIONAL APPROACH FOR INVESTMENT DECISIONS

It is important to recognize that the total risk approach looks at the *total business risk for the firm* by evaluating the portfolios of investments for a firm in relation to a corporate trade-off (typically in terms of a subjective utility function and not the functional capital market line trade-off given by the CAPM) between risk and return. Any individual project is reviewed in relation to its marginal impact on the total return (expected value) and total risk (standard deviation) of the firm as a whole. It is then management's task to judge the best firm portfolio in terms of a total risk perspective. Therefore, some of the approaches for single project evaluation (e.g. simulation/risk analysis/Hillier model, etc.) reviewed in earlier chapters are useful as input information for evaluation in terms of a total risk perspective.

The total risk approach should clearly be useful in situations in which the CAPM approach may be shaky, e.g. bankruptcy. Further, it is extremely valuable for firms whose shares are not traded in markets, and this would tend to be the case for a large number of small to medium-size private companies.

Perhaps the most sensible suggestion for the practical analyst is that whenever there is uncertainty about the decision context (e.g. when the CAPM assumptions do not apply), a *total risk* analysis should be carried out. In addition, it might also be useful to carry out other approaches, such as an incremental risk analysis, as a back-up and a guideline. The results of such alternative approaches can then be discussed with management, and advice given when different approaches offer conflicting suggestions about whether to accept or reject a particular investment.

While we believe that the CAPM approach is an increasingly useful one, we also feel that risk simulation procedures provide insights about total risk, about cash flow forecasting (particularly in relation to strategic management), and about the risk classes of projects. Such additional information is usually very valuable in relation to financial decision-making.

We would like to stress the importance of using several approaches in decision-making contexts. Indeed, the need to develop flexible, interactive capital investment decision-making procedures becomes increasingly evident when we confront case-study evidence (as in Chapter 6) of the practical implementation of risk concepts in decision-making.

This discussion should not be closed, however, without reminding readers of the survey evidence presented earlier regarding the implementation of financial decision-making techniques. Although techniques such as DCF are now widely used, it took considerable time and managerial education before they were successfully adopted. Though the treatment of risk is becoming necessary in such contexts, the implementation of risk analysis procedures lags far behind the theoretical developments of risk analysis and the CAPM. The role of the practical analyst must surely be to educate the manager about the assumptions and merits of each approach, and to develop procedures which are both theoretically sound and also capable of implementation by practising managers.

COMMENTS UPON A CAPM-TYPE APPROACH TO PROJECT APPRAISAL

We have seen that, if we accept the CAPM assumptions, a project with an expected rate of return in excess of that required from the CAPM formula should always be adopted since it will increase the value of the firm. Putting the argument another way, the approach requires that we must be able to determine a required rate for a given project or project class, so that we can then discount that project's expected future cash flows at a discount rate properly adjusted for risk (in a CAPM beta sense). If the NPV so obtained from this discounting process is then positive, we should accept the project but reject it if the NPV is negative.

It is important to note that in order to set a discount rate for a particular investment or project, we must have information about the risk class of that investment. One method of approaching this task is to attempt to screen projects into risk classes on a three-point scale, high, medium, and low risk. High-risk projects would be volatile in terms of cost changes and changes in economic activity, whereas low-risk projects would, on the other hand, be relatively insensitive to such factors. This screening process, based upon judgement and on some cash flow forecasting and perhaps risk simulation output, would then enable risk premia to be established for each of the three classes. The essence of this approach is shown in Figure 3.

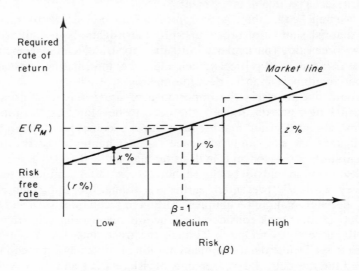

Figure 3 Establishment of risk premia

The graph shows the familiar market line (say for a particular industry of which the firm is part, or to which the project belongs) with the horizontal axis divided into low, medium, and high-risk segments. Assuming that the risk-free rate $r\%$ can be derived from prevailing rates in the market for government or gilt-edged securities, then average risk premia $x\%$, $y\%$, and $z\%$ can be estimated for the three risk classes by interpolation. The current discount rates for projects should normally be determined by adding the risk premium for the project's risk class to the risk-free rate corresponding to the life of the project (i.e. the rate on a bond of similar life) in order to obtain the appropriate *risk-adjusted rate*. Further, since the risk-free rate reflects the market's anticipation of inflation, all project expected cash flows should be forecast in *money* terms over the project's life, before being discounted at the required risk-adjusted rate to obtain the NPV. This NPV figure will indicate whether the project is acceptable, i.e. if the NPV is positive, the project should be accepted.

Whilst the comments above are not intended to be definitive, they will form some of the basis for our suggested project appraisal procedure in Chapter 7. We should note here, however, that there are problems in establishing risk classes and risk premia (for an alternative approach see the postscript) and in using risk-adjusted rates to allow for the risky environment. In addition, the treatment of inflation in capital budgeting needs to be consistent in order to avoid double counting i.e. calculations must be performed using either real cash flows and real discount rates, or alternatively, money cash flows and nominal discount rates.

SUMMARY

In this chapter we have indicated some directions for achieving a synthesis of conventional risk analysis approaches with CAPM-based approaches. Whilst we favor CAPM structures, we believe that conventional risk analyses are important in cash flow forecasting, in risk positioning, and in contexts where the CAPM assumptions do not apply. We shall develop these points further in Chapter 7, which suggests an operational risk analysis approach.

POSTSCRIPT TO CHAPTER 5

We present here for those readers who have perused the earlier AZTECH electronics case (Appendix to Chapter 2), an evaluation of project worth in terms of the CAPM approach.

AZTECH: CAPM Evaluation

The required rate of return (R) is a function of both the systematic risk of the project and the risk premium required by investors in a firm.

$$R = R_F + \beta(E(R_M) - R_F)$$

where R_F = return on riskless asset;
R_M = market rate of return;
β = systematic risk of project.
Aztech should accept all projects whose anticipated rate of return exceeds the required rate of return, R. These projects will increase the value of the firm

i.e. accept if $IRR > R$
$\qquad$ NPV at discount rate = $R > 0$.

Estimates of β (obtained from financial data sources given below)
For the FIRM: Aztech 1.3 (internally estimated)
For the INDUSTRY: Electronics Industry 1.6 (see Rosenberg and Guy (9), Foster (4))

	Before taxes	After taxes $(T = 0.4)$
assuming from case data R_F	8.3	5
and $E(R_M)$	20	12
Required return:		
$\beta = 1.6$	27.02	16.2
$\beta = 1.3$	23.51	14.1

(*Note*: T is the tax rate.)

206

Referring back to the data in Chapter 2, only decision-maker 4 would reject any project, even for $R = 27.02$. He rejects Project 2 for all values of R and Project 10 (IRR = 26.74) if $R = 27.02$.

REFERENCES

1. Brigham, E. F., *Financial Management: Theory and Practice* (2nd ed.), Hinsdale, Ill: Dryden Press, 1979.
2. Copeland, T. E., and Weston, J. F., *Financial Theory and Corporate Policy*, Reading, Mass., Addison-Wesley, 1979.
3. Fama, E. F., *Foundations of Finance*, New York, Basic Books, 1976. (See, for example, Chapter 5.)
4. Foster, G., *Financial Statement Analysis*, Englewood Cliffs, New Jersey, Prentice-Hall, 1978.
5. Franks, J. R., and Broyles, J. E., *Modern Managerial Finance*, Chichester: John Wiley and Sons, 1979.
6a. Lintner, J., 'The Valuation of Risk Assets and the Selection of Risky Investments in Stock Portfolios and Capital Budgets', *Review of Economics and Statistics*, **47**, February 1965, 13–37.
6b. Lintner, J., 'Security Prices, Risk, and Maximal Gains from Diversification', *Journal of Finance*, **20**, December 1965, 587–616.
7. Mullins, D. W. Jr., 'Does The Capital Asset Pricing Model Work?' *Harvard Business Review*, January/February **1982**, 105–115.
8. Myers, S. C. and Turnbull, S. C., 'Capital Budgeting and the Capital Asset Pricing Model: Good News and Bad News'. *Journal of Finance*, Vol **32**, No. 2, May 1977, 321–333.
9. Rosenberg, B., and Guy, J., 'Prediction of Beta from Investment Fundamentals': — Part 2 'Alternative Prediction Methods', *Financial Analysts Journal*, July/August **1976**, 62–76.
10. Sharpe, W. F., 'Capital Asset Prices: A Theory of Market Equilibrium under Conditions of Risk', *Journal of Finance*, **19**, September 1964, 425–442.
11. Van Horne, J. C., *Financial Management and Policy (5th ed.)*, Englewood Cliffs, New Jersey, Prentice-Hall, 1980.
12. Weston, J. F., 'Investment Decisions Using the Capital Asset Pricing Model', *Financial Management*, Spring 1973, 25–33.

Chapter 6

Case Studies of the Application of Risk Analysis

INTRODUCTION

The purpose of this chapter is twofold. Firstly, it attempts to provide the reader with an insight into some application areas, and secondly, by encouraging the reader to resolve some of the main issues in each case, it aims to demonstrate that one of the most valuable ways to learn is 'by doing'. Therefore, the case studies are first described, and then certain questions relevant to each case are posed. A commentary and discussion are also given for each case, so that the reader has the opportunity subsequently to review the important issues as perceived by the authors. However, in these commentaries we are not attempting to suggest that there is necessarily one best way to approach each of the problems, or that the solution presented is always the most appropriate one. It is our hope that through the careful study of such problems, the reader will become more sensitive to the problems of application and implementation, and will require in future that appraisal approaches are adapted sensibly to contextual and organizational needs. Whilst readers will naturally evaluate the merits of the different appraisal approaches, we would like to suggest some sensible guidelines for the management of the appraisal process in practice, and these guidelines will be dealt with in Chapter 7.

Finally, we would like to add that a series of further cases will be available as a companion volume to this text. The companion volume has been developed in an attempt to provide case situations which will enable the reader to derive more awareness and expertise in the application of risk analysis.

The case studies to be presented in this chapter are as follows:

(a) *The World Bank Irrigation Project*
   An example of risk analysis applied to the resolution of an irrigation investment project for economic development.
(b) *The Egg'N Foam Case*
   An example of the evaluation of alternative methods of manufacture of a new type of egg container.
(c) *The Digger Case*
   An example of the evaluation of a mining investment decision situation.

(d) *The MUCOM Case*

An example of a risk analysis in the manufacture of small arms, in which *multiple attributes*, e.g. cost, time, and performance of the system, have to be considered in the context of the decision process.

WORLD BANK CASE

The case described in this section is concerned with the determination of the net economic benefits associated with an irrigation project in an underdeveloped country. At the level of analysis identified in this simplified version of the problem, three main crops are planted within the country and the main issue centres around the trade-off between the increased production of the three crops and the costs associated with the irrigation project investment.

In the first part of the case some basic input data and a project description are presented. The input data are given either in probabilistic form (with a three-point chance event distribution) or in terms of single-point estimates where appropriate. This is followed by a description of the basic model and the various problems then posed are discussed in a concluding commentary.

As an example of a risk analysis, this case problem demonstrates many of the technical features of the approach. However, since the problem has already been well-structured and defined the issues of problem finding and structuring are not treated here.

CASE PROBLEM DATA. A WORLD BANK IRRIGATION PROJECT

Input	Outcomes	Probabilities
1. Initial Investment Cost	1,600	0.25
$= B_1$ (£)	2,000	0.50
	2,400	0.25
2. Life of Investment	5	0.33
$= N$ (years)	10	0.33
	15	0.33
3. Price of Commodity 1	2.4	0.33
$= Z_1$ (£)	3.0	0.33
	3.6	0.33
4. Price of Commodity 3	3.5	0.20
$= Z_3$ (£)	5.0	0.60
	6.5	0.20
5. Wages in Alternative Employment	1	0.30
$= W$ (£)	2	0.40
	3	0.30
6. Production — Crop 2	30	0.33
$= X_2$ (tons)	50	0.33
	70	0.33

7. Production — Crop 3 $= X_3$ (tons)	14	0.33
	20	0.33
	26	0.33
8. Price output coefficient for Crop 2 $= b$	0.06	0.30
	0.10	0.40
	0.14	0.30
9. Random effect (weather, etc.) $= e_1$ (tons)	-10	0.30
	0	0.40
	$+10$	0.30
10. Random effect (world supply, etc) $= e_2$ (£)	-0.4	0.30
	0	0.40
	$+0.4$	0.30
11. Initial Acres in production, Crop 1 $= A^0$	10	
12. Initial yield per acre Crop 1 (tons/acre) $= Y^0$	10	
13. Initial price Crop 2 $= Z_2^0$	10	
14. Annual costs (£) $= C_a$	70	

DESCRIPTION

Annual net returns consist of revenues obtained from the increased production of 3 crops (1, 2, 3). Both the number of acres put into production and the yield per acre of Crop 1 largely depend on wages farmers can earn in an alternative employment. The price of Crop 2 is assumed to be negatively correlated with the output of Crop 2 by the project. Prices of commodities 1 and 3 are not affected by the project's output. There are random effects (weather and world supply) that affect production of 1 and prices of 2. Annual costs are constant.

THE MODEL

(1) Acres in Production of Crop 1, (A) are a function of wages in alternative employment (W) $(A) = 10 - (\bar{W})$

(2) Yield per Acre of Crop 1, (Y) is a function of (W) $(Y) = 10 - 2(\bar{W})$

(3) Production of Crop 1, (X_1) $(X_1) = (\bar{A})\,(\bar{Y}) + (\bar{e}_1)$

(4) Gross revenue from Crop 1, $(S_1) = (\bar{Z}_1)(\bar{X}_1)$

(5) Price of Crop 2, (Z_2), is a function of the output of 2 and a random effect $(Z_2) = 10 - (b)(X_2) + (e_2)$

(6) Gross revenue from Crop 2, (S_2) $(S_2) = (Z_2)(X_2)$

(7) Gross revenue from Crop 3, (S_3) $(S_3) = (Z_3)(X_3)$

(8) Annual net benefit (B) $(B) = (S_1) + (S_2) + (S_3) - 70$

210

PROBLEM

A. (1) Flow chart the model.
   (2) Determine the best, most likely, and worst values of S_3.
   (3) Determine all the possible values of S_3.
   (4) Suppose Z_3 had been uniform; discuss the nature of the resulting discrete distribution.

B. Determine the present value of the benefits and the internal rate of return, using best estimates of all the inputs. (Use a discount rate of 8% for present value calculations.)

C. Determine present values *and* internal rates, assuming more conservative estimates for each of the inputs, as follows:
   (1) decrease (Z_1), (Z_3), (X_2), (X_3) and (N) by 10%;
   (2) increase (W), (B), (b) by 10%;
   (3) set (e_1) at -5 and (e_2) at -0.2.

D. Simulate with a Monte-Carlo program the distribution of present value *or* internal rate of return; determine their expected values.

E. Discuss the meaning of these results and any difference between the expectations found in (D) with those found in (B) and (C).

F. How would you go about determining the sensitivity of the results to changes in the *distribution* of the variables?

COMMENTARY

A(1) Flow Diagram for the World Bank Case
(for say 200 iterations or trials (I)

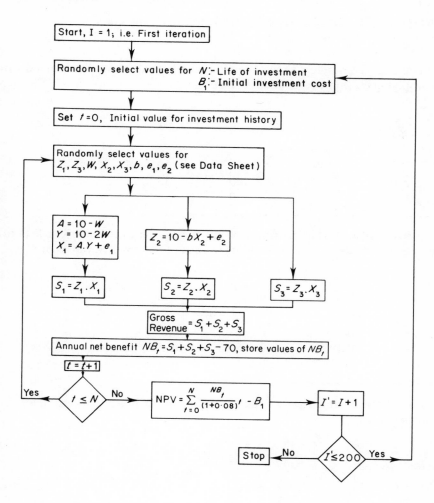

Start, I = 1; i.e. First iteration

Randomly select values for N_i- Life of investment
B_i- Initial investment cost

Set $I = 0$, Initial value for investment history

Randomly select values for
$Z_1, Z_3, W, X_2, X_3, b, e_1, e_2$ (see Data Sheet)

$A = 10 - W$
$Y = 10 - 2W$
$X_1 = A \cdot Y + e_1$

$Z_2 = 10 - bX_2 + e_2$

$S_1 = Z_1 \cdot X_1$

$S_2 = Z_2 \cdot X_2$

$S_3 = Z_3 \cdot X_3$

Gross Revenue $= S_1 + S_2 + S_3$

Annual net benefit $NB_I = S_1 + S_2 + S_3 - 70$, store values of NB_I

$I = I + 1$

Yes — $I \leq N$ — No

$NPV = \sum_{I=0}^{N} \frac{NB_I}{(1+0\cdot08)^I} - B_1$

$I' = I + 1$

Stop ← No — $I' \leq 200$ — Yes

The logic of the flow diagram is such that we use the model of the project to run (or simulate) 200 samples (or iterations) of possible realizations of the project if it were to be implemented. At each iteration, once the *life* of the investment and its *cost* have been selected by a random sampling process, the project's NPV is calculated. This is done by first random sampling to obtain values for the uncertain project variables and then using these values to calculate the *net cash flows* (NB) for each year of the project's life. Finally, the use of the

212

well-known capital budgeting formula for NPV, assuming an 8 percent cost of capital, generates an NPV as output for each iteration.

Thus, from a series of 200 iterations, we obtain 200 values for NPV and these can be reduced into the form of a probability distribution for NPV.

A(2) Determine the Best, Most Likely, and Worst Values of S_3

$$S_3 = Z_3.X_3$$

The matrix given below shows the nine possible values for S_3 obtained from multiplying the values of Z_3 and X_3 together.

		X_3	
Z_3	14	20	26
3.5	49	70	91
5.0	70	100	130
6.5	91	130	169

Associated with this matrix of values for S_3, we can similarly calculate a matrix of probabilities corresponding to each of the possible values of S_3:

		X_3	
Z_3	0.33	0.33	0.33
0.2	0.066	0.066	0.066
0.6	0.198	0.198	0.198
0.2	0.066	0.066	0.066

From these two matrices we can develop the probability distribution for S_3 as shown below:

S_3

Outcome	Probability
49	0.066
70	0.264
91	0.132
100	0.198
130	0.264
169	0.066
	0.990 [$\simeq$ 1 by rounding]

Best Outcome is 169 with probability 0.066.

Worst Outcome is 49 with probability 0.066.

Most likely *Outcomes* are 70 and 130 (this bi-modal result derives basically from the underlying discrete distribution assumptions for Z_3 and X_3.)

A(3) Determine all the Possible Values of S_3

The set of all possible values for S_3 is defined by the probability distribution given in note A(2).

A(4) Suppose Z_3 had been Uniform

If Z_3 had the form of an uniform distribution then each of the uncertain values for Z_3 would have had a 1/3 chance of occurrence. This means that each of the nine values of S_3 now has a 1/9 (1/3 × 1/3) chance of occurrence.

The probability distribution for S_3 is as below:

$$S_3$$

Outcome	Probability	
49	1/9	
70	2/9 →	
91	2/9 →	3
100	1/9	modal
130	2/9 →	values
169	1/9	

B. Determine the Present Value and IRR Using an 8 percent Cost of Capital and 'Best Estimate' Values

Assuming that we use expected values for each of the inputs as follows:

$B_1 = 2000$
$N = 10$
$Z_1 = 3$
$Z_3 = 5$ *Then* we can calculate
$W = 2$ $S_1 = 144$;
$X_2 = 50$ $S_2 = 250$;
$X_3 = 20$ $S_3 = 100$;
$b = 0.1$ $B = 424$
$e_1 = 0$
$e_2 = 0$

Therefore,
$$\text{NPV} = -2000 + \sum_{t=0}^{10} \frac{424}{(1 + 0.08)^6}$$
$$= 845.08$$

$$\text{IRR} = 16.5\%$$

C. Sensitivity Analysis

The results using conservative estimates are NPV = −113.5, IRR = 6.7 percent.

The same method of calculation is used as that shown in Section B.

D. The Following Pages Give the Results of 500 Iterations of the Monte-Carlo Simulation for This Project

The summary results are given below:

NPV: Mean = 637.21
      S.D. = 824.59
IRR: Mean = 12.4%
      S.D. = 9.2%

NPV Simulation Results
Number of trials? 500

Lowest value	Highest value
−996.321	2325.74

Interval size? 300
Lower limit of distribution? −1000
Upper limit of distribution? 2600

Probability distribution

Interval end	Prob	Cum. Prob.
−1000	0	0
−700	.052	.052
−400	.092	.144
−100	.108	.252
200	.104	.356
500	.04	.396
800	.08	.476
1100	.194	.67
1400	.164	.834
1700	.08	.914
2000	.062	.976
2300	.022	.998
2600	.002	1

Mean	Variance	Std. Dev.
637.21	679957	824.595

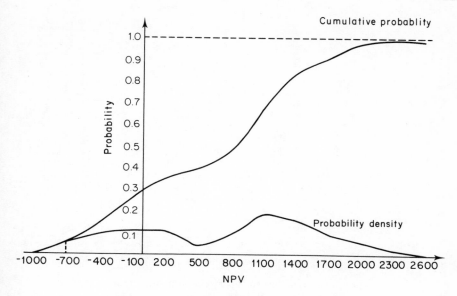

Net present value for irrigation project graph

Internal rate of return. Results
Number of trials? 500

Lowest value   Highest value
−.1115   .3155

Interval size? .05
Lower limit of distribution? −.15
Upper limit of distribution? .35

Probability distribution

Interval end	Prob.	Cum. Prob.
−.15	0	0
−.1	.002	.002
−.05	.04	.042
0	.112	.154
.05	.084	.238
.1	.086	.324
.15	.182	.506
.2	.292	.798
.25	.176	.974
.3	.024	.998
.35	.002	1

Mean	Variance	Std. Dev.
.1236	.852849E−2	.923498E−1

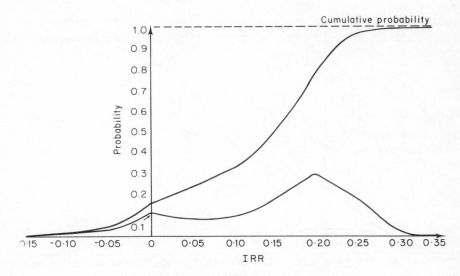

Internal rate of return for irrigation project graph

E. Discussion of Results

The result in B is based on single-point estimates for each of the variables in the model and gives a single-point estimate for the profitability of the project.

The results in C also rely on single-point estimates but in this case those variables, which are perceived as being significant in relation to the profitability of the project, are adjusted by arbitrary increments to determine a rough indication of their effect on the project's profitability. This is a very crude form of sensitivity analysis.

The results in D, on the other hand, are derived by performing 500 simulation trials and, on each trial, randomly selecting a value for each variable according to its probability of occurrence, and combining these values to derive an NPV or IRR worth measure. As a feature of this process a probability measure for a given outcome can be assessed.

As was stated earlier, the result in B represents, in effect, one branch of a large probability tree of possible outcomes and, further, the likelihood of this result is small (being the multiplication of the probabilities of each variable used to calculate the result for Part B). Therefore, it is not surprising to see it differ from the results in D which give the entire distribution for NPV and IRR. In addition, comparing the results in C with D we can draw the same conclusion since the C results reflect the left 'tail' of the entire distribution derived in D.

F. Sensitivity of the Results

Monte-Carlo simulation, or risk analysis, is in essence a comprehensive form of sensitivity analysis. It is therefore, not worthwhile to carry out further sensitivity tests unless there is good reason to suspect either that some of the original probability judgements were unsatisfactory, or that the structure of the problem has not been correctly specified in the risk analysis model.

CONCLUSIONS

In general, the World Bank project shows up many of the basic features of the risk analysis approach. However, it makes a number of strong assumptions about the mutual independence of the uncertain variables and assumes that the model structure has been well specified.

In later cases, and in the companion volume, we examine the validity of such assumptions in further detail.

THE CCA COMPANY'S EGG'N FOAM PROJECT

The Egg'N Foam project at CCA represented a large investment, a totally new market area, and a completely new product for CCA. CCA had been developing Egg'N Foam, a plastic package as a competitive substitute for paper egg cartons, for several years, refining its product design and operating a pilot plant in Nesquehoning, Pennsylvania. The project involved substantial amounts of uncertainty.

The project team selected to work on the Egg'N Foam decision consisted of representatives from the Research and Development Division, Plastics Division, and Corporate Controller's Office. People from these departments had been associated with the Egg'N Foam project for a considerable period of time and were quite familiar with the development, production, and marketing aspects of this product.

The following section discusses the step-by-step approach used by the project team to study the attractiveness of investing more funds in Egg'N Foam.

THE RISK ANALYSIS PROCESS

Developing the Flow Chart

The first step in applying risk analysis to Egg'N Foam was to construct a flow chart of the investment analysis. The process started with assessing the basic economics of the investment project and entering each element in a simple chart. The initial Egg'N Foam flow chart shown in Chart 1 consisted of six elements representing: (1) the total market size for egg cartons, (2) CCA's foam market share, (3) selling price, (4) manufacturing cost, (5) total overheads, and (6) investment base.

218

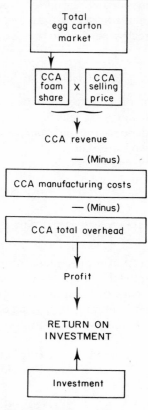

Chart 1 Initial flow chart
Egg'N Foam

The initial flow chart was then expanded backward to encompass a large set of input factors. This involved establishing a value for each factor, analyzing the determinants of that value, questioning the validity of the determining factors and, where possible, exploding the elements into further detail. The final product was a flow diagram of all the factors relevant to determining the profitability of Egg'N Foam.

The final flow chart for Egg'N Foam is considerably more detailed than the initial chart (see Exhibit I). The manufacturing costs, overhead costs, and investment base were expanded into a substantial number of inputs. On the other hand, the marketing elements (i.e. market size,* market share, and

---

*For the purpose of this study, the total market for egg cartons has been divided into five regions. Each represents a market that could be covered by the output from *one* Egg'N Foam plant. The West Coast was excluded from the analysis because entering this market was considered to be a separate decision not related to building plants in the other four regions. Egg'N Foam cartons cannot be shipped to the West Coast as the freight costs are too high.

price) were expanded into only a small amount of detail because sufficient market data were not available at that time.

Stating the Assumptions

When the flow chart was completed, assumptions underlying each of the factors were stated explicitly. This step was particularly important in that it placed a limit on the amount of detail required to substantiate the data inputs. For example, if the project team assumed CCA would capture a 10 percent share of the carton market, little data would be needed to estimate CCA's sales volume. As this exemplary assumption demonstrates, however, the magnitude that assumptions can take reveals the need to verify their reliability. Invalid assumptions can result in misleading and inaccurate conclusions from investment analysis. Thus, verification of assumptions is an integral and important part of the phase of stating the assumptions.

On the Egg'N Foam project, the team was able to verify the validity of most of the data, such as equipment rates supplied by Research and Development Division people and forecasts of total egg production supplied by the US Department of Agriculture. With some data, however, we felt that further study was necessary to determine the accuracy of the data and assumptions, such as the percentage of eggs that are cartoned and Egg'N Foam's sales volume and price. Exhibit II lists all of the assumptions underlying the most important input factors of the flow chart.

Analyzing Sensitivity

The next step in the analysis was to construct a nonprobabilistic computer model of the flow chart using the basic data shown in Exhibit III. The model was built for a single plant since each region represents a similar size market that would support a single plant operation. The model performed all the calculations indicated by the flow chart and provided answers in terms of the return on investment and cash flows.

The model was also used to determine the sensitivity of investment returns and cash flows to changes in input variables. The team was able quickly to answer questions such as 'What would happen to the discounted rate of return if the price dropped by $0.50 per thousand cartons?' or 'What would happen if the thermoformer cycle time were improved to 4-1/2 seconds?'. The results of the sensitivity analyses on Egg'N Foam are shown in Chart 2. Changes in two factors — caliper (or thickness) and demand — had a dramatic effect on the rate of return, whereas changes in the value of other factors turned out to have only minor impact on profitability. The high sensitivity of the investment return to changes in caliper and demand indicated the extreme importance of the accuracy of the assumed sales volume of Egg'N Foam.

The sensitivity analysis was also valuable because it permitted the team to experiment on the computer with different equipment combinations and plant

220

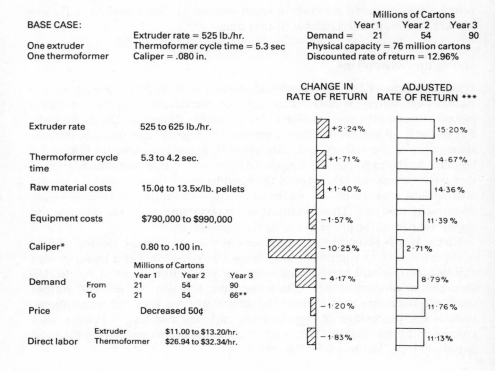

BASE CASE:

Extruder rate = 525 lb./hr.
One extruder   Thermoformer cycle time = 5.3 sec
One thermoformer   Caliper = .080 in.

Millions of Cartons

	Year 1	Year 2	Year 3
Demand =	21	54	90

Physical capacity = 76 million cartons
Discounted rate of return = 12.96%

		CHANGE IN RATE OF RETURN	ADJUSTED RATE OF RETURN ***
Extruder rate	525 to 625 lb./hr.	+2·24%	15·20%
Thermoformer cycle time	5.3 to 4.2 sec.	+1·71%	14·67%
Raw material costs	15.0¢ to 13.5x/lb. pellets	+1·40%	14·36%
Equipment costs	$790,000 to $990,000	−1·57%	11·39%
Caliper*	0.80 to .100 in.	−10·25%	2·71%

Demand

Millions of Cartons

		Year 1	Year 2	Year 3		
Demand	From	21	54	90	−4·17%	8·79%
	To	21	54	66**		

Price	Decreased 50¢	−1·20%	11·76%

Direct labor	Extruder	$11.00 to $13.20/hr.	−1·83%	11·13%
	Thermoformer	$26.94 to $32.34/hr.		

*Caliper Increase reduces the physical capacity of the plant considerably
**Sales volume drops from 76 to 66 in year 3
***Adjusted to use one extruder to two thermoformers

Chart 2 Sensitivity of investment return to changes in major input factors

sizes to identify the optimal plant operation. When applied to Egg'N Foam, the sensitivity analysis suggested that one extruder could support two thermoformers instead of one thermoformer, and also demonstrated the feasibility of building larger plants containing two extruders and four thermoformers.

Developing Investment Alternatives

After the sensitivity analysis was performed, the single plant model was used as a building block in constructing investment strategies for Egg'N Foam.* The team developed four alternative strategies for CCA in the egg carton market. Two strategies involved building superplants, each containing two extruders and four thermoformers, while the other two strategies called for small plants containing one extruder and two thermoformers.

*The Appendix lists the input data that were used for each strategy.

The difference between the two superplant strategies** and between the two small plant strategies is speed of market entry. One of the superplant strategies and one of the small plant strategies represent a slow, conservative investment pace, requiring the addition of thermoformers only after the demand for the output of existing equipment is firmly established. Conversely, the other strategies assume that CCA would act as quickly as possible to acquire equipment, hire and train the necessary manpower, and open the plants. The four strategies are shown in Chart 3, expressed in terms of the timing and sequence of equipment installation by plant location.

Assigning the Probabilities

The team's next step was to come up with probability information on input factors. Subjective probabilities were developed for the five inputs of the model that had either a significant impact on profitability or a considerable degree of uncertainty: extruder rate, thermoformer cycle time, caliper, price, and demand.

The probability distributions in Exhibit IV represent the best judgement of the CCA personnel most knowledgeable about Egg'N Foam. To understand fully the graphs shown in the exhibit, the following discussion points out the important characteristics of each probability distribution.

Extruder Rate

Information from CCA's production specialists, as well as from outside extruder manufacturers, indicated that extruders brought to the market after 1970 would have higher throughput rates due to advances in design. Therefore, two probability curves were developed, one for the period 1968 to 1970 and the other for the years 1970 to 1975. The width of both distributions is rather tight around the expected value for each distribution, which means that CCA people had a high degree of confidence that the extruders would operate at the expected pounds of foam per hour. Further, shapes of the extruder probability curves are almost identical, indicating that CCA people had the same confidence in the performance of existing and future extruder designs.

Thermoformer Cycle Time

The same advances are expected for the thermoformers. Improved equipment should be available by 1971, so two different probability distributions were necessary. The first one covers the years 1968 to 1970 and ranges from 6.0 to 4.5 seconds with an expected value of 5.3. The distribution for the 1971 to 1975 thermoformer design ranges from a 6.0 to a 3.0 second cycle time with an

---

**Superplant strategy assumes construction of two plants to serve the four regions, while the small plant strategy assumes construction of four plants.

222

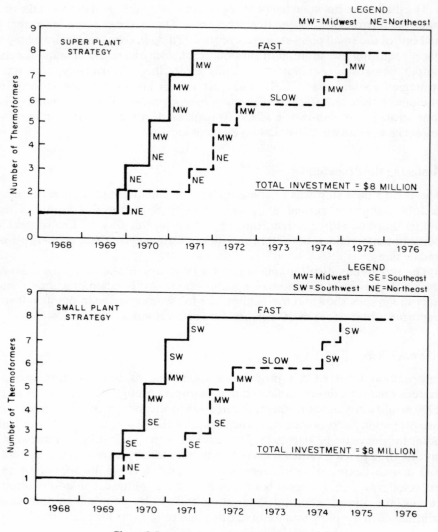

LEGEND
MW = Midwest   NE = Northeast

Chart 3 Investment strategies Egg'N Foam

expected value of 4.2 seconds. The shapes of the two curves differ, however, because CCA's people had greater confidence in the performance of 1968 equipment than future thermoformer designs.

Caliper

Similarly, two probability distributions were developed for the thickness of foam sheets to be processed by thermoformers, as shown in Exhibit IV. In this case, however, CCA production people were less confident in their predictions. The probability distribution shows that the caliper could fall anywhere between .090 and .078 inches thickness with equal likelihood. The flatness and width of both probability curves indicate the lack of confidence in CCA's ability to produce foam of uniform caliper.

Price

The project team developed probability distributions for price in each of the years between 1968 and 1975 and predicted the expected value would drop $0.30 per thousand cartons each year. The probability distributions for 3 of the 7 years are shown in Exhibit IV, and are representative of the remaining price curves.

Demand

Estimates of demand were developed for each strategy, for each plant, and for each year (the base data for means and standard deviations are shown in the appendix) based on the assumption that CCA can capture 10 percent of the egg carton market or 360 million cartons* by 1974 with the fast strategy or by 1978 with the slow strategy. For the fast strategy there is a greater probability of deviation from the expected demand than for the slow strategy.

THE REMAINING ISSUES

The next steps, which are to be undertaken by the students before reviewing the subsequent commentary, are:

1. Evaluate the effectiveness of the analyses and role of the CCA project team.
2. Prepare a flow chart for evaluation of any of the strategies.
3. Outline an approach to the selection of a strategy for implementation of the Egg'N Foam project.
4. Determine the risks involved in the alternatives.**
5. Make recommendations to management as to the strategy to be chosen, and outline the risks and contingency courses of action.

*The 360 million cartons represent a 10 percent share of the markets in four regions: East, Southeast, Midwest, and Southwest.

**Develop and/or assume distributions of any variables that are necessary, using available information.

SIZE OF CARTON MARKET

1. U.S.D.A. statistics on egg production by state are correct
2. Estimates from the editor of the Poultry Tribune are correct on eggs cartoned as percentage of total egg production
3. Statistics of U.S. Economics Corporation are correct
4. Total market is divided into five regions determined by:
     — Probable organization of CCA field sales force
     —Size of areas where a 10 percent share would be the equivalent of a small size plant
5. Foam will have better merchandising appeal than pulp or paper and therefore foam will tend to replace Pillopost, Case Ace, and folding cartons over the next 10 years
6. By 1978, share of market by carton type will have changed as follows:
     — Paperboard from 45% to 5%
     — Pulp from 53% to 50%
     — Foam from 2% to 45%

CONTINUING COSTS

1. Straight-line depreciation is used for calculating the return on investment. Double declining balances are used for calculating depreciation for tax purposes and the discounted cash flows
2. Life of the equipment is equivalent to current standards allowed by the Internal Revenue Service
     — Building 30 years
     — Production equipment 7 years
     — Trucks 5 years

MARKET SHARE

1. The market under consideration is the potential number of foam egg cartons sold through existing channels of distribution in four regions (West Coast is excluded)
2. CCA will be able to produce a high-quality foam carton which is acceptable to customers and will close satisfactorily on existing egg packers' machines
3. Product characteristics of Egg'N Foam will be competitive to Pillopost
4. CCA can successfully sell foam egg cartons through existing channels of distribution (to each type of customer in the market)
5. CCA's sales volume will be penalized by building plants in later years
6. CCA will sell out a plant's capacity regardless of when the plant is built
7. CCA will have captured 10 percent of the assumed carton market by 1978 (360 million cartons)
8. No additional carton suppliers are expected to become a significant factor in the egg carton market in the next 10 years
9. Diamond National will enter the market with its own foam carton some time before 1978 as opposed to considerably lowering their pulp carton prices
10. Colored foam will not be a factor in the market before 1978
11. CCA will equalize freight paid by customers when foam cartons are shipped into other regions

---
DIRECT COSTS
---

1. Significant cost savings can be achieved by building super plants
2. No major changes will take place in the manufacturing concept
3. In an Egg'N Foam plant no other products than foam egg cartons will be produced
4. CCA will produce its own foam sheets
5. CCA foam will have uniform quality and density characteristics
6. Through-put rates of the extruder and thermoformer will improve over time due to advancements in design and manufacturing knowledge
7. Inflation in future years has been excluded since it should affect both revenues and costs

---
PRICE
---

1. Foam cartons will sell at the Pillopost price level
2. Pillopost prices are expected to decline over the years
3. Market volume for foam cartons will drop sharply at prices above Pillopost level
4. Diamond National will be the price leader; price competition will be moderate
5. Price-volume discount schedule is unlikely to change significantly over the next decade
6. No transfer price for foam is considered

SELLING EXPENSES
---

1. Egg'N Foam distribution will be handled by the Plastics Division's Marketing Department
2. Selling costs include:
   —Unrecovered charges (design and plates, speculative art work, customer machinery)
   —Supplies
   —Dues and subscriptions
   —Advertising and promotion
3. There will be a one-time start-up cost

Exhibit II Major assumptions underlying Egg'N Foam projections

YIELD PERCENTAGES

Extruder garbage loss: 1.0%   Thermoformer mold loss: 1.0%   Printer loss: 2.5%
Extruder reclaimable scrap: 7.0% Thermoformer buttends loss: 1.0%   Printer reclaimable scrap: 1.5%
                                  Thermoformer reclaimable scrap: 13.0%

EFFICIENCIES

	EXTRUDER	THERMOFORMER
Mechanical efficiency	90%	90%
Scheduling efficiency	95%	100%

MATERIAL PRICES

Foam pellets: $0.15/lb
Supplies: $1.01/thousand cartons

MANUFACTURING COSTS*

	ONE EXTRUDER	TWO EXTRUDERS
Extruder variable costs	$15.35	$25.29
Thermoformer variable costs	22.21	38.94
Continuing costs	$237,350	$393,600

*The cost for three thermoformers is equal to the cost for one plus the cost for two.
The cost for four thermoformers is equal to twice the cost of two.

MANUFACTURING PROCESS

Extruders will work on a four-shift basis (7-day week): thermoformers on a three-shift basis (5-day week)

EQUIPMENT SPEEDS AND SPECIFICATIONS

	1968	1969	1970	1971	1972	1973	1974
Price/thousand cartons	$26.00	$25.50	$25.00	$24.50	$24.00	$28.50	$23.00
	$26.90	$27.00	$26.90	$26.80	$26.70	$26.60	$26.50
Extruder Rate (lb./hr.)	420–600	520–700					
Caliper (inches)	.080–.087	.078–.087					
Thermoformer Cycle Time* (seconds)	6.0–4.5	6.0–3.0					

*Thermoformers will use a twelve-up mold

EGG CARTON MARKET

1968	1978
3.5 billion cartons	4.7 billion cartons

Continuing costs include:
— Plant overhead
— Office expenses
— Property tax
— Mold amortization
— Depreciation
— Other production expenses

Direct costs include:
— Material
— Labor
— Supplies
— Maintenance

Selling costs include:
— Sales force salaries
— Payroll taxes, employee benefits
— Travel and entertainment (25% of salaries)
— Telephone and telegraph
— Office rent
— Unrecovered charges
— Supplies
— Dues and subscriptions
— Advertising and promotion

A small plant sales force includes:
— ½ sales manager
— 3 salesmen
— 2 packaging machinery service

A large plant sales force would include:
— 1 sales manager
— 5 salesmen
— 3 packaging machinery service

Exhibit III Fixed input data — Egg'N Foam risk analysis model

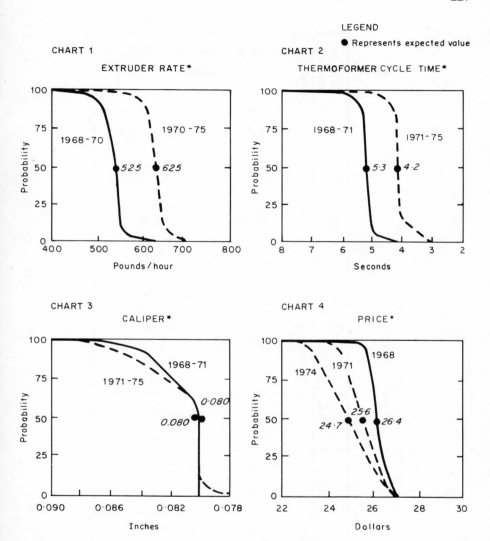

The probability distributions for these input factors are the same for each of the four strategies.

Exhibit IV Probabilities assigned to major input factors

Appendix 1 Variable input data — Egg'N Foam risk analysis model
Strategy: Super fast

Plant Location: *Nesquehoning*

Year	Building	Equipment ($000)	Trucks	Working capital	No. Extruders	No. Thermo-formers	Selling expenses ($000)	Mean demand (Carton Millions)	Standard deviation (Carton Millions)
1	720	671	20	250.0	1	1	70.0	22	30
2	0	120	0	201.2	1	1¼	121.7	41	30
3	720	701	10	401.2	2	3½	180.0	86	30
4	0	0	0	0	2	4	204.1	134	30
5	0	0	0	0	2	4	204.1	180	30
6	0	0	0	0	2	4	204.1	180	30
7	0	0	0	0	2	4	204.1	180	30
8	0	0	0	0	2	4	204.1	180	30
9	0	0	0	0	2	4	204.1	180	30
10	0	0	0	0	2	4	204.1	180	30
11	0	0	0	0	2	4	204.1	180	30
12	0	0	0	0	2	4	204.1	180	30
13	0	0	0	0	2	4	204.1	180	30
14	0	0	0	0	2	4	204.1	180	30
15	0	0	0	0	2	4	204.1	180	30

229

Plant Location: *Cairo*

Year	Building	Equipment ($000)	Trucks	Working capital	No. Extruders	No. Thermo-formers	Selling expenses ($000)	Mean demand (Carton Millions)	Standard deviation (Carton Millions)
1	0	0	0	0	0	0	0	0	30
2	0	0	0	0	0	0	0	0	30
3	720	791	20	451.2	½	½	70.0	9	30
4	720	701	10	401.2	1¾	3	180.0	54	30
5	0	0	0	0	2	4	204.1	115	30
6	0	0	0	0	2	4	204.1	139	30
7	0	0	0	0	2	4	204.1	180	30
8	0	0	0	0	2	4	204.1	180	30
9	0	0	0	0	2	4	204.1	180	30
10	0	0	0	0	2	4	204.1	180	30
11	0	0	0	0	2	4	204.1	180	30
12	0	0	0	0	2	4	204.1	180	30
13	0	0	0	0	2	4	204.1	180	30
14	0	0	0	0	2	4	204.1	180	30
15	0	0	0	0	2	4	204.1	180	30

Appendix 2 Variable input data — Egg'N Foam risk analysis model
Strategy: Super slow

Plant Location: *Nesquehoning*

Year	Building	Equipment	Trucks	Working capital	No. Extruders	No. Thermo-formers	Selling expenses	Mean demand	Standard deviation
		($000)					($000)	Carton Millions	
1	720	671	20	250.0	1	1	70.0	22	10
2	0	0	0	50.0	1	1	100.0	36	10
3	0	120	0	151.2	1	2	121.7	54	10
4	720	581	10	250.0	1½	2½	150.0	79	10
5	0	120	0	151.2	2	4	204.1	106	10
6	0	0	0	0	2	4	204.1	138	10
7	0	0	0	0	2	4	204.1	180	10
8	0	0	0	0	2	4	204.1	180	10
9	0	0	0	0	2	4	204.1	180	10
10	0	0	0	0	2	4	204.1	180	10
11	0	0	0	0	2	4	204.1	180	10
12	0	0	0	0	2	4	204.1	180	10
13	0	0	0	0	2	4	204.1	180	10
14	0	0	0	0	2	4	204.1	180	10
15	0	0	0	0	2	4	204.1	180	10

Plant Location: *Cairo*

Year	Building	Equipment	Trucks	Working capital	No. Extruders	No. Thermo-formers	Selling expenses	Mean demand	Standard deviation
	($000)	($000)					($000)	Carton Millions	Carton Millions
1	0	0	0	0	0	0	0	0	10
2	0	0	0	0	0	0	0	0	10
3	0	0	0	0	0	0	0	0	10
4	720	791	20	451.2	1	1½	0	16	10
5	0	0	0	0	1	2	100.0	50	10
6	720	701	10	401.2	2	3½	121.7	78	10
7	0	0	0	0	2	4	180.0	102	10
8	0	0	0	0	2	4	204.1	126	10
9	0	0	0	0	2	4	204.1	160	10
10	0	0	0	0	2	4	204.1	180	10
11	0	0	0	0	2	4	204.1	180	10
12	0	0	0	0	2	4	204.1	180	10
13	0	0	0	0	2	4	204.1	180	10
14	0	0	0	0	2	4	204.1	180	10
15	0	0	0	0	2	4	204.1	180	10

Appendix 3 Variable input data — Egg'N Foam risk analysis model
Strategy: Small fast

Plant Location: *Nesquehoning*

Year	Building	Equipment	Trucks	Working capital	No. Extruders	No. Thermo-formers	Selling expenses	Mean demand	Standard deviation
		($000)					($000)	Carton Millions	
1	720	671	20	250.0	1	1	70.0	21	21
2	0	120	0	201.2	1	1¼	121.7	41	21
3	0	0	0	0	1	2	121.7	57	21
4	0	0	0	0	1	2	121.7	90	21
5	0	0	0	0	1	2	121.7	90	21
6	0	0	0	0	1	2	121.7	90	21
7	0	0	0	0	1	2	121.7	90	21
8	0	0	0	0	1	2	121.7	90	21
9	0	0	0	0	1	2	121.7	90	21
10	0	0	0	0	1	2	121.7	90	21
11	0	0	0	0	1	2	121.7	90	21
12	0	0	0	0	1	2	121.7	90	21
13	0	0	0	0	1	2	121.7	90	21
14	0	0	0	0	1	2	121.7	90	21
15	0	0	0	0	1	2	121.7	90	21

Plant location: *Southeast*

Year	Building ($000)	Equipment ($000)	Trucks	Working capital	No. Extruders	No. Thermo-formers	Selling expenses ($000)	Mean demand (Carton Millions)	Standard deviation (Carton Millions)
1	0	0	0	0	0	0	0	0	21
2	0	0	0	0	0	0	0	0	21
3	720	791	20	451.2	1	1½	100.0	27	21
4	0	0	0	0	1	2	121.7	62	21
5	0	0	0	0	1	2	121.7	90	21
6	0	0	0	0	1	2	121.7	90	21
7	0	0	0	0	1	2	121.7	90	21
8	0	0	0	0	1	2	121.7	90	21
9	0	0	0	0	1	2	121.7	90	21
10	0	0	0	0	1	2	121.7	90	21
11	0	0	0	0	1	2	121.7	90	21
12	0	0	0	0	1	2	121.7	90	21
13	0	0	0	0	1	2	121.7	90	21
14	0	0	0	0	1	2	121.7	90	21
15	0	0	0	0	1	2	121.7	90	21

Plant location:*Midwest*

Year	Building	Equipment ($000)	Trucks	Working capital	No. Extruders	No. Thermo-formers	Selling expenses ($000)	Mean demand	Standard deviation
								Carton Millions	
1	0	0	0	0	0	0	0	0	21
2	720	0	0	0	0	0	0	0	21
3	0	671	20	300.0	½	½	50.0	9	21
4	0	120	0	151.2	1	2	121.7	40	21
5	0	0	0	0	1	2	121.7	70	21
6	0	0	0	0	1	2	121.7	90	21
7	0	0	0	0	1	2	121.7	90	21
8	0	0	0	0	1	2	121.7	90	21
9	0	0	0	0	1	2	121.7	90	21
10	0	0	0	0	1	2	121.7	90	21
11	0	0	0	0	1	2	121.7	90	21
12	0	0	0	0	1	2	121.7	90	21
13	0	0	0	0	1	2	121.7	90	21
14	0	0	0	0	1	2	121.7	90	21
15	0	0	0	0	1	2	121.7	90	21

Plant location: *Southwest*

Year	Building	Equipment ($000)	Trucks	Working capital	No. Extruders	No. Thermo-formers	Selling expenses ($000)	Mean demand (Carton Millions)	Standard deviation (Carton Millions)
1	0	0	0	0	0	0	0	0	
2	0	0	0	0	0	0	0	0	
3	720	791	20	0	1	1½	0	0	21
4	0	0	0	451.2	1	2	100.0	21	21
5	0	0	0	0	1	2	121.7	57	21
6	0	0	0	0	1	2	121.7	71	21
7	0	0	0	0	1	2	121.7	90	21
8	0	0	0	0	1	2	121.7	90	21
9	0	0	0	0	1	2	121.7	90	21
10	0	0	0	0	1	2	121.7	90	21
11	0	0	0	0	1	2	121.7	90	21
12	0	0	0	0	1	2	121.7	90	21
13	0	0	0	0	1	2	121.7	90	21
14	0	0	0	0	1	2	121.7	90	21
15	0	0	0	0	1	2	121.7	90	21

Appendix 4 Variable input data — Egg'N Foam risk analysis model
Strategy: Small slow

Plant Location: *Nesquehoning*

Year	Building	Equipment	Trucks	Working capital	No. Extruders	No. Thermo-formers	Selling expenses	Mean demand	Standard deviation
	($000)	($000)					($000)	Carton Millions	Carton Millions
1	720	671	20	250.0	1	1	70.0	21	7
2	0	0	0	50.0	1	1	70.0	36	7
3	0	120	0	151.2	1	2	121.7	54	7
4	0	0	0	0	1	2	121.7	72	7
5	0	0	0	0	1	2	121.7	90	7
6	0	0	0	0	1	2	121.7	90	7
7	0	0	0	0	1	2	121.7	90	7
8	0	0	0	0	1	2	121.7	90	7
9	0	0	0	0	1	2	121.7	90	7
10	0	0	0	0	1	2	121.7	90	7
11	0	0	0	0	1	2	121.7	90	7
12	0	0	0	0	1	2	121.7	90	7
13	0	0	0	0	1	2	121.7	90	7
14	0	0	0	0	1	2	121.7	90	7
15	0	0	0	0	1	2	121.7	90	7

Plant location: *Southeast*

Year	Building	Equipment	Trucks	Working capital	No. Extruders	No. Thermo-formers	Selling expenses	Mean demand	Standard deviation
	($000)	($000)					($000)	Carton Millions	Carton Millions
1	0	0	0	0	0	0	0	0	7
2	0	0	0	0	0	0	0	0	7
3	720	0	0	0	0	0	0	0	7
4	0	671	20	300.0	½	½	70.0	7	7
5	0	120	0	151.2	1	2	121.7	34	7
6	0	0	0	0	1	2	121.7	66	7
7	0	0	0	0	1	2	121.7	90	7
8	0	0	0	0	1	2	121.7	90	7
9	0	0	0	0	1	2	121.7	90	7
10	0	0	0	0	1	2	121.7	90	7
11	0	0	0	0	1	2	121.7	90	7
12	0	0	0	0	1	2	121.7	90	7
13	0	0	0	0	1	2	121.7	90	7
14	0	0	0	0	1	2	121.7	90	7
15	0	0	0	0	1	2	121.7	90	7

Plant location: *Midwest*

Year	Building	Equipment	Trucks	Working capital	No. Extruders	No. Thermo-formers	Selling expenses	Mean demand	Standard deviation
	($000)						($000)	Carton Millions	
1	0	0	0	0	0	0	0	0	7
2	0	0	0	0	0	0	0	0	7
3	0	0	0	0	0	0	0	0	7
4	720	0	0	0	1	1	70.0	16	7
5	0	671	20	300.0	1	1½	100.0	50	7
6	0	120	0	151.2	1	2	121.7	69	7
7	0	0	0	0	1	2	121.7	90	7
8	0	0	0	0	1	2	121.7	90	7
9	0	0	0	0	1	2	121.7	90	7
10	0	0	0	0	1	2	121.7	90	7
11	0	0	0	0	1	2	121.7	90	7
12	0	0	0	0	1	2	121.7	90	7
13	0	0	0	0	1	2	121.7	90	7
14	0	0	0	0	1	2	121.7	90	7
15	0	0	0	0	1	2	121.7	90	7

Plant location: *Southwest*

Year	Building	Equipment	Trucks	Working capital	No. Extruders	No. Thermo-formers	Selling expenses	Mean demand	Standard deviation
	($000)						($000)	Carton Millions	
1	0	0	0	0	0	0	0	0	7
2	0	0	0	0	0	0	0	0	7
3	0	0	0	0	0	0	0	0	7
4	0	0	0	0	0	0	0	0	7
5	0	0	0	0	0	0	0	0	7
6	0	0	0	0	0	0	0	0	7
7	720	0	0	0	½	½	0	3	7
8	0	671	20	300.0	1	2	100.0	18	7
9	0	120	0	151.2	1	2	121.7	42	7
10	0	0	0	0	1	2	121.7	66	7
11	0	0	0	0	1	2	121.7	90	7
12	0	0	0	0	1	2	121.7	90	7
13	0	0	0	0	1	2	121.7	90	7
14	0	0	0	0	1	2	121.7	90	7
15	0	0	0	0	1	2	121.7	90	7

COMMENTARY ON EGG'N FOAM CASE

1. Evaluate the Effectiveness of the Analysis and the Role of the CCA Project Team

Objectives

The case records that 'the first step ... was to construct a flow chart'. This certainly seems a questionable approach. Perhaps it would have been more sensible to precede the process of problem identification by specifying and clarifying CCA's objectives.

Further, the team seems to have considered heavily technologically oriented strategies, i.e. concentration on plant size and speed of introduction for the 'go/no go' project decision. Little emphasis was placed on interpreting the demand picture, which seems to suggest that marketing related strategies have either not been considered or have been assumed away.

It also seems that the project team were uncertain about the criteria by which choice should be made in relation to the available strategies. Internal rate of return and return on investment are both mentioned in the case, yet neither is really suitable. The latter because it takes no account of the time value of money, and the former because the cash flows from the projects occur at an uneven rate over time and this is particularly true with the so-called 'slow' alternatives. Such uneven rates can lead to problems of multiple rates of return and their subsequent interpretation. Some thought, therefore, must be directed toward the criterion for strategy choice and the development of an approach for measuring risk in relation to the strategic alternatives.

Once such clarification of objectives and criteria has been achieved the team could then have: first, identified and approved a set of feasible strategies; second, measured each strategy against management's risk profile; third, made appropriate recommendations about preferred strategies and then allowed management, through a process of policy dialogue, to compare 'Egg'N Foam' strategies, and also the relationship of the 'Egg'N Foam' project to others in hand within the organization. Such a decision-policy analytic effort would have directed effort in a more purposeful manner and have achieved the beneficial organizational effects of reducing the team's orientation, through its composition, with production and R & D and moving it towards a deeper treatment of marketing and financial considerations.

So far, this commentary has been critical of much of the team's organization. Yet some features of their approach are sound. In particular, it is good to have many of the project team's assumptions explicitly stated in Exhibit II. Further, the sensitivity analysis in Chart 2 is also useful as a means of screening the key areas of uncertainty for subsequent inclusion in a risk analysis.

In relation to the assumptions regarding Exhibit II, some further observations can be made. First, why do CCA assume that they will produce their own foam sheets when purchasing from an outside source might be a worthwhile alternative? Second, what correlation effects should be included in the model in relation to price elasticity, demand, production rates, etc? Should correlation effects be more explicitly articulated in the CCA risk-evaluation model? Third, why did CCA take market decisions as given and reduce the CCA decision to an evaluation of four production strategies?

It appears that the greatest weakness is in the area of the marketing assumptions, and the level of empirical or research support for these assumptions. Listed below are some of the areas in marketing which could be questioned:

(i) Market share will be 10 percent by 1978. (Should there not be a spread of possible values?)

(ii) No manufacturer other than Diamond National will come in before 1978.

(iii) Paper carton manufacturers will not react violently to their share being cut in ten years from 50 to 5 percent (Why wouldn't they start a price war? Can they afford to do so?)

(iv) Pricing must be at Pillopost level. Why not consider the possible adoption of penetration pricing policies?

(v) Market forecasts are assumed correct. Has any attempt been made to check their forecast accuracy?

(vi) Selling will be done by the plastics marketing department. It would appear that the transfer price will become an important motivating factor and might indicate that a separate department for marketing Egg'N Foam in the carton market be set up.

(vii) The standard deviations for demand in early years are clearly inaccurate and should be re-evaluated.

Overall it would seem sensible for greater attention to be paid to the influence of competition and competitive reaction on the Egg'N Foam decision. One possible approach would be to develop a number of marketing scenarios and, if appropriate, carry out a simulation of each scenario. For example, scenarios of the following kind could be developed:

(i) Steady price.

(ii) Price war initiated by Diamond National or others.

(iii) Price slowly declining through time.

(iv) A price war started by CCA to discourage other market entrants.

Two other financial management assumptions need further justification. First, working capital cannot be regarded as a certain need. The amount required will depend upon the accuracy of demand predictions (e.g. a stock pile-up may occur), the speed of payments by debtors and many other as yet unknown factors. Second, the influence of inflation cannot be ignored. It may

241

hit foam harder than pulp, or vice versa, seriously changing the competitive balance within CCA.

In conclusion, it would appear that the team's effectiveness might improve if its composition were better balanced by the addition of some marketing personnel. Further, in the process of policy development, the questioning of assumptions and inputs should proceed sensibly and lead to a more effective specification for the model. The final risk analysis output could then be considered as an input in the subsequent management dialogue concerning strategic information.

2. Prepare a Flow Chart for Evaluation of any of the Strategies

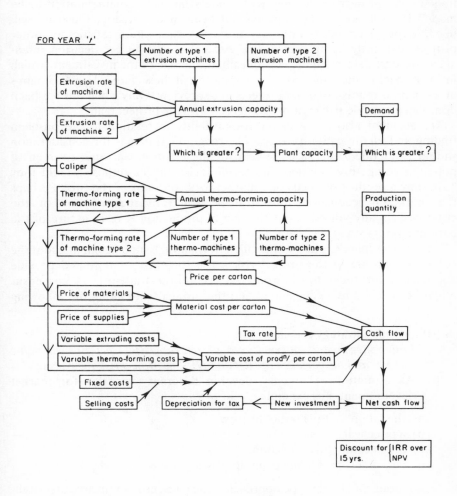

Egg'N Foam logical flow chart

3. Outline an Approach to the Selection of a Strategy for Implementation of the Egg'N Foam Project

It is appropriate in considering strategic implementation to examine the tasks which would be better performed by management rather than the project team. The project team should generate appropriate alternative strategies in line with management policy, and subsequently carry out some form of strategic evaluation using risk measures agreed jointly with management. Management's task should be to define the range of strategies to be considered and to direct the project group in the decision-making task.

Management's primary initial task is to define the type of decision. For example, do they wish the team to come up with a 'go/no go' recommendation for the project or do they wish some strategic recommendation to be made? If a 'go/no go' decision has not been made already, the team will need to be given information on the risk/return characteristics of other projects currently being considered. Assuming a 'go/no go' decision, management must determine the cost of capital, the size of the investment (which in turn might alter the cost of capital) and how large Egg'N Foam's investment is relative to other projects under review. Only when this has been done can a sensible risk measure be agreed with the project team.

Management also has a heavy responsibility in relation to the problem finding and identification process. The range of strategies for consideration should be defined after a close scan of the environment and a screen of potential competitive market and technological uncertainties. Should they have only a production focus or a market focus or a mix of the two? Perhaps the marketing/production mix strategy would overcome many of the criticisms already voiced about the overly production/R & D nature of the current strategy set.

The project team's role is to provide information to management about the risk/return profile in the project risk sense for each strategy and provide approaches for them to confront the risk/return trade-off. A consensus might be reached by management and the project team along the following lines:

(i) For each strategy calculate:
   Initial investment, internal rate of return (IRR), net present value (NPV), and the variance of IRR and NPV as project risk measures.

(ii) As a matter of urgency develop different scenarios for market development. For example,

(a) the failure of the market to grow;
(b) a price war;
(c) tough competitive reaction;
(d) consumers preferring paper to plastic cartons.

Through a Delphi-type approach some consensus subjective probabilities could be obtained for the likelihood of occurrence of each scenario. At the same time, risk/return measures as outlined in (i) could be developed for each scenario.

(iii) Cut out strategies which fail to meet criteria specified by management. Some of these might be:

(a) expected IRR is too low;

(b) chance of falling below the cost of capital is more than some pre-specified level (say 25 percent).

(c) initial investment exceeds company's resources or puts 'too many eggs in one basket'.

(d) initial investment is too small for the company.

The remaining strategies would be presented to management in terms of their risk profiles and risk/return characteristics. Management must then examine firm risk and determine the required rate of return by means of a comparison with projects in this industry for similar levels of risk. This balancing of firm risk against project risk is management's task and some analytical guidelines have been presented in Chapters 4 and 5 of this book. In addition, management is paid to take decisions and make wise judgements by balancing financial characteristics against other attributes and factors which may be important in relation to the organizational and behavioral characteristics of the firm.

4. Determine the risks involved in the alternatives

Assumptions made in the Final Analysis

(1) Growth in Demand over Fifteen Years

	Strategy			
Year	1	2	3	4
1	22	22	21	21
2	41	36	41	36
3	95	54	95	54
4	188	79	188	79
5	295	122	295	140
6	319	188	319	206
7	360	258	360	252
8	360	282	360	288
9	360	306	360	312
10	360	340	360	336
11	360	360	360	360
12	360	360	360	360
13	360	360	360	360
14	360	360	360	360
15	360	360	360	360
Standard Deviation	60	20	84	28

(2) The assumption in the simulation analysis has been to use a 5 percent discount rate (risk-free rate) in the calculation to avoid 'double counting' in relation to the incorporation of uncertainty in the analysis.

(3) It is not possible to obtain IRR's for each strategy, particularly slow strategies, because of sign changes in the cash flow pattern. Therefore, the summary results are only given in terms of NPV.

Summary of Results

A

Strategy	Point estimate (NPV) ($m)	Simulation Mean ($m)	Coefficient of variation
1	4.122	3.530	0.238
2	0.850	0.736	0.607
3	2.899	0.943	1.456
4	−1.377	−1.698	−0.402

Notes: (a) Discount rate is 0.05 (assumed riskless rate).
(b) Point estimate is NPV calculated with most likely value for each input variable.
(c) Coefficient of variation is the ratio of the standard deviation to the mean.

B

Strategy	Probability NPV > 0	NPV such that probability of 0.95 of exceeding that value ($m)
1	0.992	2.0
2	0.944	0
3	0.882	−2.0
4	0	−3.0

Note: Strategy 1 = super fast; Strategy 2 = super slow;
Strategy 3 = small fast; Strategy 4 = small slow.

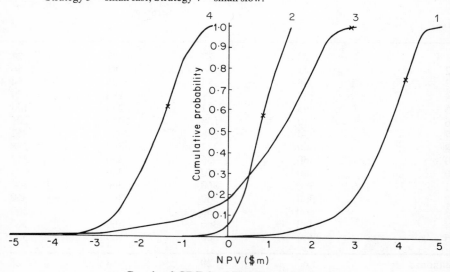

Graph of CDF for NPV for each strategy

5. Make recommendations to managements

Commentary on Results

The point estimate is the NPV which would have been calculated if uncertainty had been ignored. It should be equal to the mode of the simulation distribution.

The coefficient of variation measures the degree of dispersion in the NPV estimates for each strategy. Part of the risk (as measured by dispersion in estimates) can be eliminated by appropriate portfolio management. The remaining undiversifiable risk should thus determine the risk premium required for such a project. It is not possible to make a decision on the project as a whole without additional information on the undiversifiable risk of the project. We do not know whether the average return on alternative investment opportunities with the same degree of undiversifiable risk can be expected to be higher or lower than the expected return on the best strategy for Egg'N Foam. However, it should be possible to 'screen' out some of the strategies and make some *preliminary* recommendations prior to more detailed investigation of required rates of return.

A necessary condition to be satisfied by each strategy is that it has a positive NPV at the riskless rate of discount. The probability of NPV > 0 can be used as a measure of confidence in the decision to accept a strategy at this stage in the analysis. Strategy 4 can be eliminated immediately.

Another necessary condition is that no strategy should have a significant default risk for the company. Default risk can only be measured relative to the assets of the company in a portfolio framework. An indication of default risk can be obtained by looking at the NPV which has a particular probability of being exceeded, e.g. the NPV with a probability of 0.95 of being exceeded.

Strategy 1 dominates Strategy 2 by all selection criteria. The two slow strategies have been eliminated. The choice remains between Strategies 1 and 3, i.e. super or small plant size. Strategy 1 dominates again.

Strategy 1 (super fast) is recommended. As a contingency plan, Strategy 2 is the next best alternative if in the first four years the probabilities of fast or slow demand growth are revised towards slow growth.

Note that no final judgement can be made about this project without further analysis and debate. In particular, the required date of return for such a project could be determined with the aid of the capital asset pricing model. The NPV calculated using this required risk-adjusted rate should be positive in order to make project acceptance worthwhile.

DIGGER & SONS

Digger & Sons are in the sand and gravel business. They are an established firm with pits in various parts of south-eastern Australia. They are always looking for opportunities to expand, and tend to find that their financial and managerial resources are sufficient for any expansion they commonly contemplate, and that the dearth of new sites in their part of the country is the limiting factor. Their established customers are in Sydney and they do not want to shift their business out of the city.

The Development Director, whose responsibility is to find new deposits to renew the reserves of the business, comes to the Board with a problem. He has found a gravel site on the outskirts of the city. The Local Council, which owns the land, is willing to allow gravel mining on the site. It must have the land back within seven years or at the end of the mineral development, whichever is earlier, for further building. The site is very substantial and the Council is asking a stiff price for the right to work the land, payable as an initial lump sum of A$96,000. The Council wants a quick decision.

The site, called Flag Hills, will produce gravel which is primarily used for road construction. The State Government is currently stepping up its road construction program and will offer a three-year contract for a large quantity. On renewal for a further three-year period, the contract is likely to be for a rather smaller annual amount at a lower price, though the exact amount is unknown at the moment.

Two other members of the Board have a special interest in the Development Director's problem. These are the Marketing and Finance Directors. The Marketing Director is responsible for confirming the preliminary market estimates for new ventures. The Finance Director is required to assess their relative profitability and present this analysis to his colleagues. For this assessment to have any validity, he needs to know not only the Marketing Director's view on the most likely sales achievement, but also the range of possible outcomes and the likelihood of any part of those ranges being achieved.

The three directors form a sub-committee of the Board to report on the prospect. The Board would like to see a number of indices of profitability, as they believe each tends to cast a different light on the problem.

The sub-committee must report in the form of a general description of Flag Hills' desirability and a recommendation as to what action the company should follow. It has prepared the appended Initial Report, which summarizes its members' assessments of several aspects of the Flag Hills proposal. A notable feature of the sub-committee's initial assessments is the uncertainty as to the outcome of contract renewal negotiations at a later date. As a co-opted member of the sub-committee, you are requested to:

(1) Estimate the desirability of going ahead with the Flag Hills pit, according to several accepted indices, bearing in mind the uncertainty of your estimates.
(2) Prepare estimates of the effect on the desirability of the pit of variation in those aspects of the proposal which you think are crucial (for example, the effect of varying the cost of capital or the size of the renewal contract).

(3) If there is time before the next meeting of the sub-committee, it would be desirable to prepare some analysis of the following contingencies (suggested by the Group Manager — Planning):
   (a) the Council agreeing to waive the A$96,000 lease fee in favor of a royalty of 15 to 25 percent of total revenue from the pit;
   (b) producing 100,000 tpa for the full seven years, which would increase operating costs per ton by about 5 percent and which might involve a $5000 annual increase in the marketing budget for seven years, in current prices.

APPENDIX A: INITIAL SUB-COMMITTEE REPORT ON THE FLAG HILLS PIT

I The Market

Our basic expectation is that the promised contract for road gravel will be at the rate of 96,000 tons a year for three years at the current price of 85⅓¢ a ton ex-quarry. This contract can be signed before starting construction, so that we see no reason for seriously examining any alternative forecast.

At the time for renewal our most likely estimate is that the tonnage contracted for will fall to 75,000 tons per annum at an ex-quarry price of 80¢ a ton (disregarding price increases resulting from inflation). However, the range of possibilities we forsee is as follows:

Range of possible tonnage   60,000–95,000 tpa
Range of possible prices   75¢–90¢ (ignoring inflation)

II Costs

The capital cost will be as follows:

Fixed Assets	A$80,000
Lease	A$96,000
Working Capital	A$15,000
Total Capital	A$191,000

At the conclusion of the Flat Project, a further A$10,000 at present prices will be incurred in making good the surface of the land before returning the site to the Council. This will be spent at the end of the last year of operation.

Operating costs will be 22¢ a ton direct, at the initial contract level. The increase in administrative overhead, etc. attributable to this project will be

248

about A\$2,000 a year in most years. Both figures are expressed in present prices (i.e. the dollar amounts can be expected to increase with inflation).

We believe our cost estimating is sufficiently good to make a study of the effects of an overrun or higher operating costs unnecessary.

III Finance

No permanent loan capital can be raised for this project due to its short life. However, we have been promised an A\$80,000 increase in our 10 percent overdraft facilities on the condition that we repay this increase after three years. All other finance will be from the company's equity cash resources. Projects of similar risk elsewhere earn 12 percent after tax. The Finance Director thinks that the most likely return over the next eight years for this level of risk is slightly higher (about 14 percent), with minimum and maximum rates of 8 and 18 percent. These rates are all nominal rates: i.e. they do not allow for the inflation rate of 4 percent pa which most analysts predict (real rates are 4 percent less).

IV Taxes

The company tax rate is 46.0 percent. (For the sake of this case, tax is paid over to the Government in cash at the end of the year following that in which the profits on which it is assessed are earned.) Depreciation and depletion are on a straight-line (prime cost) basis over six years. The fixed assets qualify for the Australian Government's investment allowance, which is 40 percent of the investment. The allowance takes the form of a deduction from taxable income in the year of commencement. Digger pays enough tax on its other earnings to fully absorb the allowance and any other tax deductions in the year in which they arise.

APPENDIX B: DPMSIM FINANCIAL EVALUATION PROGRAM

To assist in this and similar problems, DPM Consultants have prepared the DPMSIM Financial Evaluation Program. The program allows for four assumptions concerning the behavior of cash flows and discount rates.

(1) that they are known (and take on fixed values); or
(2) that they are uncertain and follow a 'rectangular distribution' (which can be described by the minimum and maximum feasible values, with all interim values being equally likely); or
(3) that they are uncertain and follow a 'triangular distribution' (which can be described by the minimum and maximum values and the most likely value); or
(4) that they are uncertain and follow a 'normal distribution' (which can be described by mean and variance).

Each year's cash flow can be believed to follow any one of the three distributions; neither the cost of capital nor any one cash flow need have the same distribution as any other.

Inputs to the DPMSIM program are of the form required in Appendix C. It is possible to run more than one simulation 'trial', varying (if necessary) your beliefs about the cash flows or the discount rate. A separate input form is required for each trial. Please note that, in this program, you enter parameters of the distributions of the *cash flows*, not their component parts (e.g. selling price).

APPENDIX C: DPMSIM FINANCIAL EVALUATION PROGRAM INPUT SHEET

Trial No._____

	Distribution[1] type	Input 1 [2]	Input 2 [2]	Input 3 [2]
Cash Flows:(CF)				
Year 0				
1				
2				
3				
4				
5				
6				
7				
8				
9				
10				
Cost of Capital				

(1)　= 1 for fixed (known amount);
　　　= 2 for rectangular distribution of amount;
　　　= 3 for triangular distribution of amount;
　　　= 4 for normal distribution of amount.

(2)　If (1) = 1, input 1 is the fixed amount;
　　　If (1) = 2, inputs are the minimum and maximum amounts;
　　　If (1) = 3, inputs are the minimum, most likely and maximum amounts;
　　　If (1) = 4, inputs are the mean and variance.
(3)　Year 0 is the time of the initial outlay; year 1 is the end of one year after the initial outlay and experiences the first cash inflows.

DIGGER & SONS — COMMENTARY

The following are computer print-outs for six trials of the case. The basic criteria and results for each trial are summarized in Table 1. Some details of the calculations and assumptions for the first of these trials follow.

Table 1

Trial	Basic criteria	Payback (years)	IRR (%)	NPV A$
1	A$96,000 lump sum given COC	3.925	12.2	16,374 (SD* 982)
2	A$96,000 lump sum increase COC 5%	3.925	12.2	Negative
3	15% Royalty given COC	1.909	36.0	69,496 (SD 585)
4	15% Royalty increase COC 5%	1.909	36.3	51,551 (SD 450)
5	25% Royalty given COC	1.858	35.6	65,115 (SD 745)
6	25% Royalty increase COC 5%	1.858	35.3	48,510 (SD 586)

*SD denotes Standard Deviation.

It should be noted that the results in Table 1 strongly favor the royalty payment over the lump-sum option. This information provides planners and managers with valuable guidelines for the negotations with the Council. It would appear that Digger should attempt to negotiate a royalty-based contract.

Details of Cash Flow Assessments for one Alternative Scenario (Trial 1 above)

A$96,000 lump sum payment.
No royalty.
Original production figures.
Given cost of capital distribution.

Assumptions.

1. The means of financing a project are independent of the evaluation of that project.
2. Inflation in project appraisal is treated in a consistent manner: i.e. nominal cash flows with nominal discount rates; or real cash flows with real discount rates, as has been done in this case. Therefore discount rates are:

$$18 - 4 = 14\%$$
$$14 - 4 = 10\%$$
$$8 - 4 = 4\%$$

3. Working capital is repaid at the end of the project.

4. The results are a simulation. This means that further replications with the same input data may give slightly different answers.

Calculations — Trial 1

Year 0   A\$

Capital costs — \$191,000 (as per Appendix A)   = +191,000

Year 2

Investment allowance: 40% × .46 × 80   = +14,720

Years 1–3 (CF at 85⅓¢ price):

Contribution: 96,000 × (85 1/3 − 22) = 60,800

− expenses   − 2,000   = +58,800

Years 2–4 (taxes one year in arrears):

CF   58,800

Depreciation & Depletion (176/6)   29,333

    —————

    29,467

tax (46% of 29,467)   = −13,555

Years 4–5 (CF)

(a) Min. 60,000 (75 − 22)   31,800

  − expenses   2,000   = +29,800

(b) Mod. 75,000 (80 − 22) − 2,000   = +41,500

(c) Max. 95,000 (90 − 22) − 2,000   = +62,600

Years 5–7 (tax one year in arrears):

(a) Min. tax .46 (29,800 − 29,333) = .46 (467)   = − 215

(b) Moderate .46 (41,500 − 29,333) = .46 (12,167)   = − 5,597

(c) Max. tax .46 (62,600 − 29,333) = .46 (33,267)   = −14,843

Year 7

− 10,000 (restoration) + 15,000 (Working Capital)   = + 5,000

Year 8

Tax saving on restoration (46% of 10,000)   = + 4,600

Given the above calculations the financial evaluation input sheet (see Appendix C) would be constructed as shown in the following table for Trial 1. Thus, net cash flows are obtained by adjusting gross cash flows to take account both of the tax payments and of the year in which they are paid.

For example, Year 2 net cash flows are obtained in the following manner:

CONTRIBUTION + INVESTMENT ALLOWANCE − TAX

i.e.   58,800   +   14,720   −13,555

    =59,965

TRIAL 1: DPMSIM FINANCIAL EVALUATION PROGRAM
INPUT SHEET

	Distribution[1] type	Input 1 [2]	Input 2 [2]	Input 3 [2]
Net Cash Flows:				
Year 0	1	−191,000		
1	1	+58,800		
2	1	+59,965		
3	1	+45,245		
4	3	+16,245	+27,945	+49,045
5	3	+29,585	+35,903	+47,757
6	3	+29,585	+35,903	+47,757
7	3	−9,843	−597	+4,785
8	1	+4,600		
9				
10				
Cost of Capital	3	.04	.10	.14

(1) = 1 for fixed (known amount);
= 2 for rectangular distribution of amount;
= 3 for triangular distribution of amount;
= 4 for normal distribution of amount.

(2) If (1) = 1, input 1 is the fixed amount;
If (1) = 2, inputs are the minimum and maximum amounts;
If (1) = 3, inputs are the minimum, most likely and maximum amounts;
If (1) = 4, inputs are the mean and variance.

(3) Year 0 is the time of the initial outlay; year 1 is the end of one year after the initial outlay and experiences the first cash inflows.

Note that in this Trial the uncertainty about the cash flows in Years 4–7 and about the cost of capital has been described in terms of the triangular distribution.

The simulation results for Trial 1 giving the derived payback, IRR and NPV distributions are shown on the following pages. The results for the remaining five Trials summarized in Table 1 are then shown on subsequent pages. The purpose of showing the Trials in such detail is to provide the reader and the student with actual output to facilitate both replication and understanding of the process.

DETAILS OF SIMULATION MODEL FOR TRIAL 1

PERIOD 0 CF FIXED AT	-191000.					
PERIOD 1 CF FIXED AT	58800.					
PERIOD 2 CF FIXED AT	59965.					
PERIOD 3 CF FIXED AT	45245.					
PERIOD 4 CF TRIANGULARLY DISTRIBUTED.	MIN	16245.	MODE	27945.	MAX	49045.
PERIOD 5 CF TRIANGULARLY DISTRIBUTED.	MIN	29585.	MODE	35903.	MAX	47757.
PERIOD 6 CF TRIANGULARLY DISTRIBUTED.	MIN	29585.	MODE	35903.	MAX	47757.
PERIOD 7 CF TRIANGULARLY DISTRIBUTED.	MIN	-9843.	MODE	-597.	MAX	4785.
PERIOD 8 CF FIXED AT	4600.					

COST OF CAPITAL TRIANGULARLY DISTRIBUTED.	MIN	0.040	MODE	0.100	MAX	0.140

DIGGER & SONS INPUT DATA

254

SUMMARY PLOTS OF THE OGIVE (CUMULATIVE PROBABILITY) CURVES FOR (1) PAYBACK
PERIOD, (2) IRR AND (3) NPV

(1) PAYBACK PERIOD

SUMMARY OF DISTRIBUTION

DECILE	VALUE
.1	3.698
.2	3.754
.3	3.820
.4	3.862
.5	3.915
.6	3.969
.7	4.014
.8	4.098
.9	4.192

MEAN   3.925

STANDARD DEVIATION   0.184

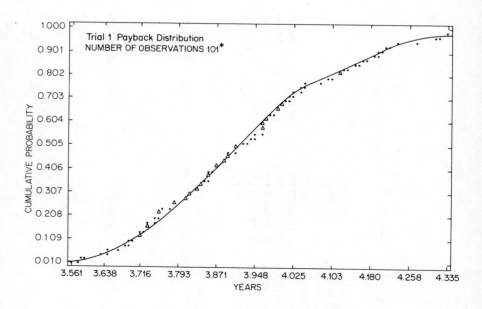

(*Note that not all observations are plotted.)

(2) INTERNAL RATE OF RETURN

SUMMARY OF DISTRIBUTION

DECILE	VALUE
.1	0.093
.2	0.103
.3	0.112
.4	0.116
.5	0.122
.6	0.127
.7	0.131
.8	0.139
.9	0.147

MEAN	0.122
STANDARD DEVIATION	0.020

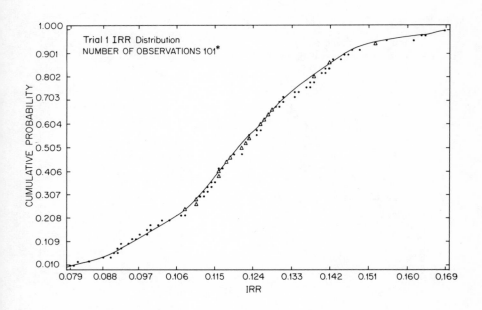

Trial 1 IRR Distribution
NUMBER OF OBSERVATIONS 101*

(*Note that not all observations are plotted.)

(3) NET PRESENT VALUE

SUMMARY OF DISTRIBUTION

DECILE	VALUE
.1	15306.076
.2	15465.392
.3	15757.679
.4	15967.600
.5	16143.024
.6	16327.876
.7	16513.994
.8	17375.107
.9	18128.816

MEAN   16374.700

STANDARD DEVIATION   981.701

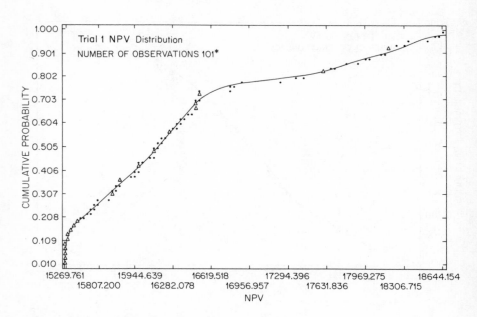

(*Note that not all observations are plotted.)

DETAILS OF SIMULATION MODEL FOR TRIAL 2

PERIOD 0 CF FIXED AT   -191000.
PERIOD 1 CF FIXED AT   58800.
PERIOD 2 CF FIXED AT   59965.
PERIOD 3 CF FIXED AT   45245.

PERIOD 4 CF TRIANGULARLY DISTRIBUTED.	MIN	16245.	MODE	27945.	MAX	49045.
PERIOD 5 CF TRIANGULARLY DISTRIBUTED.	MIN	29585.	MODE	35903.	MAX	47757.
PERIOD 6 CF TRIANGULARLY DISTRIBUTED.	MIN	29585.	MODE	35903.	MAX	47747.
PERIOD 7 CF TRIANGULARLY DISTRIBUTED.	MIN	-9843.	MODE	-597.	MAX	4785.

PERIOD 8 CF FIXED AT   4600.

COST OF CAPITAL TRIANGULARLY DISTRIBUTED.	MIN	0.090	MODE	0.150	MAX	0.190

SUMMARY PLOTS OF THE OGIVE CURVES FOR (1) PAYBACK, (2) IRR AND (3) NPV

(1) PAYBACK PERIOD

SUMMARY OF DISTRIBUTION

DECILE	VALUE
.1	3.698
.2	3.754
.3	3.820
.4	3.862
.5	3.915
.6	3.969
.7	4.014
.8	4.098
.9	4.192

MEAN   3.925

STANDARD DEVIATION   0.184

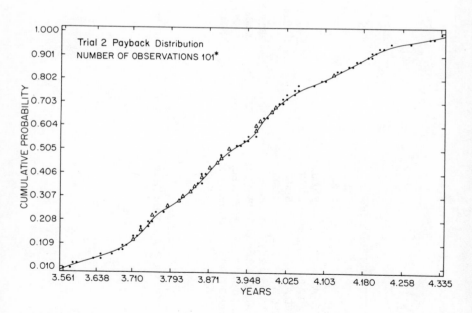

(*Note that not all observations are plotted.)

(2) INTERNAL RATE OF RETURN

SUMMARY OF DISTRIBUTION

DECILE	VALUE
.1	0.093
.2	0.103
.3	0.112
.4	0.116
.5	0.122
.6	0.127
.7	0.131
.8	0.139
.9	0.147

MEAN	0.122
STANDARD DEVIATION	0.020

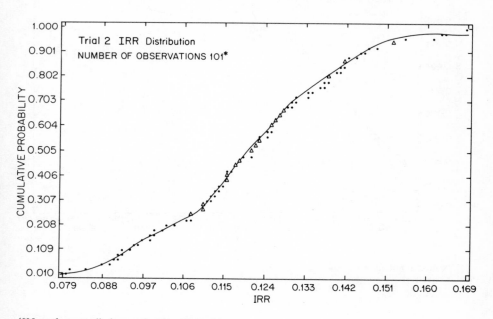

(*Note that not all observations are plotted.)

(3) NET PRESENT VALUE

SUMMARY OF DISTRIBUTION

DECILE	VALUE
.1	-9420.642
.2	-9298.485
.3	-9055.286
.4	-8882.867
.5	-8726.168
.6	-8573.863
.7	-8442.157
.8	-7628.867
.9	-6944.950

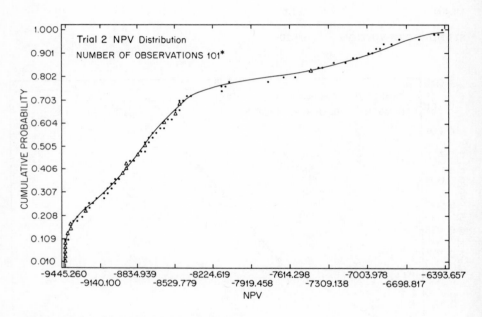

(*Note that not all observations are plotted.)

DETAILS OF SIMULATION MODEL FOR TRIAL 3

PERIOD 0 CF FIXED AT	-95000.					
PERIOD 1 CF FIXED AT	46512.					
PERIOD 2 CF FIXED AT	53332.					
PERIOD 3 CF FIXED AT	38612.					
PERIOD 4 CF TRIANGULARLY DISTRIBUTED.		MIN	15150.	MODE	24600.	MAX	41857.
PERIOD 5 CF TRIANGULARLY DISTRIBUTED.		MIN	18580.	MODE	23683.	MAX	30012.
PERIOD 6 CF TRIANGULARLY DISTRIBUTED.		MIN	18580.	MODE	23683.	MAX	30012.
PERIOD 7 CF TRIANGULARLY DISTRIBUTED.		MIN	-11763.	MODE	-3817.	MAX	530.
PERIOD 8 CF FIXED AT	4600.					

COST OF CAPITAL TRIANGULARLY DISTRIBUTED.   MIN 0.040   MODE 0.100   MAX 0.140

262

SUMMARY PLOTS OF THE OGIVE CURVES FOR (1) PAYBACK, (2) IRR AND (3) NPV

(1) PAYBACK PERIOD

SUMMARY OF DISTRIBUTION

DECILE	VALUE
.1	1.909
.2	1.909
.3	1.909
.4	1.909
.5	1.909
.6	1.909
.7	1.909
.8	1.909
.9	1.909

MEAN 1.909

STANDARD DEVIATION 0.003

(2) INTERNAL RATE OF RETURN

SUMMARY OF DISTRIBUTION

DECILE	VALUE
.1	0.336
.2	0.344
.3	0.348
.4	0.353
.5	0.358
.6	0.363
.7	0.371
.8	0.379
.9	0.387

MEAN 0.360

STANDARD DEVIATION 0.018

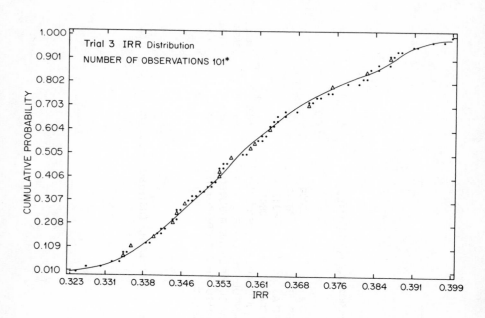

(*Note that not all observations are plotted.)

(3) NET PRESENT VALUE

SUMMARY OF DISTRIBUTION

DECILE	VALUE
.1	68892.797
.2	68998.786
.3	69118.312
.4	69184.508
.5	69216.867
.6	69300.266
.7	69787.789
.8	70071.055
.9	70522.945

MEAN	69496.602
STANDARD DEVIATION	585.047

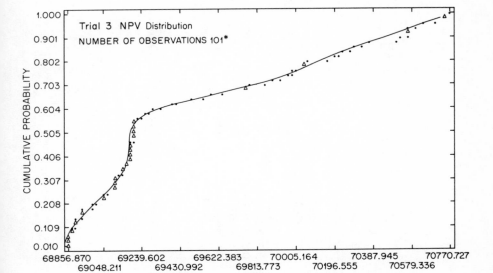

(*Note that not all observations are plotted.)

DETAILS OF SIMULATION MODEL FOR TRIAL 4

Trial 4

PERIOD 0 CF FIXED AT   -95000.
PERIOD 1 CF FIXED AT   46512.
PERIOD 2 CF FIXED AT   53332.
PERIOD 3 CF FIXED AT   38612.

	MIN		MODE		MAX
PERIOD 4 CF TRIANGULARLY DISTRIBUTED.	MIN	15150.	MODE	24600.	MAX	41875.
PERIOD 5 CF TRIANGULARLY DISTRIBUTED.	MIN	18580.	MODE	23683.	MAX	33012.
PERIOD 6 CF TRIANGULARLY DISTRIBUTED.	MIN	18580.	MODE	23683.	MAX	33012.
PERIOD 7 CF TRIANGULARLY DISTRIBUTED.	MIN	-11763.	MODE	-3817.	MAX	530.

PERIOD 8 CF FIXED AT   4600.

	MIN	MODE	MAX
COST OF CAPITAL TRIANGULARLY DISTRIBUTED.	MIN 0.090	MODE 0.150	MAX 0.190

SUMMARY PLOTS OF THE OGIVE CURVES FOR (1) PAYBACK, (2) IRR AND (3) NPV

(1) PAYBACK PERIOD

(2) INTERNAL RATE OF RETURN

SUMMARY OF DISTRIBUTION

SUMMARY OF DISTRIBUTION

DECILE	VALUE	DECILE	VALUE
.1	1.909	.1	0.340
.2	1.909	.2	0.348
.3	1.909	.3	0.354
.4	1.909	.4	0.357
.5	1.909	.5	0.361
.6	1.909	.6	0.367
.7	1.909	.7	0.373
.8	1.909	.8	0.380
.9	1.909	.9	0.388

MEAN 1.909

MEAN 0.363

STANDARD DEVIATION 0.003

STANDARD DEVIATION 0.018

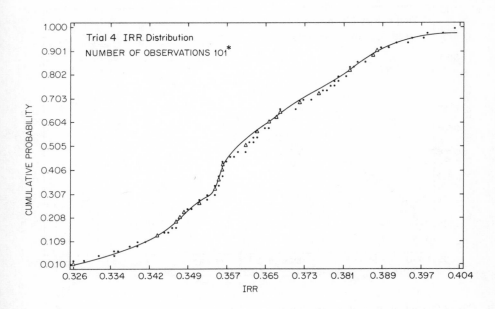

(*Note that not all observations are plotted.)

(3) NET PRESENT VALUE

SUMMARY OF DISTRIBUTION

DECILE	VALUE
.1	50991.035
.2	51041.953
.3	51131.078
.4	51304.211
.5	51573.855
.6	51710.652
.7	51912.184
.8	52069.770
.9	52175.312

MEAN   51551.191

STANDARD DEVIATION   450.122

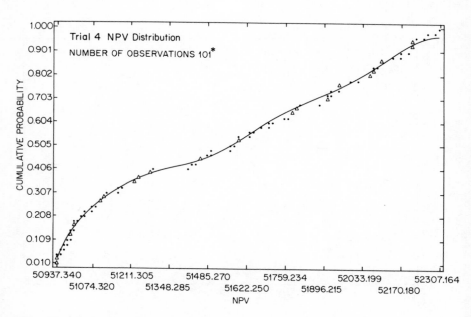

(*Note that not all observations are plotted.)

DETAILS OF SIMULATION MODEL FOR TRIAL 5

						Trial 5
PERIOD 0 CF FIXED AT	-95000.					
PERIOD 1 CF FIXED AT	53040.					
PERIOD 2 CF FIXED AT	48905.					
PERIOD 3 CF FIXED AT	34185.					
PERIOD 4 CF TRIANGULARLY DISTRIBUTED.	MIN	14415.	MODE	22365.	MAX	37090.
PERIOD 5 CF TRIANGULARLY DISTRIBUTED.	MIN	16150.	MODE	20443.	MAX	28395.
PERIOD 6 CF TRIANGULARLY DISTRIBUTED.	MIN	16150.	MODE	20443.	MAX	28395.
PERIOD 7 CF TRIANGULARLY DISTRIBUTED.	MIN	-7830.	MODE	-1057.	MAX	2600.
PERIOD 8 CF FIXED AT	4600.					
COST OF CAPITAL TRIANGULARLY DISTRIBUTED.	MIN	0.040	MODE	0.100	MAX	0.140

SUMMARY PLOTS OF THE OGIVE CURVES FOR (1) PAYBACK, (2) IRR AND (3) NPV

(1) PAYBACK PERIOD

SUMMARY OF DISTRIBUTION

DECILE	VALUE
.1	1.858
.2	1.858
.3	1.858
.4	1.858
.5	1.858
.6	1.858
.7	1.858
.8	1.858
.9	1.858

MEAN	1.858

STANDARD DEVIATION	0.003

(2) INTERNAL RATE OF RETURN

SUMMARY OF DISTRIBUTION

DECILE	VALUE
.1	0.334
.2	0.340
.3	0.346
.4	0.351
.5	0.358
.6	0.362
.7	0.365
.8	0.371
.9	0.376

MEAN	0.356

STANDARD DEVIATION	0.016

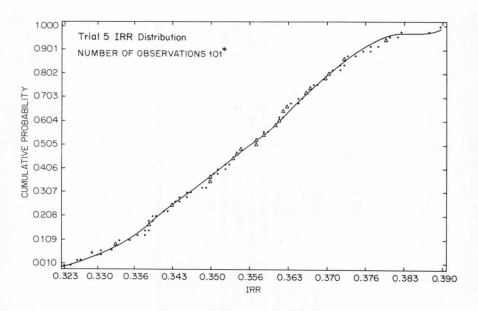

Trial 5 IRR Distribution
NUMBER OF OBSERVATIONS 101[*]

(*Note that not all observations are plotted.)

(3) NET PRESENT VALUE

SUMMARY OF DISTRIBUTION

DECILE	VALUE
.1	64456.258
.2	64574.047
.3	64657.469
.4	64725.859
.5	64800.898
.6	64859.992
.7	65198.477
.8	65871.141
.9	66460.422

MEAN   65115.520

STANDARD DEVIATION   745.492

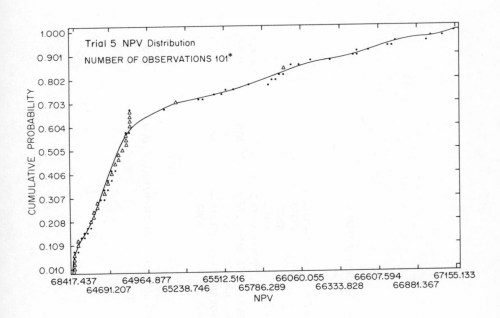

(*Note that not all observations are plotted.)

DETAILS OF SIMULATION MODEL FOR TRIAL 6

PERIOD 0 CF FIXED AT	-95000.				
PERIOD 1 CF FIXED AT	53040.				
PERIOD 2 CF FIXED AT	48905.				
PERIOD 3 CF FIXED AT	34185.				
PERIOD 4 CF TRIANGULARLY DISTRIBUTED.	MIN	14415.	MODE	22365.	MAX	37090.
PERIOD 5 CF TRIANGULARLY DISTRIBUTED.	MIN	16150.	MODE	20443.	MAX	28395.
PERIOD 6 CF TRIANGULARLY DISTRIBUTED.	MIN	16150.	MODE	20443.	MAX	28395.
PERIOD 7 CF TRIANGULARLY DISTRIBUTED.	MIN	-7830.	MODE	-1057.	MAX	2600.
PERIOD 8 CF FIXED AT	4600.				

COST OF CAPITAL TRIANGULARLY DISTRIBUTED.	MIN	0.090	MODE	0.140	MAX	0.190

SUMMARY PLOTS OF THE OGIVE CURVES

(1) PAYBACK PERIOD

(2) INTERNAL RATE OF RETURN

SUMMARY OF DISTRIBUTION

SUMMARY OF DISTRIBUTION

DECILE	VALUE	DECILE	VALUE
.1	1.858	.1	0.329
.2	1.858	.2	0.337
.3	1.858	.3	0.345
.4	1.858	.4	0.348
.5	1.858	.5	0.353
.6	1.858	.6	0.357
.7	1.858	.7	0.361
.8	1.858	.8	0.368
.9	1.858	.9	0.375

MEAN 1.858   MEAN 0.353

STANDARD DEVIATION 0.003   STANDARD DEVIATION 0.017

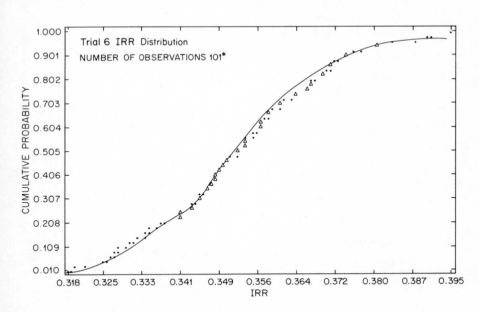

(*Note that not all observations are plotted.)

(3) NET PRESENT VALUE

SUMMARY OF DISTRIBUTION

DECILE	VALUE
.1	47968.164
.2	48167.434
.3	48274.629
.4	48290.109
.5	48301.762
.6	48469.715
.7	48723.641
.8	49158.605
.9	49454.367

MEAN   48510.539

STANDARD DEVIATION   586.016

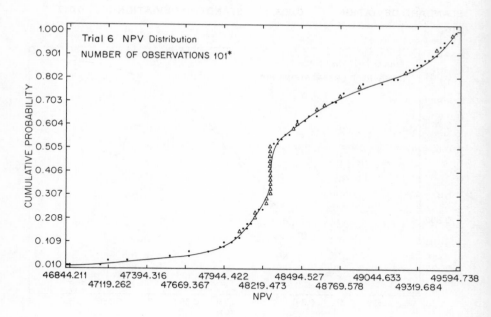

(*Note that not all observations are plotted.)

Postscript to Digger

The previous graph plots and tables show how the projected results of six alternative scenarios for the Flag Hills project can be generated. It should be noted that both risk analysis and sensitivity analysis approaches are used. Sensitivity analysis helps to identify key project assumptions and uncertain variables whilst risk analysis enables outcome distributions to be produced for each alternative scenario.

MUCOM CASE

INTRODUCTION

In early 1970, MUCOM undertook a study of methods for modernizing the manufacture of small arms ammunition. Recent engineering developments opened up the possibility of constructing modules that would achieve substantially higher average rates of production than those presently employed. A preliminary analysis done in conjunction with a small arms modernization team located at the Frankford Arsenal identified ten feasible configurations for a module incorporating the latest in manufacturing technology.

Members of the team recognized that there were a substantial number of uncertainties that must somehow be taken into account in making a choice of design. In consultation with a specialist in risk analysis, they were able to identify two major sources of uncertainty: those arising from the nature of the development process, and those associated with performance of a module once it is developed and put into operation. In addition, the module designs they were considering would be rendered obsolescent if any of a number of future developments occurred; e.g. adoption of new types of cartridges such as caseless ammunition, the development or advent of new types of weapons that would change radically the configuration of small arms ammunition, significant force structure changes that might increase or decrease rates of ammunition usage, and possible shortages of raw material that might necessitate radical changes in cartridge design.

The team set out to do an analysis that would:

(1) take these uncertainties into account in an explicit, unambiguous way
(2) consider the trade-offs between costs, development time, and module performance; and
(3) blend probabilities and preferences together to yield a meaningful preference ordering of alternatives.

Manufacturing Process

The manufacturing process consists of several basic tasks performed sequentially; sub-modules performing these tasks are:

(1) case manufacture;
(2) primer insert;
(3) ball bullet rotary;
(4) load and assembly;
(5) ball bullet in line;
(6) tracer bullet rotary;

In addition to on-line sub-modules performing manufacturing operations, a module may have several off-line sub-modules such as inspection equipment, computer controlling devices, and packing units.

Alternatives

At the outset the team decided to limit the set of new design alternatives they would consider to three:

    I. serial connection of sub-modules with *no* stand-by redundancy;
   II. stand-by redundancy of one sub-module on all sub-modules with marginal expectation of efficiency* less than 95 percent;
  III. stand-by redundancy necessary to bring each sub-module task up to a minimum of 80 percent marginal efficiency.

Prior to choosing among designs, they could perform a variety of bench tests which would enable them to refine their judgements about attributes of each sub-module. Before doing so, they wished to evaluate the relative merits of these three alternatives. They conjectured that this evaluation would generate enough information for them to determine whether or not a more detailed investigation of other alternatives was warranted. The possibility of a new manufacturing design being rendered obsolete in the near future suggested that they consider continuing with the present method of production for a period of time and *then* introduce a new design. Nevertheless, they decided to postpone consideration of such strategies, reasoning that if an initial investigation of alternatives demonstrated that continuing with the present method is best when obsolescence of a new design is ignored, then this same strategy must be best if obsolescence is taken into account.

The efficiency of a design clearly depends on the policy adopted for maintaining buffer inventory at the interface between each pair of sub-modules in series within a module. At this stage in analysis, the team saw no clear-cut way of determining what constitutes an optimal inventory policy for a new design, but recognized that a lower bound on efficiency would be generated by a policy of *no* inventory between sub-modules while an upper bound would be generated by the assumption that inventory between

---

*The team defined 'efficiency' of a sub-module as the percent of total manufacturing time the sub-module is operable.

sub-modules is unlimited. They decided to consider the implications of both assumptions.

Attributes

After some reflection, the team decided to characterize the outcome of a choice of development strategy in terms of:

(1) average production rate (in pieces per minute) of the module when in operation;
(2) proportion of production found defective;
(3) efficiency (percent of manufacturing time the module is in operation);
(4) variable manufacturing cost per unit of production;
(5) costs of development, construction, and installation;
(6) time to completion of development, construction, and installation.

None of these attributes were known with certainty to the team. It was clear to them however, that (a) the first four listed above were functionally interrelated, and that (b) for purposes of analysis one could in principle combine the first three into a single attribute, rate of production of *acceptable* pieces per two-shift day. Although it might make assessment of the *uncertainties* somewhat more difficult, a reduction in the number of distinct attributes of a generic outcome would make it much easier to establish a preference ordering of outcomes.

Performance

Since the team was composed of experts in ammunition manufacturing, it undertook an evaluation of the range of achievable values of rate of production of acceptable pieces per two-shift day under each alternative.

They began by considering each sub-module (including interface and transfer elements) separately. To guide them in quantifying their judgements, the team discussed each operation performed by a sub-module and categorized it as 'current state of the art', as 'a modest advance in state of the art', or as 'a significant advance in state of the art' (see Table 1).

The engineers who designed the sub-modules had in mind a target production rate of 900 acceptable pieces per minute. Since many of the sub-modules incorporated components whose design and construction required a 'significant advance in the state of the art', there was in fact considerable uncertainty about the *actual* rate of production of acceptable pieces which could be produced. The team decided to break down the assessment of uncertainties about the rate of production of acceptable pieces per two-shift day into two parts; an assessment of the probabilities of percent of total manufacturing time each sub-module will be in operation, and an assessment of the average *proportion* of defective pieces produced by each sub-module when operating close to the maximum production rate it is designed to achieve.

276

Table 1 Sub-module: case manufacture

	Current state of the art	A modest advance in state of the art	Significant advance in state of the art
Cup Orient & Inspect & Feed		X	
Eject	X		
1st Draw		X	
Eject	X		
Final Draw		X	
Eject	X		
Heading			X
Inspect		X	
Eject & Transfer		X	
Head Turn			X
Venting & Piercing	X		
Eject	X		
Orient	X		
Cleaning	X		
Body Anneal	X		
Cooling	X		
Orient	X		
Eject	X		
Taper, Plug & Trim		X	
Inspect		X	
Eject	X		
Orient	X		
Clean, Stress Relief			X
Mouth, Neck Anneal	X		
Cooling	X		
Orient	X		
Case, Flaw Detect			X
Eject	X		
Component Transfer	X		

One team member said: 'In my judgement, the higher the production rate when we have the module operating, the more down time we're going to have, on the average. There will be more tool wear, jamming, breakage. We've somehow got to consider this.' A second team member responded: 'We're really interested in efficiency times rate of production per minute times the proportion of production that's acceptable. Within the range of possible production rates that may pop up given our design specs, I really don't think that there's much dependency between these two variables.' Unable to resolve this difference of opinion, the team agreed to explore the implications of both points of view.

Their initial step towards this end was to ascertain for each sub-module the range of possible values for the efficiency and the range of possible values for the proportion of defective pieces per minute in operation. They broke down

Table 2a Assessments of Efficiency. Sub-module: Case Manufacture

	Highest	Lowest	Most likely	Median
Cup Orient & Inspect & Feed	100	100	100	100
Eject	100	100	100	100
1st Draw	98	90	95	96
Eject	100	100	100	100
Final Draw	95	85	90	88
Eject	100	100	100	100
Heading	93	83	88	87
Inspect	99	99	99	99
Eject & Transfer	99	97	98	98
Head Turn	95	85	90	90
Venting & Piercing	93	83	88	90
Eject	100	100	100	100
Orient	99	97	98	98
Cleaning	99	99	99	99
Body Anneal	99	99	99	99
Cooling	99	97	98	98
Orient	99	97	98	98
Eject	100	100	100	100
Taper, Plug & Trim	95	85	90	92
Inspect	99	97	98	98
Eject	100	100	100	100
Orient	99	97	98	98
Clean, Stress Relief	99	97	98	98
Mouth, Neck Anneal	99	99	99	99
Cooling	99	97	98	98
Orient	99	97	98	98
Case, Flaw Detect	99	97	98	98
Eject	100	100	100	100
Component Transfer	99	97	98	98

each sub-module into its component operations and agreed upon ranges for individual operations. (Examples are shown in Tables 2a and 2b.)

The risk analyst working with the team then asked each team member, without consulting with other team members, to record for each component of each sub-module his judgement of (1) the *most likely* value of efficiency and (2) the value of efficiency such that it was equally likely that the efficiency *actually observed* once the module was in operation would be above or below that value. Subsequently, members compared their assessments and after considerable debate, were finally able to agree on the assessments. (see Table 2a).

A similar assessment procedure was followed for the average proportion of acceptable pieces. It yielded results similar to those displayed in Table 2b.

Table 2b Assessments of average proportion of defective pieces. Sub-module: Case Manufacture

	Highest	Lowest	Most likely	Median
Cup Orient & Inspect & Feed	0	0	0	0
Eject	0	0	0	0
1st Draw	.02	0	.005	.005
Eject	0	0	0	0
Final Draw	.03	0	.005	.01
Eject	.	.	.	.
Heading	.	.	.	.
Inspect	.	.	.	.
Eject & Transfer	.	.	.	.
Head Turn	.	.	.	.
Venting & Piercing	.	.	.	.
Eject	.	.	.	.
Orient	.	.	.	.
Cleaning	.	.	.	.
Body Anneal	.	.	.	.
Cooling	.	.	.	.
Orient	.	.	.	.
Eject	.	.	.	.
Taper, Plug & Trim	.	.	.	.
Inspect	.	.	.	.
Eject	.	.	.	.
Orient	.	.	.	.
Clean, Stress Relief	.	.	.	.
Mouth, Neck Anneal	.	.	.	.
Cooling	.	.	.	.
Orient	.	.	.	.
Case, Flaw Detect	.	.	.	.
Eject	.	.	.	.
Component Transfer	.	.	.	.

Time

When the team attempted to quantify their judgements about the time required for development and construction of each sub-module, much to the dismay of the risk analyst, they found that agreement on a single set of probabilities couldn't be reached. A typical set of probability judgements elicited for the case manufacture sub-module is shown in Table 3.

Again the question of whether or not there were important dependencies between times to completion of different sub-modules arose. Team members agreed that in fact there were, but weren't sure how to take them into account.

After generating three sets of probability assessments for each sub-module, the team concluded that, discounting differences in judgement *between* team

Table 3 Probability of successful completion in t months or less

No. 1		No. 2		No. 3	
Months	Prob.	Months	Prob.	Months	Prob.
25	0	22	0	20	0
25	.60	25	.50	25	.60
30	.85	28	.85	28	.75
36	1.00	31	1.00	31	1.00

Table 4 Schedule

1. Begin case manufacturing module development immediately.
2. Begin ball bullet rotary nine months from start.
3. Begin primer insert eight months from start.
4. Begin tracer bullet rotary nine months from start.
5. Begin load and assembly sub-module immediately.

Table 5 Probability of successful interfacing in t months or less

No. 1		No. 2		No. 3	
Months	Prob.	Months	Prob.	Months	Prob.
4	0	6	0	6	0
8	.40	8	.60	8	.45
10	.75	10	.80	12	.85
14	1.00	12	1.00	16	1.00

members, substantial differences in time to completion of sub-modules were almost certain to arise. By scheduling start-up delays, they could strongly influence the time to completion of a module; however, time to completion of the complete module would still be an uncertain quantity. In their judgement the assessment of probabilities for *total* time to completion of a module under each of the three strategies was a crucial ingredient of the analysis, so to fix ideas they agreed to explore the implications of a delay schedule as shown in Table 4.

Once all sub-modules were satisfactorily completed they would have to be interfaced. The team's probability assessments of the time required to complete the interfacing are shown in Table 5.

Costs

A detailed cost study performed by the Cost Analysis Division showed that while the development and construction costs of each of the alternatives were highly uncertain, conditional upon knowing the time to completion, installa-

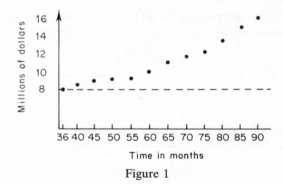

Figure 1

tion, and demonstration of a module, cost could be estimated with reasonable accuracy. Consequently, the team chose to regard these costs of an alternative as a function of time. Some additional computation yielded a set of graphs of cost versus time like that shown in Figure 1 for alternative I with no buffer inventory.

ASSESSMENT OF PREFERENCES

While responsibility for a final choice of design rested with higher authority, the team wished to make a recommendation in its report that reflected the team members' preferences among alternatives in a coherent way. Thus, at the outset the risk analyst saw as one of his tasks development of a *utility function* defined for all *achievable* performance, cost, and time triplets that would reflect the team's *ordinal* preferences among such triplets, and that could also be used to determine preferences among alternatives with uncertain outcomes.

Rather than have the team work from the very start as a group, the risk analyst first spent time with individual members discussing the issues involved in assessing preferences. These discussions led him to conclude that for the initial analysis of alternatives the *probability* of achieving good pieces an average of nine hundred or more per minute over a two-shift day could serve as an adequate index of the desirability of an alternative's potential performance. While, in the judgement of each of the team members, achieving an average greater than nine hundred good pieces per minute was quite desirable, 'nine hundred' was a critical level of performance; if it was not reached, the project would not be judged highly successful. Recognizing that a more sophistica' d analysis would take performance directly into consideration, the risk analyst felt that the ensuing simplification of the process by which preferences among alternatives was to be established accruing from use of 'probability P of nine hundred or more' as a numeraire was worthwhile. (Each possible consequence of choice of an alternative could then be written as a triplet (P,T,C) where P remained *fixed* for that alternative.)

He brought the team members together in order to determine the important features of the *team's* attitude towards taking risks, and began the discussion by asking questions such as:

> Suppose I *fix* the probability of achieving 'nine hundred or more' at $P = .9$. Which do you prefer, a cost-time pair* ($18, 72 mos.) or ($22, 65 mos.)?
>
> Does your preference among these two pairs change if I change P to .8? to .7? How about to .98?

The responses validated the risk analyst's conjecture: to a first approximation, the team's preferences ordering of cost-time pairs did *not* depend on the value of P — as long as P was above some low value. The 'low value' seemed to be in a small neighborhood of .5.

He concluded the discussion and began planning for the next meeting. In his notebook he sketched a block diagram (Figure 2), outlining how he intended to quantify the team's preferences. In a margin appeared: 'As time to completion increases, team is willing to spend an increasingly large increment of dollars to reduce time by one month'. Underneath this comment a rough graph like that in Figure 3 was drawn.

A review of the data collected by the team and the Cost Analysis Division's study showed that the minimum time to completion that could possibly be obtained with any of the alternatives under consideration was thirty-six months, while the maximum was ninety months; similarly the range of costs that might be obtained was found to be twelve to twenty-four million dollars. By posing a series of questions to the team like:

> For what value of time T to completion would you be indifferent between the cost-time pair (18,50) and (20,T)?

the risk analyst generated four sets of indifference points as shown in Figure 4.

In order to carry out step 3 shown in Figure 2, he needed a value of P for each alternative.

Computation of Probabilities

In addition to P the risk analyst needed for each alternative the *joint* probability of each achievable cost-time pair. A number of issues immediately arose:

1. The probability assessments recorded (for each sub-module) of efficiency and proportion defective when in operation were *marginal*

---

*Cost is expressed in millions of dollars and time in months.

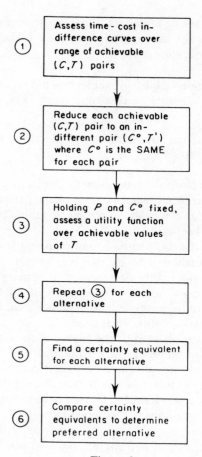

Figure 2

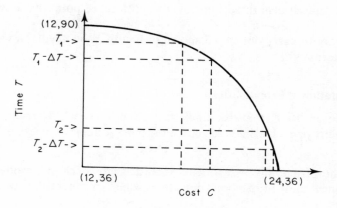

Figure 3

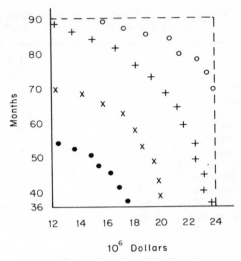

Figure 4 Time-cost indifferences

probability assessments. Under what conditions could the probability distribution of the average rate of acceptable pieces per minute over a two-shift day be determined from these assessments?

2. The team had not yet determined whether or not for a given alternative there was probabilistic dependency between average production rate and the time required for development installation and demonstration. Should they bother to?

3. The marginal probabilities assessed for time to complete the interfacing did not account for differences between alternatives: interfacing may take longer when there are many redundant sub-modules built into the system.

4. What should he do about differences between team members' probability distributions of times to completion of sub-modules? Of interfacing times?

Rather than attempt to resolve these issues immediately, the risk analyst decided to explore the implications of *assuming* independence of all uncertain quantities mentioned above. Using each team member's probability assessments of 'times', he generated by computer simulation a set of probabilities as shown in Tables 6a and 6b.

Conditional Preference Assessments and Certainty Equivalents

With these probabilities in hand, he returned to the problem of determining the team's preferences among uncertain alternatives. Using the indifference curves shown in Figure 4, he reduced *each feasible* cost-time pair to an *indifferent* pair with cost fixed at sixteen million dollars. Then using the datum of Table 6a, he asked the team to respond to questions such as:

284

Table 6a Marginal probability of nine hundred acceptable PPM or more in two-shift day (team member No. 1)

	Buffer inventory?	Prob.
Ia.Serial connection, no stand-by redundancy	Yes	.66
Ib.Serial connection, no stand-by redundancy	No	.52
IIa.Stand-by redundancy of one sub-module where efficiency ≤ .95	Yes	.82
IIb.Stand-by redundancy of one sub-module where efficiency ≤ .95	No	.70
IIIa.Stand-by redundancy to raise each sub-module task to at least .80 efficiency	Yes	.91
IIIb.Stand-by redundancy to raise each sub-module task to at least .80 efficiency	No	.74

Fix P at .70. Consider an alternative yielding a fifty-fifty chance of (.70, $16, 90 mos.) or (.70, $16, 36 mos.). For what certain value of 'time' T would you be indifferent between the uncertain alternative and one that yielded (.70, $16, T) with certainty?

From the responses, he constructed a set of six *conditional utility functions**. Graphs of a typical pair of such functions are shown in Figure 5.

Using team member No. 1's probability judgements about 'time' (as shown in Table 6b) he computed the *expected utility* of each alternative in Table 6a. For example, to compute the expected utility of alternative IIIa in Table 6a he computed the sum

$$\sum_{t=36}^{90} p^{(1)}(t)u(t)$$

where $p^{(1)}(t)$ is the probability assigned by team member No.1 to a 'time' of t months and where $u(t) = u(.91, \$16, t)$ as found in Figure 5.

A similar set of calculations using team members No.2 and No.3 probabilities led to an array of expected utilities as shown in Table 7.

By inverse interpolation, the analyst determined a *certainty equivalent* in units of time for each of the expected utilities displayed in Table 7 (see Table 8). (One of the team members asked the risk analyst why he had bothered to compute certainty equivalents since he had already computed expected utilities.

---

*A function which, conditional upon P and cost being *fixed*, would impute a preference ordering among uncertain alternatives in which *only time* was an uncertain quantity.

Table 6b Probabilities of time to completion and installation of first module

Time	(Team member No. 1) Prob.	(Team member No. 2) Prob.	(Team member No. 3) Prob.
36	0	0	.01
37	.0	0	0
38	.01	0	0
39	.02	.01	.02
40	.01	.02	.04
41	.01	.03	.04
42	.02	.03	.02
43	.02	.03	.05
44	.03	.05	.04
45	.04	.06	.
.	.	.	.
.	.	.	.

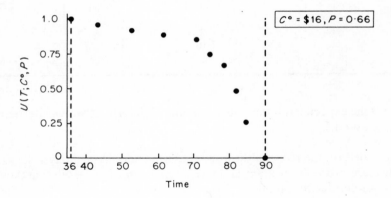

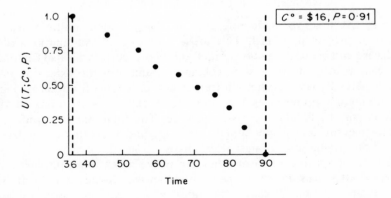

Figure 5

Table 7 Conditional expected utilities

Alternative	No. 1	No.2	No. 3
Ia	.34	.39	.37
Ib	.32	.36	.34
IIa	.72	.70	.68
IIb	.69	.69	.67
IIIa	.67	.74	.79
IIIb	.65	.71	.73

Table 8 Certainty equivalents (months)

Alternative	No. 1	No. 2	No. 3
Ia	85	81	82
Ib	87	84	86
IIa	63	65	61
IIb	68	68	67
IIIa	(60)	(55)	(52)
IIIb	65	66	67

'Don't the expected utilities you've computed determine which alternative is best?' he asked.)

As this juncture, the risk analyst wondered what additional analysis he should ask the team to do. While many issues remained unsettled, he felt that they had made considerable progress.

COMMENTARY ON THE MUCOM CASE

Earlier in the text we made reference to the so-called multiple attribute problem in project appraisal. This arose both in our examinations of the Aztech case and in our discussion of methods of project appraisal in Chapter 3.

The case is in many ways self-explanatory, and uses the extension of the Raiffa (7) BRLT (basic reference lottery ticket) procedure for determining the decision-maker's preferences for alternatives expressed in terms of three attributes, viz, performance, cost, and time. The final aim is to reduce the triplet to an equivalent single-valued numeraire, and to use that numerarie as a means of discrimination amongst alternatives.

This type of approach is useful but can prove much more difficult as the number of attributes increases. In such instances, Keeney and Raiffa's (5) more recent volume discusses methods which can be used to assess multi-attributed utility functions which have different functional forms, e.g., additive, linear, multiplicative. Generally some assumptions must be made about the nature of this function in order to make measurement a practical possibility. The appropriateness of assuming a particular functional form in practical contexts is a modelling choice for the analyst and usually represents a trade-off between effective model specification and measurement feasibility.

A brief introduction to alternative forms of multi-attributed utility functions is presented below so that the reader can judge the appropriateness of each form in applied contexts of the MUCOM type (see also Hull, Moore and Thomas (3)).

Multi-attributed Utility

From the viewpoint of general theory there is virtually no difference between a multi-dimensional and a uni-dimensional utility function. Both are single-valued functions expressing preferences and attitudes to risk over a set of possible outcomes. The use of more than one variable to describe outcomes is a matter of convenience. However, when measurement is considered, new practical problems arise simply because the number of possible outcomes has increased by at least one order of magnitude. Consider, for example, using Raiffa's method to evaluate a corporate decision-maker's utility function for asset position, market share, and turnover. This would involve specifying a number of different levels for each variable and then, for the outcomes described by each possible combination of levels, determining the equivalent standard gambles on the best and worst outcomes, i.e. it would involve asking the corporate decision-maker at least one question for every point on a three-dimensional grid. This sort of approach is clearly out of the question. Some assumptions must be made about the nature of the utility function in order to make measurement a practical possibility. In this section we discuss separately four different assumptions:

(1) A linear utility function.
(2) An additive utility function.
(3) A lexicographic utility function.
(4) A utility function with some other specific property.

1. Linear Utility Functions

Linearity is the simplest assumption applicable when each dimension lends itself to direct quantification on a scale of measurement (e.g. \$, minutes, inches, share of market, etc.). It states that

$$u(x_1, x_2, \ldots, x_n) = \sum_{i=1}^{n} a_i x_i, \tag{1}$$

where u is the utility function, x_i is the value of the variable corresponding to the ith dimension and a_i are constants $(i = 1, \ldots, n)$.

Linearity implies that there is a constant rate of trade-off between one dimension and another (i.e. a_j units of variable x_i are always equivalent to a_i units of variable x_j). In the example given above involving the corporate decision-maker, this means that he would be willing to make a series of statements of the form:

> No matter what the value of my asset position, market share and turnover I would always consider a 1 percentage unit increase in market share and a $100,000 increase in assets equally valuable.

The measurement of a linear utility function involves determining a number of such trade-offs. If there are N dimensions, then only N-1 trade-offs need to be evaluated. Unless N is very large the measurement process is not therefore very tedious once linearity has been established.

It is interesting to note that in spite of its restrictive properties the linear utility assumption is often made implicitly in studies in economics and operational research. Cost benefit analyses, for example, almost invariably assume that all costs and benefits, whatever the units they are measured in, can be traded-off at fixed rates for money. These assumptions are unlikely to be perfectly true and the extent of their validity should always be investigated.

2. Additive Utility Functions

Additivity is a slightly more general assumption than linearity. It states that

$$u(x_1, x_2, \ldots, x_n) = \sum_{i=1}^{n} u_i(x_i)$$

where u_i is a function of the variable x_i corresponding to the ith dimension.

There are a number of ways of viewing this assumption. Tests for its validity have been constructed by Adams and Fagot (1), Luce and Tukey (6), and Fishburn (2a,b,c,d). Basically it implies that the factors are valuewise independent or that the utility of the whole equals the sum of the utilities of the parts. In terms of trade-offs it requires that the rate of trade-off between two variables depends only on the values of those variables and not on that of the others. The corporate decision-maker in the example given above would therefore subscribe to a series of statements of the form:

> Whatever my turnover, increasing my market share from 20 percent to 21 percent would always have the same value to me as increasing my asset position from $5,000,000 to $5,300,000.

One particularly simple example of an additive utility function is given when all the factors are binary (i.e. discrete with only two levels). For if we set:

$v_i = u_i$ (more desirable level of factor i)
$\quad -u_i$ (less desirable level of factor i)

then it is clearly sufficient to determine the relative values of the v_i ($i = 1, \ldots ,$ n). This problem is precisely analogous to that of determining the uni-dimensional utility function of a factor that can have n discrete levels. All the discrete factor uni-dimensional methods (i.e. direct rating, standard gamble, and ordered metric methods) can therefore be used. In addition, as it is in effect possible to add outcomes in this case, a number of other powerful methods involving, for example, comparing $v_1 + v_3$ with $v_2 + v_4 + v_5$ are possible.

The problem of measuring binary utilities arises a great deal in the public sector where resources are competing to satisfy a number of objectives. Stimson (8) for example considered the problem of allocating resources in a Health Service to satisfy seven objectives. First, he asked subjects to rank the objectives. Then he asked a number of questions of the form: 'would you prefer the objective you have ranked first to a combination of the objectives you have ranked second, third and fifth?' Finally, subjects were asked to rate each objective on a scale from 0 to 100. Of the eleven subjects only one remained consistent throughout. However, a further eight were prepared to change their decisions in the light of inconsistencies pointed out to them.

Unfortunately, measuring the general additive utility is considerably more complicated than this. In equation (1) u_i can clearly be interpreted as the uni-dimensional utility function when all the variables except x_i are kept fixed (i.e. when x_i is the only variable describing the outcomes). However, it is not sufficient simply to determine the u_is individually by the uni-dimensional methods. For each u_i would then only be determined up to a linear transformation, and linear transformations of each u_i do not necessarily give a linear transformation of $\Sigma_{i=1}^n u_i$. It is clear that the dimensions must be rated in importance relative to each other in some way. Turban and Metersky (9) provide a practical example of how this might be accomplished in a study where forty 'measures of effectiveness' of a defense system have to be combined into one utility measure.

In some situations (e.g. the asset position, the market share turnover example) rating dimensions in importance relative to each other may not be a very natural procedure for the decision-maker. Establishing trade-offs between the dimensions may be more efficient. Fishburn (2d) lists a number of methods for this. They fall into two general categories:

(a) Methods where one u_i is assumed to be known and is used to determine another u_i (known as 'Scaling Methods').
(b) Methods where two u_is are determined simultaneously (known as 'Flight of Stairs Methods).

In (a) questioning is generally aimed at trading-off increases in one dimension with decreases in another. In the corporate decision-maker example given above, suppose that the u_i corresponding to assets has already been determined. Questioning would then take the form:

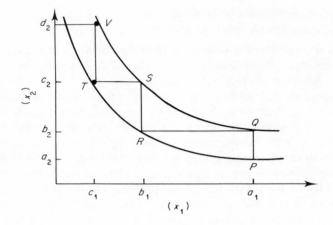

Exhibit 1 Indifference curves

If initially you have assets of A and a market share of B, to what value would your market share have to be increased in order to compensate for a decrease in the level of your assets to C?

Either A and B are kept fixed and C is varied, or B and C are kept fixed and A is varied. In the first case an 'indifference curve' is obtained; in the second case a 'transformation curve' is obtained. In both cases at least part of the u_i function corresponding to market share is known at the end of the process.

In (b) two indifference or transformation curves must be used simultaneously. To illustrate the method consider the situation where it is required to estimate a utility function $U(x_1, x_2) = u_1(x_1) + u_2(x_2)$. We may suppose that the two indifference curves shown in Exhibit 1 have already been obtained.

Let P, Q, R, S, T, V be the points indicated in Exhibit 1 (the choice of P is arbitrary). Let $P = (a_1,a_2)$, $Q = (a_1,b_2)$, $R = (b_1,b_2)$, $S = (b_1,c_2)$, $T = (c_1,c_2)$, $V = (c_1,d_2)$.

The difference in utility between any outcome represented by a point on the upper curve and any outcome represented by the corresponding point on the lower curve is constant. It follows that

$$U(a_1,a_2) - U(a_1,b_2) = U(b_1,b_2) - U(b_1,c_2) = U(c_1,c_2) - U(c_1,d_2)$$

and using $U(x_1,x_2) = u_1(x_1) + u_2(x_2)$ we obtain

$$u_2(a_2) - u_2(b_2) = u_2(b_2) - u_2(c_2) = u_2(c_2) - u_2(d_2)$$

showing that u_2 can be plotted entirely from the vertical distances between the two curves. Similarly u_1 can be plotted entirely from the horizontal distances between the curves.

Unfortunately this method has one drawback. If a reasonable number of points are to be plotted on u_1 and u_2, the indifference curves must be relatively close together. The whole analysis then becomes very sensitive to the precise shapes of the two curves.

There are many variations on the methods given here. Two levels of a discrete factor can be used to scale a continuous factor; a discrete factor can be rated using an already scaled continuous factor; the methods in (b) can be extended to embrace three or more factors simultaneously. Up to now, however, the methods have been put to relatively little practical use. The main reason for this is undoubtedly that the conceptual difficulties, measurement problems, and general level of uncertainty in a given business situation all increase by an order of magnitude as soon as a second variable is introduced. However, many questions of public policy such as where to site an airport, whether to build a road, etc. although involving several factors (comfort, cost, time saved, etc.) have one great simplifying feature: for a given decision the outcomes are deterministic or nearly deterministic. It seems likely therefore that this type of problem will be the first to use more complicated structures in the future.

3. Lexicographic Utilities

Lexicographic utilities describe situations where one factor is of overwhelming importance, and in a choice between two outcomes a second factor is taken into account only when there is a tie on the first. It might be supposed, for example, that a housewife buys butter on the attractiveness of its packaging only when no other difference between two brands is apparent, or that a family when selecting a car considers the number of doors to be of prime importance, and only takes other attributes into account when distinguishing between cars with the same number of doors, etc. In the business context, lexicographic utilities must be looked upon as a useful conceptual tool for isolating important factors and eliminating very poor outcomes from further consideration. Measurement problems are more akin to those arising from uni-dimensional situations and do not appear to present any special extra difficulties.

4. Other Utility Structures

As already pointed out, general utility structures of the form:

$$\text{Utility} = F(x_1, x_2, \ldots, x_n)$$

are likely to be of little practical use. The only alternative structure not already mentioned is that described by Keeney (4a,b). The basic assumption is that trade-offs between gambles on only one of the variables are independent of the values of the other variables. This is slightly less strict than additivity and Keeney shows that in the two-dimensional case it leads to the functional form:

$$u(x_1,x_2) = u_1(x_1) + u_2(x_2) + Ku_1(x_1)u_2(x_2) \tag{2}$$

This is of great theoretical importance and, as Keeney points out, is not in principle a great deal more difficult to measure than the additive structure.

A 'linear' version of (2) has been used by Yntema and Klem (10) who attempted to measure how safe it is for a pilot to land in terms of three dimensions: ceiling, visibility, and fuel left. Experienced pilots were asked questions of three basic types:

(a) Which of these two situations would you prefer?
(b) Where would you rate this situation on a scale stretching between the best and worst possible situations?
(c) How large is the difference between a ceiling of 5000 and 1000 ft as compared with the difference between 5000 and 100 ft?

From the answers the following functional form was evaluated:

$$\text{Utility} = A + Bx + Cy + Dz + Exy + Fyz + Gxz + Hxyz \tag{3}$$

where x measures ceiling, y measures visibility, z measures fuel left and A, B, C, D, E, F, G, H are constants.

The experiment was successful in that the fractional disagreement between a pilot and equation (3) was found to be of the same general size as the fractional disagreement between two pilots. Yntema and Klem made a number of observations on the experiment, the most interesting of which is that questions of type (c) above involved too great an abstraction and most pilots always converted it to a question of type (b).

REFERENCES

1. Adams, E. W., and Fagot, R. F., 'A Model of Riskless Choice', *Behav. Sci.*, **4**, 1959, 1–10.
2a. Fishburn, P. C., 'Independence in Utility Theory with Whole Product Sets', *Operations Res.*, **13**, 1965, 28–45.
2b. Fishburn, P. C., 'Independence, Trade-offs, and Transformations in Bivariate Utility Functions', *Man. Sci.*, **11**, A, 1965, 792–801.
2c. Fishburn, P. C., 'A Note on Recent Developments in Additive Utility Theories for Multiple Factor Situations', *Operation Res.*, **14**, 1966, 1143–8.
2d. Fishburn, P. C., 'Methods of Estimating Additive Utilities', *Manag. Sci.*, **13**, A, 1967, 435–53.
3. Hull, J. C., Moore, P. G., and Thomas, H., 'Utility and its Measurement', *Journal of the Royal Statistical Society*, A, Vol. **136**, Pt. 2, 1973, 226–247.
4a. Keeney, R. L., 'Quasi-separable Utility Functions', *Naval Res. Log. Q.*, **15**, 1968, 551–64.
4b. Keeney, R. L., 'Utility Functions for Multi-attributed Consequences', *Manag. Sci.*, **18**, A, 1972, 276–87.
5. Keeney, R. L., and Raiffa, H., *Decisions with Multiple Objectives: Preferences and Value Trade-Offs*, New York, John Wiley, 1976.
6. Luce, R. D., and Tukey, J. W., 'Simultaneous Conjoint Measurement: A New Type of Fundamental Measurement', *Jour. Math. Psychol.*, **1**, 1964, 1–27.
7. Raiffa, H., *Decision Analysis*, Reading, Mass., Addison-Wesley, 1968.
8. Stimson, D. H., 'Utility Measurement in Public Health Decision-making', *Manag. Sci.*, **16**, B, 1969, 17–30.

9. Turban, E., and Metersky, M. L., 'Utility Theory Applied to Multivariable System Effectiveness Evaluations', *Manag. Sci.*, **17**, B, 1971, 817–28.
10. Yntema, D. B., and Klem, L., 'Telling a computer how to Evaluate Multi-dimensional Situations', IEEE Trans. Human Factors Electronics, HFE-6, 1965, 3–13.

Chapter 7

The Management of the Risk Analysis Process: Suggested Procedures and Implementation Problems

INTRODUCTION

It seems appropriate at this point to synthesize the main ideas discussed so far, and to provide the reader with a suggested framework for risk analysis and the management of the resource allocation process. In doing this, it is important to stress the limitations of the available procedures, as well as anticipate the problems which may be present when attempting to implement risk analysis. First, let us look at the role of simulation and the CAPM in risk analysis.

THE ROLE OF RISK SIMULATION IN RISK ANALYSIS

At this stage it is appropriate to review some of the earlier flow diagrams (see Chapter 2) which showed schematically the nature of the decision analysis approach, and the versions of risk analysis and basic DCF type appraisal which are embedded within such an approach.

We should recognize that it is quite logical and valuable to use simulation as a much wider and complex form of sensitivity analysis in project appraisal. However, we must also be specific about the role of simulation in risk analysis, and provide guidelines about how it should be used.

First, one of the major advantages of the decision analytic treatment of investment decisions is the focussing of managerial effort on structuring and understanding the problem. We emphasize, once again, that this preliminary pre-decisional effort, the modelling and structuring phase, is the most important and yet often the least researched phase of all. In our experience, it is clear that up to 60 percent of the time and effort in any analysis should be spent on structuring, and we have provided some basic suggestions in earlier chapters (see also Bunn and Thomas (2)).

Second, simulation can only be used as a solution approach once this model of the problem has been developed. What risk simulation then achieves is a description of the project's intrinsic risk picture, and this enables a manager to develop a better understanding of the project's nature, the problems associated with cash flow forecasting, and the existence of important uncertain variables, e.g. cost overruns influencing the project's financial viability. Therefore, this output does not, as it stands, provide any insight into the relationship of this single project with the broader portfolio of the firm's activities, or the shareholders' other investments. The impact of the project on the portfolio, i.e. the firm's total risk, can be handled by simulating all possible portfolios of projects that the firm can hold. Alternatively, an incremental analysis approach could be used to assess the impact of a single project on the existing portfolio.

Third, the issue of project impact on the valuation of the firm is difficult to determine from the risk simulation decision analysis type of approach. There is a theoretical problem with imposing management's utility function, or attitude towards risk, on the distributions of portfolio NPV. This is because, for a publicly quoted firm at least, it is the market's perception of risk (and not the manager's) which is the relevant risk dimension for determining the value of a project.

This does not seem to us sufficient reason for abandoning the use of simulation or analytical approaches for developing NPV distributions. Lessard and Bower (7) for example, argue that the use of a particular technique in a capital budgeting process depends upon our ability to translate it into a form in which senior executives can relate to their intuition, judgement and experience. A similar sentiment is also echoed in published surveys of financial decision-making. The challenge to risk analysts is to frame the output of risk analysis procedures in a manner which makes sense to the manager, and provides him with clear judgemental insight into the problem.

We believe that simulation (and the analytical forms of risk analysis) have many positive advantages for managers. First, if managers are presented with a probability distribution of rate of return, they can then examine the project's intrinsic business risk, and screen the project into a number of firm relative risk classes, say, low, medium, or high. This screening would subsequently provide an input into the process of developing appropriate adjustments for risk in discounting calculations and, what is even more important, allow a manager to get a 'handle on' or 'feel' for the influence of uncertainty upon the project.

Second, simulation is useful as a sensitivity analysis vehicle and therefore for developing project understanding. Third, simulation is extremely important as a device for future cash flow forecasting, and in understanding the impacts particular variables have upon such cash flow forecasts. Further, sensible probabilistic earnings projections can be developed for the project and/or the firm.

However, it is also important to note that there is one problem in using the simulated distribution of NPV in a risk-screening process. That is the issue of which discount rate should be used in the calculation? If a risk-adjusted rate is used, then further allowance for risk will merely lead to double counting. If a risk-free rate were used, then the meaning of the NPV distribution is unclear.

However, such problems are not unique to simulation approaches: there are also some problems associated with the CAPM. In particular the assumptions of the CAPM pose problems for the capital budgeting process, some of which were examined in Chapter 5. For example, the single time period aspect of the CAPM may limit its application in the context of multi-period projects, that is, projects which involve cash flows occurring in several time periods.

As a consequence of the application problems which may occur with both the *risk simulation* and *systematic risk* approaches (recognizing that the latter conveys a higher potential for relevant risk recognition in terms of the valuation of the firm), we will argue in the next section for a mix of the two approaches in investment decision-making. Using a financial measure of NPV for project worth based upon expected cash flows discounted at some risk-adjusted rate may be difficult to apply because such a method requires a knowledge of the project's risk class and its required rate of return. The simulation process in which cash flow profiles are generated can help as a first-stage form of risk screening for the risk evaluation process.

In the next section, therefore, we pose a positive role for risk simulation procedures in risk evaluation, and develop a multi-stage procedure for financial evaluation.

A SUGGESTED PROCEDURE FOR APPRAISAL OF PROJECTS IN TERMS OF RISK ANALYSIS

Recalling some of the arguments in Chapter 1, we assume here that the risk identification stage has been completed, and that we require to estimate and evaluate the risky situation.

We propose here a two-stage procedure. The first stage involves *risk determination and positioning*, and the second stage involves a project *risk evaluation* process. The schematic diagrams for each follow, and are similar in structure to those given in Chapter 1. Having examined the various approaches for risk analysis in previous chapters, we now offer an alternative approach. This approach consists of a mixture of conventional risk analysis and risk simulation, but includes too the modern asset pricing theories of finance.

During Stage I (see Figure 1) we seek to identify the risk associated with the project. During this phase we believe that a probabilistic type of risk simulation should be used to forecast the likely cash flows and earnings projections, (narrowly for the project and more broadly for the firm as a whole). This is in order that the manager can develop an understanding of the project's intrinsic riskiness. By the use of sensitivity analysis in association with this forecasting procedure, the manager can also gain an increased understanding of the relationships between factors affecting project cash flows.

The basic idea at this stage is that the manager develops a procedure to screen projects into ranges of perceived risk from low to high. Simulation is a

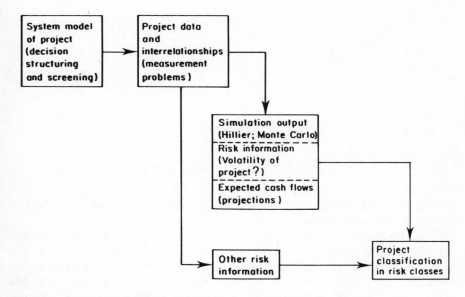

Figure 1 Risk determination and positioning phase

fundamental part of this screening process, and as a consequence, it is extremely important for a manager to learn how to interpret the output of risk simulations, so that projects can be meaningfully classified into risk bands. From time to time, other information about risk is also valuable, and this can be culled from evidence of the experience of other comparable firms undertaking similar projects. Such information will provide additional back-up for establishing a project's risk class.

We should note that the purpose of simulation at this point is both to develop project understanding, and also to classify projects according to the degree of perceived non-diversifiable risk of each type of project. Such non-diversifiable risk refers to the project's exposure to the spectrum of economic risks and, in particular, the project's volatility in relation to project cost and revenue expectations. Thus, a high-risk project would be one highly sensitive to cost and revenue variations in relation to economic activity.

Stage 2 (see Figure 2) of the process is to identify the appropriate risk-adjusted rate which should be associated with each project risk class. This rate should take account of the relevant capital market risk premium according to the CAPM approach, noting that it may be difficult to determine betas for projects or divisions of a company in order for the basic CAPM formula to apply.* The final risk-adjusted rate should then be the sum of the after tax

---

*The suggested procedures are to identify β's (betas) for firms carrying out similar projects and with similar financial structures. Thus, for example, in a pharmaceutical investment situation, a firm would look for β's for firms investing in projects in essentially similar pharmaceutical areas.

298

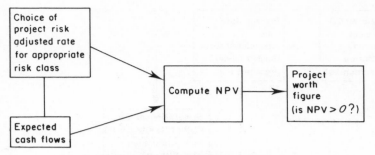

Figure 2 Project evaluation process

risk-free rate (obtained, say, from returns on government stocks) and the risk premium calculated for each risk class.

The procedure for calculating a project's NPV would then involve discounting the project's period-by-period expected cash flows by the risk-adjusted rate previously calculated. The NPV figure obtained from this calculation can predict the likely marginal net effect of a project on the firm's value. Only if the NPV figure is positive can we say that the project will increase the value of the firm.

Stage 1 and Stage 2 together give us a procedure in which simulation is a necessary first step for risk evaluation of projects. Indeed such a procedure should be able to provide a basic approach which can be accommodated within the firm's managerial decision-making process. We turn to such managerial issues briefly in the next section.

MANAGERIAL ISSUES IN INVESTMENT DECISION-MAKING

A simplified initial structure to conceptualize managerial decision-making for capital investment is shown in Figure 3. Basically, the risk analyst provides the manager with a project worth measure, the NPV, and some sensitivity analyses connected with the NPV measure which the manager or his team may request. There is a managerial desire to capture risk more formally in the decision process, yet to have available for decision purposes, simple, intuitive measures of worth which can be relatively easily understood. We believe our Stage 1 process views simulation results as a managerial framework for understanding the influence of uncertainty on projects. Thus, Stage 1 is a broad risk-screening phase, before a 'collapsed' measure, NPV, is obtained in Stage 2.

However, it should also be remembered that appraisal processes are dynamic and change rapidly with experience, intangible or unquantifiable factors, and new information. Top managers look at three main factors in their decision process. First, *project risk* which is identified in the risk analysis process and which leads to the NPV measure. Second, *project interdependencies* with the other activities of the firm. This is handled partially through a

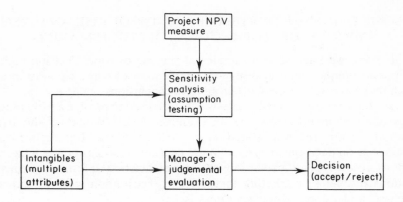

Figure 3 Decision-making process

positive NPV value which indicates a potential increase in the firm's market valuation, and partially by managerial assessment of the relationships between projects. Managers should be especially concerned about whether such an addition would fit well in terms of the firm's growth and strategy path. Third, managers also need to consider *other attributes*; that is, attributes other than purely financial measures. Such factors might include strategic issues, the need to develop new products and to maintain expertise and employee morale within the organization.

We believe that many organizations may find it useful to divide responsibility, on a mutually agreeable basis, in the conduct of the investment decision-making process. It may be sensible, for example, for the project sponsor or functional manager to carry out a risk simulation, thereby undertaking some preliminary risk screening for the project. If the project does not fail on this *screen*, it should be passed for further appraisal, say, by the divisional manager who might perform the risk-adjusted NPV calculations and any relevant sensitivity analyses jointly with the financial manager. The divisional and functional managers would then be in a position to discuss the results with top management, and during a final *project appraisal* task, may consider any additional information which might need to be reviewed. Included in the discussion at this stage might be the issue of satisfying a number of alternative goals. Management, at this level, would probably wish to judge the potential impact of the project on the firm's future value and growth. It is perhaps also appropriate to mention at this point that a problem which does sometimes occur, is that of bias associated with such judgement tasks. It is to be hoped that such biases can be lessened by sensible interactive decision processes. However, it is possible that such interactive decision-making may introduce other biases. For example, lower-level managers may distort information channels and bias the assessment of risk classes, in order to influence the ultimate decision.

300

SOME EVIDENCE ON THE USEFULNESS OF RISK ANALYSIS APPROACHES IN PRACTICAL DECISION-MAKING

In this book we have given examples of the use of some decision and risk analysis techniques, and also given an indication of some circumstances in which they have been used. Certain general conclusions can be drawn.

First, that decision and risk analysis has been used to resolve a wide range of types of decision problems. As an example, Geoff Wells* of the British Imperial Group recently stated at a Social Science Research Council Conference on decision analysis, that the decision analysis approach has been used to resolve plant expansion and rationalization questions, industrial relations problems, marketing logistics and distribution studies, computer purchase, and a series of policy/strategy issues.

Second, that increasing use is being made of decision analysis in the public as well as the private sector, although at least in terms of current reported applications in the literature, more often in relation to tactical, operational level, rather than strategic, decision problems. Rex Brown, a prominent decision and risk analysis consultant, at the same Social Science Research Council Conference, in reviewing the use of decision analysis stated:

> Decision analysis may well turn out to be one of the most influential aids towards the world's conduct of its affairs. Certainly the pace of application has perceptibly quickened during this past decade at upper levels of government and industry in the United States.
>
> The first major field of application was business. Probably a third of the five hundred largest US businesses now make some use of decision analysis, many of them at main board level. To take just one organization, at least three senior executives at Ford Motor Company have based major decisions on systematic analysis: one used it in the decision to drop convertibles; another to evaluate a move into the tire business; the third to adjust prices on tractors.

Third, despite the ever-increasing volume of literature on the subject, practical guidelines for the implementation of the decision and risk analysis approach have probably not received sufficient attention. Clearly, there are behavioral dimensions in the implementation of such approaches in the organizational context. For example, managers complain that these approaches are time-consuming rather than time-saving, and that very often they offer no support in problem formulation but only in post-formulation analysis. In the succeeding paragraphs, some insights are given into the issues of implementation.

Very often individuals involved in decision-making will exert a substantial influence on how the decision is made, and therefore on the adoption of

*SSRC Conference on Decision Analysis, London Business School, January 1981.

decision aids such as risk analysis. McKenney and Keen (10), for example, suggest that in building models, or decision aids, for managers to use, cognitive styles and problem-finding perceptions of the model builder (analyst) may differ markedly from those of the group of business managers within the firm. Thus, the 'model builder' may frame and structure the problem incorrectly, and any resulting analysis may not only be worthless, but will certainly never be implemented.

Little (8) gives some helpful guidelines for model building. He lists the desirable properties of a model as follows:

(i) *Simple* (that is, the structure is well understood; input information is seen to be relevant and concise; important relationships are included and less important ones are left out; problem assumptions are clearly understood, precise and acceptable to the decision-making group).

(ii) *Robust* (the model does not produce absurd answers, and varies in a manner consistent with underlying assumptions).

(iii) *Easy to control and understand* (the user can readily establish cause-effect relationships between the inputs and outputs.

(iv) *Adaptive* (the model can be up-dated as the modelled system evolves).

(v) *Complete* (the most important phenomena are included in the model).

(vi) *Easy to communicate with* (the managers feel involved and believe they both 'own' and can work with the approach).

How, therefore, can managers be encouraged to generate that vital creativity needed for the structuring and formulation of decision options which they wish to compare?

Organizational as well as individual problems can also impede effective implementation. Carter (3) identified organizational as well as individual features which can hinder a firm's use of risk analysis. An interesting finding was that when considering the appropriate trade-off between risk and return, many managers:

... felt that financial theorists specializing in the field of capital structure had failed badly to give supportable guidance in this area.

This tends to suggest that the analysis was providing new and difficult information input, and it is possible that many managers felt that they somehow had to develop a 'feel' for the nature and meaning of the numbers included in the analysis. How can such a learning process be accelerated within the organizational context so that the approach is not abandoned before it can be usefully deployed — assuming that to be an achievable state? This is obviously an important consideration for the analyst. It may involve activity in organizational development and result in redesign of organizational structure. Another important point is that made by Brown (1), who states:

What is significant, in my opinion, is that even these companies, leaders though they are, do not show drastic changes in their general decision-making procedures as a result of decision theory analysis.

This raises the issue that there is considerable resistance to any change in the decision-making processes in organizations, even when decision analysis has been exploited and implemented. This suggests that analysts have not fully understood the nature of the organizational intervention involved in applying decision aids such as risk analysis. Attention to organizational committment must be a minimum necessary prerequisite for sound implementation.

Hammond (6) and others have identified managerial involvement as a necessary, if not sufficient, condition for the acceptance and use of new approaches and models. It is not necessarily a case of giving models to the managers, as suggested by Little (8), but more a matter of creating an approach to decision-making which also builds upon the status quo in recognizing and working with existing information and decision processes in the organization. Rados (11) sees the solution as educating managers about the role and meaning of appropriate decision aids. Whilst training is a necessary prerequisite, it is much more important that sound communication and interaction between analyst and managers be developed so that they can effectively work on the adaptation of the assumptions and structure of the problem. For example, we have found that the decision-tree approach provides a sound, logical structuring basis for communication about the underlying nature and structure of the problem. It is a 'thinking' focus for the decision-making group.

Historically, decision and risk analysis approaches were largely applied as extensions of an existing (usually deterministic) quantitative model. What was new for managers was not only the type of input information — such as probabilistic or preference data — and the distributional form of the output information, but more importantly, as applications progressed, the focussing of considerable managerial thinking into the process of identifying and structuring the problem. In the latter area there was often managerial resistance and resentment to the approach.

Grayson (4) talked about his experiences in the managerial role, and throws some light upon the usefulness of risk and decision analysis techniques in that role: '... I used absolutely none of the management science tools explicitly'. He also explores the possible reasons for not using the techniques. Briefly, these can be summarized as:

  (i) Lack of time to do the necessary analysis.
 (ii) Difficulty in obtaining the necessary information.
(iii) Resistance to new concepts (by other people).
 (iv) Long response time of decision-analysis techniques.
  (v) Simplifying assumptions, which invalidate the models and their output.

In discussing these findings, we should point out that there was an element of Grayson's work which is not common to all situations. That is, he was involved in the setting up of a new organization, the Price Commission in the

US. In an established decision-making process, some of the reasons given may carry less weight, but in our experience, are nevertheless important. The value of Grayson's guidelines lies in the definition of a set of factors which need consideration when contemplating the use, or non-use, of decision and risk analysis. In considering how these problems of implementation can best be accommodated, Grayson suggests a greater degree of integration between managers and decision-analysts, i.e. an improved analyst/manager interaction.

We believe that a dialogue type of strategic thinking framework may be extremely important for the successful introduction of risk and decision analysis approaches in organizational decision-making (Thomas (12)). We suggest that the risk analysis role in this process should be to develop an understanding about the dynamic character of the policy, strategy, or decision problem being studied. Indeed, we would go further and emphasize that adaptive mechanisms and flexibility must be consciously designed and built into the process. Thus, external and environmental factors which may, for example, threaten the future stability and existence of the organization can, to some extent, be anticipated.

We perceive this dialogue process to be both a 'thinking' structure and a flexible search process in relation to the resolution of decision problems. We see no distinction between strategy analyses, such as risk analysis, and formulation. Instead, we see them as an integral part of the policy/strategy dialogue process.

In our experience, the more extensive the previous policy dialogue, the greater the likelihood that the decision-making group will have confronted the range of organizational and other factors which will influence policy implementation. For example, 'first-pass' risk analyses can develop initial project understanding and, following further managerial dialogue, sensitivity analyses may be used to highlight perceived critical features of the problem. Continued discussion, debate, and assumption testing will be on-going, and should lead to an effective final consensus. Mason and Mitroff's (9) strategic assumptions analysis approach may also be used to achieve consensus in strategic decision processes.

CONCLUSIONS

It is a continuing difficulty in managerial research that the same, or related, aspects of management practice can be examined through such a wide variety of interdisciplinary 'lenses'. This variety can be valuable in aiding the understanding of complex situations (such as the one described here), but it has also probably added some confusion to the study of policy, strategy formulation, and planning. Viewpoints available include, at one extreme, those which regard strategic decision-making as organizational politics and, at the other extreme, those which regard strategic decision-making as a comprehensively rational process (using decision or risk analysis).

The stance taken in this chapter is that a useful measure of reconciliation can be achieved amongst the various viewpoints through a continuous policy dialogue involving analyses and assumptions. Indeed, we would argue that the decision-making process finally adopted in most organizations results from continual review, updating, and consensus through group discussion.

We would argue that the view presented here is of the 'mixed scanning' type (Etzioni (5)), and is compatible with the range of approaches suggested for problem finding, formulation, and analysis.

REFERENCES

1. Brown, R. V., 'Do Managers Find Decision Theory Useful', *Harvard Business Review*, May/June **1970**, 78–89.
2. Bunn, D. W., and Thomas, H., 'Decision Analysis and Strategic Policy Formulation', *Long Range Planning*, **10**, December 1977, 23–30.
3. Carter, E. E., 'What are the Risks in Risk Analysis', *Harvard Business Review*, July/August **1972**, 72–82.
4. Grayson, C. J., Jr., 'Management Science and Business Practice', *Harvard Business Review*, **51**, No.4, July/August 1973, 41–48.
5. Etzioni, A. 'Mixed Scanning: A Third Approach', *Public Administration Review*, December 1967, 385–391.
6. Hammond, J. S., III, 'Do's and dont's of Computer Models for Planning', *Harvard Business Review*, **52**, No.2, March/April 1974, 110–123.
7. Lessard, D. R., and Bower, R. S., 'An Operational Approach to Risk Screening', *Journal of Finance*, **28**, March 1973, 321–338.
8. Little, J. D. C., 'Models and Managers: The Concept of a Decision Calculus', *Management Science*, **16**, No. 8, April 1970.
9. Mason, R. O., and Mitroff, I. I. *Challenging Strategic Planning Assumptions,* New York, John Wiley and Sons, 1981.
10. McKenney, J. L., and Keen, P. G. W., 'How Managers' Minds Work', *Harvard Business Review*, **52**, No. 3, May/June 1974, 79–80.
11. Rados, D. L., 'Judging Mathematical Models in Marketing', *Journal of Business Administration*, **5**, No. 1, 1973, 51–61.
12. Thomas, H., 'Strategic Policy Analysis: The Role of Applied Decision Analysis in Strategic Management', Working Paper, Department of Business Administration, University of Illinois, 1981.

Chapter 8

Strategic Management and Risk Analysis: Future Growth Directions

INTRODUCTION

In the book's introduction we stressed the dual role of risk analysis, that is firstly to serve as a 'lens' for strategic thinking and secondly to stimulate input into the process of policy dialogue about the organization's strategy options and, ultimately, strategy choice.

Recent contributions to the management literature mention the importance of risk in relation to strategic management in the environment of the 1980s and 1990s, at the same time stressing the need for more adaptive forms of planning processes. The quotes below illustrate this view:

On the concept of strategy:

> For the better part of a decade, strategy has been a business buzzword ... All this may have blurred the concept of strategy, but is has also helped to shift the attention of managers from the technicalities of the planning process to substantive issues affecting the long-term well-being of their enterprises. (F. Gluck *et al.* (4))

On the need to consider risk/return in strategic planning:

> Since its emergence in the early 1970s, the portfolio technique — along with related concepts like the SBU (strategic business unit) and the experience curve — has become the framework for strategic planning in many diversified companies. Now the act has advanced enough to give a diversified company a variety of approaches when it is considering installing such a system or substituting one that evidently meets its needs better than the current portfolio.

> Conceptually, we think, the tailor-made approaches are superior because they:

> Permit inclusion of the conceptually desirable dimensions of risk and return, plus any other idiosynchratic elements viewed by management as important. (Y. Wind and V. Mahajan (14))

On risk reduction:

> Companies can no longer think in terms of diversifying risk but rather in terms of reducing it altogether. (Gluck, McKinsey and Co. Ltd. (quoted in *Business Week*, 1 June, 1981))

On risk analysis and strategic planning:

> As stated previously, 'strategic planning' is just now, but rapidly, becoming recognized as a formal discipline. Methods research is actively underway for (1) constructing alternative futures (scenarios); (2) forecasting fuzzy futures; and (3) selecting one alternative or a combination of alternatives as a basis for strategy. It is in this context that I believe risk analysis can be used to make a significant contribution. (Wagner (13))

On operational versus portfolio planning:

> Zakon sees portfolio management being replaced by 'operating' management — which calls for managers to focus again on each business as an entity in itself, rather than as part of a diversified mix. (Zakon, Boston Consulting Group (quoted in *Business Week*, 1 June, 1981))

On an 'operational' management focus:

> Companies are saying that operations have been neglected for far too long. (Wheelwright, Stanford Business School (quoted in *Business Week*, February 1981, 'Management Focusses on the Factory Floor'.))

Two broad themes emerge from this series of statements. First, that some form of strategic risk analysis is necessary in order to manage the risk content of the strategic process and also develop dialogue about uncertainty impacts and future scenarios. Second, that there is a need, in the future, to focus on a different, more mature and entrepreneurial form of strategic planning. As *Business Week* (1 June, 1981) pointed out, the questions currently being asked by companies are:

(1) How many businesses can we afford to be in without spreading ourselves too thin?
(2) What particular strengths do we as a company have that will enable us to survive in those businesses?

The strategic focus in business organizations over the last twenty to thirty years seems to have moved from operations to strategy, and back to a focus on basic operations, i.e. understanding and developing individual businesses and searching for those relatively well-defined and less risky segments within which they should operate. Increasingly, managers are being charged with a mission of consolidating and improving their organization's strengths and capabilities, whilst simultaneously taking on as little risk as possible. Clearly, there is often more concern about risk aversion, such as limiting downside risk, than there is about gaining significant rewards. In other words, the emphasis is often more on avoiding than taking risks.

THE PROCESS OF CORPORATE DEVELOPMENT

There seem to be two fundamental issues in this area. First, the determination of the set of activities to be undertaken. These might include such areas as new businesses, new products, new territories, new subsidiaries, divestment or consolidation of existing businesses, and different segments in existing businesses. The second issue is the definition of the organization's need for resources and capabilities which will enable it to carry out the chosen set of activities in an effective manner.

In addressing these two issues, one of the main problems for the organization is that it does not know precisely what will happen in the future. This uncertainty about the future means that the organization must develop planning and allied approaches to handle and cope with the effects of uncertainty. Thus, it must build in flexibility and adaptability in order to cope with contingencies, and also be prepared to anticipate changes both in competitive behavior and in the underlying economic environment.

Another major problem, particularly in current times, is that the set of activities facing the organization is often quite small. Rather than having an initial major allocation problem by being required to choose amongst a large number of items in the activity set, managers are faced more often with a search process for scarce new opportunities and creative shifts in existing industries. Managerial attention needs to be directed towards more insightful and creative thinking as a prelude to decision-making and choice.

Ultimately, however, the organization requires to find that strategic combination of activities which makes sense in both aggregate terms and also at the level of the individual business. In other words, senior managers have to understand single business strategy and the synergy between it and overall corporate strategy. In order to determine such a strategic combination, the organization's corporate development function must, therefore, generate an appropriate policy dialogue. This can be achieved by viewing the strategic options in terms of a number of alternative analytic 'lenses' and thinking processes, involving not only discussion about the ultimate *corporate development strategy* but, equally importantly, the building blocks of *evaluation of existing and new activities* and of the *examination of possible organizational activity portfolios*.

In the next section, we examine the role of one of the possible sets of analytical 'lenses' and approaches, namely, risk analysis. This is discussed in the context of the strategic management of the corporate development process.

RISK ANALYSIS AND THE CORPORATE DEVELOPMENT PROCESS

In order to structure the discussion here we will categorize the following main activities in corporate development and, in turn, examine the contribution which *risk analysis* can make in relation to these activities. The set of activities we shall define are: *existing businesses and activities*; *new activities*; *portfolios of new activities*; a *combined portfolio*; and a *development strategy*.

Existing Businesses

In essence, the examination of existing activities requires the definition of options, the resources they will consume, and the financial resources they will produce. (That is, we assume that the search and problem-finding process has already been undertaken.) In this area, therefore, the main contributions of strategic risk and decision analysis are in the areas of *financial planning and forecasting*.

Basic financial planning is a logical extension of the budgeting, cash flow, and funds flow projections normally developed within organizations. The initial stage is usually for the organization to specify its growth targets and acceptable financial policies. For example, a target of, say 12 percent annual compounded growth in earnings per share may be suggested, and policies of avoiding overly high leverage may be implemented in terms of guidelines such as the statement of a maximum value for the debt to equity ratio.

Typically, in order to forecast cash flows, we need to develop uncertainty profiles for the underlying key system variables (which might include sales, costs, prices, inflation rates, environmental factors, etc.), during the planning horizon specified for the firm. Such profiles can be obtained using procedures for probability assessment discussed in the measurement section of this book.

The next step in the procedure is to gather the assessed probabilistic information into a structural risk-simulation model of the firm's operations, in order to determine the cash flow and probability effects of both the individual variables and their combination. Such a procedure will not only develop probabilistic cash flow and budget profiles over the planning period but also, more importantly, assess the sensitivity of the profiles to individual components and combinations of those components. Examples of forecasting approaches, including those which seek to widen the forecasting process to a consideration of more 'fuzzy' futures are given by Mao (8), and Wagner (13).

Perhaps one of the main problems associated with forecasting fuzzy futures is the need to assess adequately all possible scenarios or future sequences of events which bear upon the forecast, and the assumptions which should underlie the construction of such scenarios. We have found that the probability tree, or 'fault' tree as it is commonly referred to by engineers, is a very useful aid for structuring the thinking process provided that the assessor is encouraged to think about extremes of the range of possible outcomes. This means that the 1 percent and 99 percent fractiles should be carefully considered and the assessor discouraged from 'anchoring' his thinking solely around the central values of the distribution. A number of corporate planning groups which encourage *scenario* construction for 'futures' have identified this 'anchoring' bias around 'central' or 'status quo' type values, and have modified assessment procedures to avoid asing directly for the 'most likely' scenario. Further, they have consistently reported that decision-makers find difficulty in confronting future events, despite the many suggestions, including brainstorming, which have been offered in the literature on futures research and technological forecasting. For an extensive study of real-life futures forecasting problems in a telecommunications situation see Burville and Thomas (1).

New Activities and Portfolios of New Activities

The corporate development task in this area is to search for, and identify, potential new prospects and activities for the organization. It should then be possible to discover if there are groups of new activities which it might be sensible to launch and develop simultaneously as one entity.

In developing new prospects, we have already seen in earlier sections the value both of creative search processes and of sensitivity analysis and screening approaches in identifying and reducing the number of options to be considered by the organization. Indeed, the Aztech case in Chapter 2 illustrates that a thorough risk analysis of even a relatively small set of options is extremely complex and time-consuming. It is evidently important in practice, therefore, to undertake the maximum amount of preliminary screening in order to reduce the initially envisaged set of options to a minimum set worthy of more detailed evaluation.

Aztech shows the use of two screening approaches which merit practical attention. First, the multi-attributed screening model, the Churchman–Ackoff model, expresses preferences for options in terms of linear scoring measures. It has been widely accepted as a useful screening device, and in addition has intuitive appeal for managers, largely because it is a simple and easily understood formulation of the decision problem. Second, the mean/variance approach offers an alternative form of screening under uncertainty which consists of identifying the 'efficient set' of options.

An equally important screen is the sensitivity analysis approach applied to a structural model of the new activity in order to understand more clearly the nature of uncertainty, and its impact on that activity. For a recent example of strategic sensitivity analysis see Dubourdieu and Thomas (2).

Continuing the research and development theme developed in Aztech, (in an electronics context), we can extend our discussion to the portfolio domain by means of another example. In a recent article, David Hertz (5) described the role of risk analysis in strategic decisions in the R & D area, and in subsequent paragraphs we summarize the suggested procedures.

No area of risk-taking contains more uncertainty than research and development. In this area, simulation can help the senior executive to see the nature of his choices more clearly, to weigh the uncertainties they entail, and to widen his margins of safety in R & D through project 'portfolios' designed to balance his risks. For example, a technologically-oriented firm might develop a basic strategy to capitalize on the substitution opportunities arising out of obsolescence. With the aid of an effective simulation model, the nature and probable impact of this obsolescence can be determined, and the ranking of alternative ventures can take into account the longer-term probabilities of profitable substitution.

United Aircraft Corporation, for example, employs a variety of management science methods, including technological forecasting, risk analysis, and systems dynamics models to help it shape R & D strategy. The company starts by identifying potential market needs. It develops a future-oriented scenario describing in considerable detail — technological, economic, ecological, sociological, and political—the likely long-term environment for its present and potential products. The specific effect of various alternatives on possible market needs is simulated, and from these simulations new product concepts are developed. Thus, a scenario might be developed covering world energy requirements. By modelling the growth of energy demands and the constraints imposed by resource availability and environmental considerations, a series of product needs could then be identified and a structure of product concepts proposed.

The next step is to develop and evaluate alternative R & D programs that could exploit these product concepts. The concepts are assessed from technical, technological, social, and environmental points of view, to produce recommendations for specific new products, along with useful data about their potential uses and market acceptance. These data are then used to estimate the risks of alternative R & D programs in terms of their probabilities of success.

If the success probability of a particular R & D program is high enough to warrant the commitment of the necessary resources, the company then develops quantitative models of the ventures necessary to exploit the new product results. Varying the inputs to these venture models permits management to determine which variables are most likely to influence their ultimate profitability.

Thus, the model building process at United Aircraft comprises a chain of analyses, starting with concept formation based on a broad view of the company's environment, through a series of stages culminating in the hypothetical marketing of a potential product. The next step is to determine, by means of a competitive model, what pricing policy would maximize the net present value of each venture. This model includes such variables as the initial market-share position, the market growth rate, the number of possible competitors, the slope of the manufacturing-cost learning curve, and the product life cycles of present and potential products. A computer simulation is utilized to determine the best policy; uncertainties are then introduced, their effects computed, and the estimated chances of achieving various levels of return charted in the form of risk analysis curves. This enables management to simulate the risks and returns associated with the various proposed product ventures as well as the cash-flow exposure involved at various levels of risk.

The final result is a portfolio of R & D investment possibilities, rank-ordered in terms of the trade-offs between respective rates of return and their risk-exposure characteristics. To a company whose future depends upon orderly risk-taking and continuing investment in new product possibilities, such analytical information could spell the difference between indifferent perform-ance and brilliant success.

Combined Portfolios

In a combined portfolio not all strategic decisions, of course, are subject to the overriding uncertainties that characterize the previously described R & D environment. Many decisions, though less uncertain than R & D, are complicated by the necessity of satisfying several organizational objectives.

Any organizational portfolio must, therefore, simultaneously satisfy corpo-rate objectives and also those of the divisions or strategic business units. What is needed is a planning structure that enables the organization to organize 'top-down' and 'bottom-up' objectives and develop the plans and action programs for achieving these objectives.

Let us consider an example from an international chemical company which shows how a creative family of models can deal both with complexity and uncertainty. The family of models is shown in Figure 1.

The three types of models shown in Figure 1 are discussed below.

1. Risk Analyses

These are used to test the attractiveness of diversification opportunities, as well as the potential range of future profitability for the company as a whole. They provide the basis for setting corporate and divisional profitability objectives, which are basic to the corporate decision-making process and are incorporated in the financial models.

2. A Corporate Financial Model

This linear programming model provides 'top-down' simulation of the financial consequences of alternative corporate objectives, policy guidelines, and resource allocations. It checks their consistency and assesses the potential effects of incorrect or untrue assumptions on overall corporate performance.

3. Divisional Financial Models

These simulate alternative divisional objectives from the bottom up, and test their consistency with top-down corporate objectives. Proposed resource allocations to the division, and division profitability objectives, can be varied in the simulation until an alternative consistent with corporate objectives is identified. (If this cannot be done by varying resource allocations and divisional objectives and/or realistically reappraising their underlying assumptions, then corporate objectives may need re-examination.)

312

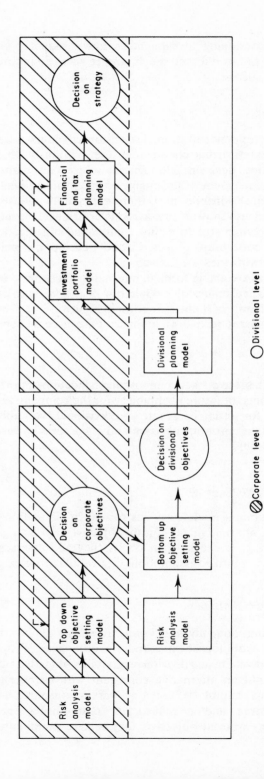

Figure 1 Family of models for portfolio planning

These models have given senior management a clear picture of the interdependencies between corporate objectives and financial policies, and enabled them to test the sensitivity of the results to changes in the assumptions. If corporate objectives turn out to be inconsistent with desired financial policies, the models provide a means of achieving the best possible compromise. In one instance, when a proposed increase in dividend payout threatened an unacceptable increase in external financing requirements, these models enabled the company to develop optimum combinations of equity and debt financing for each of several alternative dividend payout ratios.

Thus, the corporate model (essentially a set of logical statements about relationships with the business) utilizes the computer to balance asset, liability, and capital requirements within a framework of specified constraints and objectives. Meanwhile, the divisional model determines the financial consequences of various patterns of resource allocation, and their respective efficacy for the achievement of divisional profitability objectives. Alternatives within the divisional model are analyzed in terms of risks and probabilities. With the aid of two additional management science models, a set of high payoff projects is then chosen at the corporate level, aggregated in terms of planned investment expenditures, sales levels, and cash flows, and finally checked for consistency with corporate objectives. In short, by displaying the entire corporate planning mechanism as a set of interrelated decision models, management science has measurably strengthened the effectiveness of decision-makers on the top management level. For the complex, diversified enterprise especially, this last example suggests the possibility of attaining, through creative application of already available management science techniques, a really important improvement in the quality of their strategic decision-making. Consider:

(i) Corporate objectives can be dovetailed with the projected financial results of existing and planned new investment projects.

(ii) Investment decisions can be taken according to clearly defined strategic concepts. Projects with real potential for building up products and markets will not automatically be rejected just because high start-up costs make them initially unable to compete with investments in traditional product lines.

(iii) Projects can be evaluated for their 'fit' within a total portfolio, and overall portfolio performance can be significantly improved by balancing projects combining low return and low risk with projects combining high risk and high return.

(iv) Strategic planning can be effectively linked to financial planning. Given pertinent information on the risks, returns, and timing of cash flows for each investment project, the financial planner will have a clear picture of the present and planned structure of assets and will, therefore, be able to make recommendations that better fit the requirements of the company as a whole.

Development Strategy

Recommendations

At this stage, given a preferred portfolio, the organization must find an effective method of implementation which might involve training and skills development, acquiring management, businesses, other firms or finance, and changing existing organizational structures.

Successful decision and risk analyses, however, tend to have common ingredients for success which can usefully be categorized as *organizational*, *personal*, and *technical*.

From the organizational perspective, there must be commitment and enthusiasm from senior managers for the analysis to be both carried out and implemented. Many management techniques have failed to gain implementation because they have been pursued by rather isolated specialist groups; the typical operational research department is an example. It is essential for the success of strategic risk and decision analysis that there should be none of this 'arms-lengths' consultancy. In so far as the approach is mainly one of elucidating managerial expertise, it requires a close personal relationship between analyst and manager (or managerial group). Therefore, there must be sufficient time (and freedom from undue pressure) in which to carry out the analysis, and this factor alone suggests the decision and risk analyses will tend to be most effective in the resolution of those more complex tactical and strategic decision problems in which the typology of the problem structure is 'fuzzy', the organizational mechanism for decision-making unclear, and both the level of risk and the scale of the decision significant.

At the *personal* level, managers must understand the broad-brush, strategic thinking flavor of the decision and risk analysis approach, and effectively communicate their information needs in decision-making to analysts.

At the *technical level*, the major need in application is to get the manager fully to understand the nature of the problem and thus provide the analyst with an effective 'model' of the problem. In particular, the analyst must be clearly informed about the nature of the decision-making process as well as the existence of decision support and information systems so that he can tailor the decision analysis to organizational needs. As mentioned previously, we have found that the decision-tree framework provides a very effective discussion and communication vehicle, analogous perhaps to a 'thinking algorithm', for formulating and structuring the essential elements and difficulties inherent in any reasonably complex analysis of strategy.

CONCLUSIONS

We believe that we have demonstrated, not only by the examples in this chapter (and in the companion case study volume) but also by the argument put forward in the entire book, that strategic risk analysis is extremely useful as a 'lens' for viewing the whole range of questions that encompass the activities known as strategic planning and policy formulation.

In the previous chapter we referred to some articles which purported to show why risk analysis did not work. Some of their reasons are noted below:

(i) The wrong problem may be solved due to inadequate *problem structuring*.

(ii) There are many problems in assessing uncertainty and in getting managers to *confront events in the long-term future*, e.g. the future business environment.

(iii) There are organizational problems associated with the implementation of risk analysis. For example, there needs to be a conducive *organizational structure* for strategic risk and decision analysis to be proven effective. In some cases, more decentralized structures (e.g. of divisionalized form with risk analyses carried out at the division level) have proven to be effective, but the common thread for success seems to be the need for *organizational commitment*, i.e. the approach is not forced by the Chief Executive Officer (CEO) but through communication and discussion its value is perceived. Otherwise, sabotage by managers is likely to occur.

(iv) Risk analysis cannot work because it smacks of 'overkill', and the technique is generally too sophisticated for the present generation of managers.

(v) Risk analysis encourages 'tunnel vision', is not adaptive to change and does not eliminate the need for the manager to 'take a gamble' once the results of the risk analysis are known (*because* it does not specify a clear-cut decision criterion).

Each of these criticisms can be addressed in turn.

Problem Structuring

We have stressed that problem finding and the search for options are the most creative parts of the decision process. This has also been recognized by writers and consultants in the field (e.g. Kepner and Tregoe (7), Prince (10)) and is an increasingly important research area.

We believe, however, that with the simultaneous improvements in decision aids and in the number of real-life case-study applications, problem-solvers can learn more about, and avoid problems in, problem structuring. However, structuring is an 'art', not a science, and in a sense practice makes perfect, through a process of 'learning by doing'.

Uncertainty Assessment

We believe that the measurement problems in probability assessment can be overcome. Increasingly, the use of interactive programs (e.g. Schlaifer (11)) and fault trees (e.g. Fischoff, Slovic, and Lichtenstein (3)) is helping managers both to understand the assessment process and to structure complex assessments in a more effective manner.

We believe that most of the problems of probability assessment are not technical but behavioral, and feel that behavioral implications such as task difficulty, analyst-manager interaction, etc. should be carefully considered when designing the assessment procedure for use by a particular individual or group. It should be noted that research is continuing to provide insights into the behavioral aspects of probability assessment.

Strategy and Structure

Risk analysis clearly needs both organizational commitment and a sound organizational structure for effective implementation. In our experience, if strategic thinking is an acceptable norm within an organization, then strategic risk analysis can help formulate strategies which will typically be understood and subsequently implemented. In our view, structure inhibits strategy whenever the strategy concept and strategic thinking are at variance with the organization's premises and belief system (which we believe most often provides the driving force underlying the organization's decision processes). Some form of organizational design and restructuring is often necessary in order to implement risk analysis and other strategic 'lenses' because this restructuring is often a *signal* for employees about the organization's commitment to, and belief in, strategic thinking.

Risk Analysis Too Sophisticated — Leads to Overkill?

We feel that this criticism is largely unfounded. Where necessary, training is important both for the managers and the CEO of the organization in order for them to understand and appreciate the value of the risk analysis process. Such training can also indicate the types of behavioral biases that commonly occur in judgement (see Tversky and Kahneman (12)) and the heuristics (or rules of 'thumb') frequently used in judgemental tasks. Thus, training should alert the manager to the nature of risk analysis as a thinking approach for his decision problem, which does not necessarily solve it or even prescribe what should be done. Rather, it encourages communication about the problem and its underlying assumptions, and ultimately leads to a more measured and balanced decision process.

Tunnel Vision

Risk analysis is increasingly seen as a necessary and useful adjunct to a strategic planning and thinking process (Hertz and Thomas (6)). Namely, as an approach for forecast/uncertainty-based planning (Stage 2/3 of Gluck et al's (4) four stages of strategic planning) in which an understanding of project risk, cash flow projections and future scenarios is developed. Risk analysis can help strategic thinking by encouraging constructive dialogue and debate about the policy options. Thus, it is recognized that an initial risk analysis is no more than a first attempt at problem understanding. It should encourage controversy and allow members of the decision-making group to discover where basic differences exist about problem assumptions, values and uncertainties. This controversy should enable critical comment and review to be obtained, and through policy dialogue force the re-analysis, re-examination and sensitivity testing of the problem situation.

Therefore, risk analysis does not promote 'tunnel vision'. Rather, it is a useful framework for understanding, formulating and resolving ill-structured, complex policy and planning problems. Mason and Mitroff (9: 302) state a similar message:

"In our view the task of policy, planning and strategy should not consist of attempting to demonstrate the superiority of one approach or framework for all situations but rather of showing their mutual dependency... . Whatever methods are used, they should always aid in challenging strategic planning assumptions."

POSTSCRIPT

Strategic risk and decision analysis is not an argument in methodology (in finance or any other area) but rather an approach which can be used to encourage problem-solving and strategic thinking about the organization's future decisions, strategies, and growth paths. It provides a means of structuring complex problems which cannot be neatly categorized as, say, finance or marketing problems, and uses an extensive set of inputs from all relevant managers, disciplines, and external sources in its attempt to solve problems. It is, therefore, a multi-disciplinary approach which enables people to understand strategic options more fully, and to make judgements in an atmosphere of greater awareness and understanding of future scenarios.

Such analyses provide managers with one of several possible 'lenses' with which they can view the strategy formulation process. As inputs to this process of policy dialogue, they provide specific and valuable information about the impacts of uncertainty on policy options, and allow managers to judge and examine options in the light of changes in the wider social, economic, and political environment and the organization's goal structures.

REFERENCES

1. Burville, P. J., and Thomas, H., *Strategy Planning; A Public Sector Application*, London, Croom Helm, (forthcoming).
2. Dubourdieu, J. R., and Thomas, H., 'Strategic Sensitivity Analysis: The Case of an Electricity Generation Project' Working Paper, University of Illinois, 1981.

318

3. Fischoff, B., Slovic, P., and Lichtenstein, S., 'Fault Trees: Sensitivity of Estimated Failure Probabilities to Problem Representation', *Journal of Experimental Psychology Human Perception and Performance*, **4**, No. 2, 1978, 330–344.
4. Gluck, F. W., Kaufman, S. P., and Walleck, A. S., 'Strategic Management for Competitive Advantage,' *Harvard Business Review*, July/August **1980**, 154–161.
5. Hertz, D. B., 'Management Science and the Chief Executive,' *Management Decision*, **10**, Winter 1972, 253–261.
6. Hertz, D. B., and Thomas, H., 'Risk Analysis and its Role in Strategic Thinking and Dialogue', *Long Range Planning* (forthcoming).
7. Kepner, C. H., and Tregoe, B. B., *The Rational Manager*, New York, McGraw-Hill, 1965.
8. Mao, J. C. T., *Quantitative Analysis of Financial Decisions*, New York, Macmillan, 1969.
9. Mason, R. O., and Mitroff, I. I., *Challenging Strategic Planning Assumptions,* New York, John Wiley and Sons, 1981.
10. Prince,. G. M., *The Practice of Creativity*, New York, Collier, 1970.
11. Schlaifer, R. O., *Computer Programs for Elementary Decision Analysis*, Cambridge, Mass, Harvard University Press, 1971.
12. Tversky, A., and Kahneman, D., 'Judgement Under Uncertainty: Heuristics and Biases', *Science*, **185**, 1975, 1124–1131.
13. Wagner, G. R., 'Strategic Thinking Supported by Risk Analysis,' *Long-Range Planning*, **13**, June 1980, 61–68.
14. Wind, Y., and Mahajan, V., 'Designing Product and Business Portfolios,' *Harvard Business Review*, January/February **1981**, 155–166.

Index